Conversations with Ant

Literary Conversations Series

Peggy Whitman Prenshaw
General Editor

Photo credit: © Nancy Crampton

Conversations with Anthony Burgess

Edited by
Earl G. Ingersoll and Mary C. Ingersoll

University Press of Mississippi
Jackson

www.upress.state.ms.us

The University Press of Mississippi is a member of the Association of American University Presses.

Copyright © 2008 by University Press of Mississippi
All rights reserved
Manufactured in the United States of America

First printing 2008

Library of Congress Cataloging-in-Publication Data

Burgess, Anthony, 1917–1993.
    Conversations with Anthony Burgess / edited by Earl G. Ingersoll and Mary C. Ingersoll.
        p. cm. — (Literary conversations series)
    Includes index.
    ISBN 978-1-60473-095-1 (cloth : alk. paper) — ISBN 978-1-60473-096-8 (pbk. : alk. paper) 1. Burgess, Anthony, 1917–1993—Interviews. 2. Authors, English—20th century—Interviews. I. Ingersoll, Earl G., 1938– II. Ingersoll, Mary C. III. Title.
    PR6052.U638Z59 2008
    823.914—dc22

                                                                                                2008006090

British Library Cataloging-in-Publication Data available

Books by Anthony Burgess

Time for a Tiger. London: Heinemann, 1956.

The Enemy in the Blanket. London: Heinemann, 1958.

English Literature: A Survey for Students, as John Burgess Wilson. London: Longman, Green, 1958; revised edition, as Anthony Burgess, London: Longman, 1974.

Beds in the East. London: Heinemann, 1959.

The Doctor Is Sick. London: Heinemann, 1960; New York: Norton, 1960.

The Right to an Answer. London: Heinemann, 1960; New York: Norton, 1961.

Devil of a State. London: Heinemann, 1961; New York: Norton, 1962.

The Worm and the Ring. London: Heinemann, 1961, withdrawn; republished in revised edition, 1970.

One Hand Clapping, as Joseph Kell, London: P. Davies, 1961; as Anthony Burgess, New York: Knopf, 1972.

The Wanting Seed. London: Heinemann, 1962; New York: Ballantine, 1962.

A Clockwork Orange. London: Heinemann, 1962; with final chapter omitted, New York: Norton, 1963; republished with final chapter and an introduction by the author, New York and London: Norton, 1987.

Inside Mr. Enderby, as Joseph Kell, London: Heinemann, 1963.

Honey for the Bears. London: Heinemann, 1963; New York: Norton, 1964.

The Novel Today. London: Longmans, 1963; Folcroft, Pa: Folcroft, 1971.

Nothing Like the Sun: A Story of Shakespeare's Love Life. London: Heinemann, 1964; New York: Norton, 1964.

Language Made Plain. London: English Universities Press, 1964; New York: Crowell, 1965; revised edition, London: Fontana, 1975.

The Eve of Saint Venus. London: Sidgwick & Jackson, 1964; New York: Norton, 1970.

The Long Day Wanes: A Malayan Trilogy. New York: Norton, 1964—comprises *Time for a Tiger*, *The Enemy in the Blanket*, and *Beds in the East*; republished as *Malayan Trilogy: Time for a Tiger, The Enemy in the Blanket, Beds in the East*. London: Pan, 1964.

Here Comes Everybody: An Introduction to James Joyce for the Ordinary Reader. London: Faber and Faber, 1965; republished as *Re Joyce*. New York: Norton, 1965; revised edition with original title, Feltham, U.K.: Hamlyn, 1982.

A Vision of Battlements. London: Sidgwick & Jackson, 1965; New York: Norton, 1966.

Tremor of Intent: A Eschatological Spy Novel. London: Heinemann, 1966; New York: Norton, 1966.

The Novel Now: A Student's Guide to Contemporary Fiction. London: Faber and Faber, 1967; republished as *The Novel Now: A Guide to Contemporary Fiction*. New York: Norton, 1967; revised, 1971.

Enderby Outside. London: Heinemann, 1968.

Enderby. New York: Norton, 1968—comprises *Enderby Outside* and *Inside Mr. Enderby.*

Urgent Copy: Literary Studies. London: Cape, 1968; New York: Norton, 1969.

Shakespeare. London: Cape, 1970; New York: Knopf, 1970.

MF. London: Cape, 1971; New York: Knopf, 1971.

Joysprick: An Introduction to the Language of James Joyce. London: Deutsch, 1973; New York: Harcourt Brace Jovanovich, 1975.

Napoleon Symphony. London: Cape, 1974; New York: Knopf, 1974.

The Clockwork Testament; or, Enderby's End. London: Hart-Davis, MacGibbon, 1974; New York: Knopf, 1975.

Beard's Roman Women. New York: McGraw-Hill, 1976; London: Hutchinson, 1977.

A Long Time to Teatime. London: Dempsey & Squires, 1976; New York: Stonehill, 1976.

Moses: A Narrative. London: Dempsey & Squires, 1976; New York: Stonehill, 1976.

Abba Abba. London: Faber and Faber, 1977; Boston: Little, Brown, 1977.

Ernest Hemingway and His World. New York: Scribners, 1978; London: Thames & Hudson, 1978; republished as *Ernest Hemingway,* London: Thames & Hudson, 1986; New York: Thames & Hudson, 1999.

1985. Boston: Little, Brown, 1978; London: Hutchinson, 1978.

The Land Where the Ice Cream Grows, by Burgess and Fulvio Testa. London: Bonn, 1979; New York: Doubleday, 1979.

Man of Nazareth. New York: McGraw-Hill, 1979; London: Magnum, 1980.

Earthly Powers. New York: Simon & Schuster, 1980; London: Hutchinson, 1980.

On Going to Bed. London: Deutsch, 1982; New York: Abbeville, 1982.

The End of the World News: An Entertainment. London: Hutchinson, 1982; New York: McGraw-Hill, 1983.

This Man and Music. London: Hutchinson, 1982; New York: McGraw-Hill, 1983.

Enderby's Dark Lady; or, No End to Enderby. London: Hutchinson, 1984.

Ninety-Nine Novels: The Best in English Since 1939: A Personal Choice. London: Allison & Busby, 1984; New York: Summit, 1984.

Flame into Being: The Life and Work of D. H. Lawrence. London: Heinemann, 1985; New York: Arbor House, 1985.

The Kingdom of the Wicked. London: Hutchinson, 1985; New York: Arbor House, 1985.

Oberon Old and New by Burgess and J. R. Planché. London: Hutchinson, 1985.

Blooms of Dublin: A Musical Play Based on James Joyce's Ulysses. London: Hutchinson, 1986.

The Pianoplayers. London: Hutchinson, 1986; New York: Arbor House, 1986.

Homage to QWERT YUIOP: Essays. London: Hutchinson, 1986; republished as *But Do Blondes Prefer Gentlemen? Homage to QWERT YUIOP and Other Writings.* New York: McGraw-Hill, 1986.

Little Wilson and Big God: Being the First Part of the Confessions of Anthony Burgess. New York: Weidenfeld & Nicholson, 1987; London: Heinemann, 1987.

Books by Anthony Burgess

A Clockwork Orange: A Play with Music Based on His Novella of the Same Name. London: Hutchinson, 1987.

They Wrote in English. London: Hutchinson, 1988.

Any Old Iron. New York: Random House, 1989; London: Hutchinson, 1989.

The Devil's Mode and Other Stories. New York: Random House, 1989; London: Hutchinson, 1989.

You've Had Your Time: Being the Second Part of the Confessions of Anthony Burgess. London: Heinemann, 1990; New York: Weidenfeld & Nicholson, 1991.

Mozart and the Wolf Gang. London: Hutchinson, 1991; republished as *On Mozart: A Paean for Wolfgang.* New York: Ticknor & Fields, 1991.

A Mouthful of Air: Languages, Languages—Especially English. London: Hutchinson, 1992; republished as *A Mouthful of Air: Language and Languages—Especially English.* New York: Morrow, 1993.

A Dead Man in Deptford. London: Hutchinson, 1993; New York: Carroll & Graf, 1995.

Byrne. London: Hutchinson, 1995; New York: Carroll & Graf, 1997.

The Complete Enderby: Inside Mr. Enderby, Enderby Outside, The Clockwork Testament, Enderby's Dark Lady. New York: Carroll & Graf, 1996.

One Man's Chorus: The Uncollected Writings. Ed. Ben Forkner. New York: Carroll & Graf, 1998.

Contents

Introduction

Often collections of conversations with writers have been justified by the writer's not yet having been the subject of a biography. Anthony Burgess has been blessed, and cursed, by having been the subject of *two* biographies in recent years. The first—Roger Lewis's simplistic and hostile 2002 biography—has been rapidly supplanted by Andrew Biswell's 2005 biography. Biswell's title, *The Real Life of Anthony Burgess*, gives the impression (later confirmed by the book itself) that this biography is in some measure a response to Lewis's book, or more precisely a corrective to its predecessor's careless research and naive willingness to take Burgess at his word, in his memoirs as well as in the many interviews he participated in over the decades. Unlike Lewis, Biswell is much more sensitive to the almost self-conscious myth-making of a writer such as Burgess, fashioning a persona in his conversations with others and in his memoirs, a kind of extended monologue to his readers. Accordingly, the conversations in this collection demonstrate performances of Burgess in support of a self-image that readers should approach with some caution. Taken as a whole, the conversations reveal the creative factor in memory, particularly in a highly imaginative writer such as Burgess; in addition, they represent an effort to put forward a projection of how he would have his audience "read" him.

Burgess's self-image is grounded, of course, in biography. As he notes on several occasions, he lost his mother and his sister to the influenza pandemic following World War I. The Irish stepmother who came into his young life apparently stinted in her affection for her husband's child. In the same vein, his heavy-drinking father—a tobacconist as well as a piano player whose music accompanied silent films—apparently had little time for his son, not even enough to show the young Burgess where to find C on the piano keyboard. And yet Burgess includes these memories of his childhood *not* to elicit his listener or reader's sympathy but to establish the early beginnings of his fierce sense of self-reliance. Similarly, he emphasizes that he was not privileged to attend a grammar school for the children of those wealthy enough to afford its tuition, just as he would later graduate from a "red-brick" university—Manchester—rather than Oxford or Cambridge, either of which might have allowed him to develop more quickly as a composer of music (his first career aspiration) or as the writer (his second choice) he was to become when he discovered in middle age that he could pay his bills more comfortably as a writer than as a teacher in a secondary school.

Readers will also find in the conversations to follow various renditions of how he got back to England from Brunei, where he had been teaching. As he retells the "story" over the years, Burgess gradually discloses that what happened was a good deal more complicated than he had at first rendered it. He reveals that both he and his wife were very heavy drinkers, consuming a case of gin per week, and she had a penchant for being outspoken. Once during a visit, Queen Elizabeth's husband, the Duke of Edinburgh, apparently asked Mrs. Burgess a conventionally inane question to which she responded with a remark so "obscene," as Burgess terms it, that he would not repeat it on the air. The authorities wanted him out badly enough to send him back to London for the treatment of a possible brain tumor, presumably at the government's expense. There he was handed the "death sentence" of having only a year to live, a prognosis that produced not depression and despair but an outburst of creative energy. In an effort to increase his potential widow's meager legacy, he set himself the task of writing ten novels, a goal he failed to achieve, having to settle for the manuscripts of "only" five and a half. In his later years Burgess reveals that he was overwhelmed by the drudgery of teaching, and instead of falling to the floor of the classroom he may have simply lain down, essentially saying to the authorities, I'm ill; take care of me. He may well have concocted this elaborate ruse to get back to England and the imaginative construct of having only a "year to live" to motivate himself to become a full-time writer, having already proved to himself that he could write in those long, steamy afternoons while other Europeans were having their siestas.

And a "full-time writer" he certainly became. Burgess was an embarrassingly productive writer, but the embarrassment was not his. It was, one suspects, the embarrassment of the academic world and perhaps his larger readership whose assumption it has been that anyone who produced as much as Burgess could not be a "good" writer. (One thinks in this regard of the "plight" of Joyce Carol Oates, who continues to produce under the threat that her "public" has already condemned her to the realm of the "prolific.") The embarrassment may also be shared by those writers who can unpack a closet full of justifications for not producing more than they do; some even give the impression of holding back perhaps to demonstrate that each new novel is a gem that has taken years to craft. Burgess might let himself off by claiming, I just love to write; he confesses, however, that, if anything, he is a lazy writer, who had to assign himself the task of writing 1,000 words a day, seven days a week and nearly all of the 365 days of the year. Writers write, and in this context when they are not writing, they essentially have no being.

Clearly this attitude of Burgess that he was a "professional writer" runs against the grain of modernist enshrinement of literature as Art, a kind of humanist replacement for religion. It is virtually impossible to conceive of a supreme modernist such as W. B. Yeats saying, Writing is a job like carpentry. Burgess admired the work of James Joyce, but he would hardly see himself investing eighteen years of his life writing a *Finnegans Wake*, a work that in the end alienated even Joyce's supporters such as T. S. Eliot and Ezra Pound. Burgess was happy to label his work "entertainments," not Art. In addition, Burgess was a highly imaginative writer, who undoubtedly went to his grave over a dozen years ago with scores of ideas for novels and screenplays he never got to write. In contrast, one thinks of writers like Joyce and Woolf in the thirties, who may well have sensed their entrapment in the modernist strategy of forcing each new work to go beyond its predecessor and eventually writing themselves out of a job.

If anything, Burgess tended to turn the overt or implicit claim that he was too "prolific" back on his accusers with the reminder that he never benefitted from the generous support system of those who have written in the groves of academe and have not had to depend entirely upon the income from their writing to survive. As Burgess confesses to Don Swaim, he suffered from the "sin" of envy in observing how academic positions, grants, large advances on royalties, etc., made it possible for at least some American writers to write less than he was forced to—and what's more, *worry* less about paying the bills. Burgess goes so far as to admit that he considered becoming an "American writer," but he felt he probably had waited too long to make the move. Not that he would have felt any sense of disloyalty to the England of his early life.

Indeed, it is no coincidence that Burgess published a biography of D. H. Lawrence, *Flame into Being*, in 1985 for the centenary of his literary father's birth. Asked about the biography, Burgess made his kinship with Lawrence very clear. Both were outsiders in the England of their birth and younger lives. Lawrence was born near Nottingham; Burgess, in Manchester. Neither family had the resources to support a public-school education so that neither writer benefitted from the lifetime connections of an Oxbridge education. Both were fiercely independent, provocative, prone to express ideas that were guaranteed to position them outside the Establishment. The decision of Burgess to leave England, first by taking a teaching job in Malaysia, and later by moving to the Mediterranean as an independent writer, was probably influenced by Lawrence's abandonment of his native land as a nation beyond rescue from itself. As Burgess also notes in the way of comparison, Lawrence married a German baroness, while he married an Italian contessa.

Another facet of his career that these conversations highlight is the central issue of *A Clockwork Orange*. Indeed, those who are for one reason or another unfamiliar with the depth and range of his creative output are likely to ask of Anthony Burgess, What has he written besides *A Clockwork Orange*? As he indicates again and again, the fame, or more accurately the *notoriety*, of Stanley Kubrick's film adaptation of a short novel Burgess continued to dismiss as one of his least significant accomplishments made him eventually regret ever having published *A Clockwork Orange* because it became his best-known work. Burgess considered *A Clockwork Orange* a "jeu de spleen," a slight work in response to the nightmare that essentially destroyed his wife's health and the Burgess marriage. Like the story of how he was "sentenced" to a year to live, the story of his first wife's tragedy comes down to us from Burgess in differing versions. In any case, during the Second World War his wife was apparently mugged by four American G.I. deserters who caused her to miscarry, not through any sexual assault but in the attempt to wrest her wedding ring from her finger. Clearly *A Clockwork Orange* is more than a mere expression of the author's rage against his wife's attackers; indeed, it might be argued that the presence in that novel of a writer who is working on the manuscript of a work he will also one day publish as *A Clockwork Orange* cannot be dismissed as merely an early expression of postmodernist self-reflexivity, any more than it can be ignored that the writer F. Alexander and the leader of the gang of four, who rape his wife as he is forced to watch, is "another Alex."

Stanley Kubrick's decision to base his film on the truncated American edition of *A Clockwork Orange*, rather than the English edition in which Alex matures and grows bored with violence, had very large repercussions on Burgess's reputation and creative productivity. The notoriety of having written the novel that led to the Kubrick film and to Arthur Bremer's attempted

assassination of George Wallace during the campaign for the 1972 Repub-
lican presidential nomination impelled Burgess into a web of intertextuality,
as he wrote a number of novels with the writer Enderby suffering from his
creator's frustration and anger at becoming notorious by association. That
notoriety also became a burden under which Burgess was to labor as a writer
in the later (and far larger) part of his career. When he produced one of his
largest, later novels—*Earthly Powers*—he had to know that many potential
readers were expecting *A Clockwork Orange* redux, and it was his (in)famous
novel that many interviewers really wanted to talk about. In a very clear sense,
he suffered the fate of Gustav Holst, who according to legend grew to hate
The Planets because his public refused to pay attention to any of his other
compositions.

One other facet of Burgess's career often overshadowed by the *cause scan-
dale* resulting from Kubrick's film of *A Clockwork Orange* is that Burgess had
a passionate interest in education. It is worth noting that after spending six
years in the British Army in World War II he began his professional career not
as either a composer of music or as a writer but as a teacher. Reports of his
former students and colleagues indicate that he cared deeply about teaching.
After all, it was education that made it possible for the young Burgess to become a teacher and eventually a writer, and the interviews indicate his aware-
ness of how he might have been restricted to the opportunities of his lower-
middle-class origins, had it not been for his education. He was a brilliant
lecturer, as demonstrated by his visit to the University of North Carolina at
Chapel Hill, where in a single day he presented five lectures on writers ranging from Chaucer to Joyce, astounding faculty and students alike with his
knowledge and dramatic style of performing that knowledge. Perhaps the
sorest test of his teaching experience was the one-year appointment at City
College in New York, where he faced a student population that was often un-
motivated, unruly, and downright cruel to this alien with whose writing they
were unsympathetic, if they were even familiar with what he had written. His
colleague Joseph Heller remembered him thus: "His desire to teach, to bring
about a positive change in what were sometimes rather deranged minds, ex-
ceeded by far his need for self-preservation. He made himself available to
them, and the students made enormous demands on his time, excessively
so, but then wasted his time because they had only come to him for another
anti-establishment raving session. I admired the way Burgess could take even
the most hostile of these students seriously. He knew and remembered their

names. He gave serious thought to even their most absurd statements" (qtd. by Biswell 349–50). Heller goes on to say: "I have to say that in all my life, even at its most compassionate moments, I have not even come close to reaching that enormous inner generosity that characterized Anthony Burgess" (qtd. by Biswell 350).

In addition, as readers will note in the later conversations in this collection, Burgess became increasingly outspoken in expressing views that a twenty-first-century audience might find "politically incorrect." Were Burgess allowed the opportunity to respond, he might venture the opinion that much of contemporary society has moved so many views into the column of those it considers not "correct" to acknowledge, much less actually espouse, that we run the risk of becoming a monolithic culture in which there is no longer very much to talk about, once we have exhausted the doctrinaire responses to the "bad old days," now blissfully in the past. Whether we always agree with Burgess, we have to concede that his was a lively and energetic intellect and that he cared deeply about contemporary issues. Furthermore, he seems to have believed that simply shutting out issues and ideas we refuse to confront, reminiscent of the nineteenth century which often conspired not to face its "social problems," never makes anything go away.

Also unlike a number of other later twentieth-century writers Burgess seems never to have refused the request for an interview. Indeed, the fact that he granted dozens of them speaks to his obvious enjoyment in the contemporary "genre" of the literary conversation—if by that term we understand that the interviewer is reasonably well versed in the author's work and avoids the celebrity interview that often begins with the interviewer asserting something such as, I haven't read any of your work but I would like to ask you. . . . Burgess welcomed the opportunity to talk about his work as well as to raise issues he had to know would be provocative. Indeed, one suspects that the Burgess conversations often contain extreme versions of his views and ideas to unsettle his listeners or readers, to prod them into thinking, or at least into defending their own views against comments with which he may have anticipated his audience would disagree.

This collection brings together a full dozen Burgess conversations that appeared in a startling range of venues from famous and accessible literary journals such as *Paris Review* to journals such as the *Fabula* and *Delaware Literary Review*, defunct for many years. The collection begins with the Thomas Churchill conversation, appearing in January of the fateful year 1971, the year in which the Kubrick film of *A Clockwork Orange* was to change Burgess's life. The Churchill conversation is typical of the best of the interviews: although Churchill asks questions about the novel, there is none of the obsessiveness evident in the "girlie" magazine interviews after the film appeared. Similarly, the Riemer conversation, appearing in of all places the *National Elementary Principal*, allows Burgess to talk about American education in his characteristically provocative and insightful manner. The conversation supports the view that Burgess was deeply concerned about education throughout his life, and in this case he demonstrates a father's concern with the education of his young son.

The next group continues to demonstrate the range and diversity of these conversations. The first, John Cullinan's interview with Burgess for *The Paris Review*, is important because being interviewed for that magazine (and having the interview reprinted in the George Plimpton volumes of *Paris Review* interviews, *Writers at Work*) certifies that Burgess had achieved a position of significance in contemporary letters. As Cullinan indicates in the headnote, Burgess had spent a grueling day of visiting classes at the University of Wisconsin and giving readings, but he never stinted on his willingness to be questioned at length in the interview. Similarly, Charles T. Bunting's interview for *Studies in the Novel* in 1973 demonstrates Burgess's prominence on the literary scene, in part due to the Kubrick film. Like Cullinan, Bunting has interests in Burgess's work far beyond *A Clockwork Orange*. The brevity of yet another 1973 conversation—the Reilly interview originally appearing in the *Delaware Literary Review*—highlights two salient features of the others: the remarkable length of most of these conversations and the substantiality of Burgess's responses to each of the questions. Unlike many other writers who disdain the interview as a contemporary genre and often indicate their reluctance to participate by offering very brief responses, Burgess clearly enjoyed talking about his work. He even discusses work-in-progress—as, for example, *MF* with Reilly—rather than claiming superstitiousness about unfinished works as some other writers have done.

The next interviews move into the latter "half" of Burgess's career. The appearance of the Murray and Coale conversations in the *Iowa Review* and *Modern Fiction Studies*, respectively, offers further evidence of Burgess's substantial position in contemporary literature. The Coale conversation was based on lengthy interviews, serving as background for Coale's book, one of the earliest and most important critical appraisals of Burgess's writing. This

lengthy conversation provides a panoply of comments on other writers—
ranging from Gerard Manley Hopkins to William Burroughs—and issues as diverse as his Roman Catholic background and his fascination with
Buckminster Fuller, who said to him in a Danish taxi, "The universe has no
nouns. It only has verbs!"

The last interviews in this collection appeared in a five-year period at the
end of Burgess's life. They include the Joannan interview, appearing in a
little-known and short-lived French journal, *Fabula*, with its further demonstration of Burgess's interest in fiction, from the *Satyricon* to the experimentation of Nathalie Sarraute and Alain Robbe-Grillet, with Burgess's arguing
for the "big" novel of traditional writers like Balzac, Dickens, and Tolstoy as
well as modern writers such as Norman Mailer and presumably himself in his
then-recent novel *Earthly Powers*. This group also includes his conversation
with Rosemary Hartill, perhaps the most extensive revelation of his religious
views, as he neared seventy and the reality of death. It also includes Pierre
Assouline's brief interview which originally appeared in *L'Express*. Finally,
this group also includes two conversations printed for the first time. One is
Don Swaim's radio talk with Burgess, one of hundreds of literary interviews
with leading writers Swaim has conducted over the past decades. The other is
with the British media celebrity Sir Jeremy Isaacs, transcribed from his *Face
to Face* program, televised by BBC on 21 March 1989. Once again, these two
conversations reveal an author who clearly loved to talk about himself, his
writing, and the contemporary scene, one of those writers likely to tire out
the interviewer before they tire themselves.

The interviews appear here roughly in the order in which they were conducted or published/aired. Such a generally chronological order allows readers to observe the changes as well as the continuities of the author's views and
interests. The conversations appear "complete," allowing for repetitions of
comments from one conversation to another. As Andrew Biswell, his biogra-
pher points out, Burgess as storyteller often changed his rendition of the stories that make up his memories of his own personal history. As a whole, the
conversations comprise a sort of "biography" of this author's concerns and attitudes, changing, yet often surprisingly consistent.

EGI
MCI

Chronology

1917	John Burgess Wilson is born in at 91 Carisbrook Street, Manchester, England, on 25 February, son of Elizabeth Burgess Wilson and John Wilson.
1918	In November Elizabeth Burgess Wilson and daughter Muriel Wilson die in the influenza pandemic of 1917–1919, responsible for the deaths of at least 20,000,000 (perhaps as many as 50,000,000) worldwide.
1922	John Wilson marries Margaret Byrne Dwyer, owner of the Golden Eagle public house into which AB and his father move.
1923	AB begins his education at Bishop Bilsborrow Memorial School.
1928	AB wins a scholarship to Xaverian College, a selective grammar school for Roman Catholic boys.
1935	AB completes the work for his Matriculation Certificate at Xaverian College and begins his studies at Victoria University of Manchester with a concentration in literature. His first choice, music, is foreclosed to him because he lacked physics in his preparation for university. He is an active participant in the university theater productions and frequent contributor to university literary magazine.
1938	AB begins his courtship of his first wife, Llewela Jones, born in Tredegar, Wales, in 1920.
1940	AB receives his BA (Hons) from Manchester University. He begins his service in the British Armed Forces in the Entertainments Section of the 54th Division of the Royal Army Medical Corps.
1942	AB and Lynne (Llewela) marry in Bournemouth, England, on 28 January, while he is on leave.
1943	AB transfers into the Army Education Corps in Gibraltar, where he gave lectures to new recruits on "The British Way and Purpose." He also works as the film critic on the *Gibraltar Chronicle*.
1944	In April AB receives the news that his wife Lynne has been attacked

during the blackout and so brutally beaten that she has miscarried the child with which she was pregnant. Perpetual menstruation produces anaemia, and she is encouraged by physicians to drink pints of Guinness ale, leading to alcoholism.

1946   After six years of military service, AB is finally demobilized. In August he begins teaching for the Central Council for Adult Education in His Majesty's Forces, his students being members of the Royal Army Education Corps.

1948   AB accepts a second teaching post as a lecturer in Speech and Drama at Bamber Bridge Emergency Training College, where he helps to train war veterans to become schoolteachers. From 1948–50 he directs six plays at the College, ranging from T. S. Eliot's *Murder in the Cathedral* to Shakespeare's *Hamlet*, the latter using male actors, as in Shakespeare's time, since the student body at the College was all male.

1949   AB begins to draft his first extensive effort in fiction, based on his wartime experiences on Gibraltar, published in 1965 as *A Vision of Battlements.*

1952   AB directs a production of Sean O'Casey's *Juno and the Paycock* for the Adderbury Drama Group and writes his first original play, *The Eve of St. Venus.* Heinemann rejects the manuscript of his novel *A Vision of Battlements.*

1954   AB's *The Worm and the Ring,* withdrawn from bookshelves after the publisher admits it contains libelous material. He and his wife sail to Malaya, where he begins teaching at the Malay College in Kuala Kangsar. He begins writing the three novels he publishes before he returns to England five years later.

1955   AB takes a teaching post in the Malayan Teachers' Training College at Kota Bharu, Kelantan.

1956   Heinemann brings out *Time for a Tiger,* with the *nom de plume* "Anthony Burgess," Anthony being the name he assumed at his first communion and Burgess being his mother's maiden name.

1957   In addition to writing fiction, AB continues to compose music, including his "Malayan Symphony," which marked Malaya's independence. With the expiration of his three-year teaching contract with the Colonial Office, AB and his wife Lynne return to England.

1958   In January AB and Lynne fly back to Asia, where AB begins teaching at the Sultan Omar Ali Saifuddin College in Brunei Town. Heinemann brings out *The Enemy in the Blanket*. AB publishes *English Literature: A Survey for Students*, the only book to ever appear under his legal name, John Burgess Wilson.

1959   Heinemann brings out *Beds in the East*, the third novel in the Malayan trilogy. In September AB's teaching career ends when he falls to the classroom floor and refuses to move. He is flown to London, where he is diagnosed as having a possible brain tumor and given a year to live.

1959–60 In an effort, he says, to enhance Lynne's legacy he drafts five and a half novels during the year he was granted by his doctors. Apparently AB did not believe in the "death sentence" passed down on him by the medical profession. Among the novels written in the "terminal year" are *The Doctor Is Sick* (1960), based on his two months in the hospital, *The Right to an Answer* (1960), *Inside Mr. Enderby* (1963), and *One Hand Clapping* (1961), published under the *nom de plume* Joseph Kell.

1961   W. W. Norton begins to publish AB's novels with *The Right to an Answer*. In the summer, AB and his wife travel to Leningrad, U.S.S.R. AB teaches himself Russian. Before he leaves England he writes sixty pages of what will be published the next year as *A Clockwork Orange*. The manuscript is completed by year's end.

1962   Heinemann brings out *A Clockwork Orange*; the Norton edition appears the next year, minus the last (twenty-first) chapter. Heinemann also publishes *The Wanting Seed*.

1963   AB publishes *Honey for the Bears*, based on his trip to Leningrad, with Heinemann, which also brings out his *Inside Mr. Enderby*, under the name Joseph Kell. The stratagem of publishing under another *nom de plume* was the publisher's attempt to conceal the fact that AB was publishing six novels in two years. AB later regrets acceding to the stratagem. AB loses his job reviewing books for the *Yorkshire Post* when the newspaper realizes it has published AB's review of his own novel. AB and Lynne travel to Tangier, Morocco, in March, meet William Burroughs, and gather background material for *Enderby Outside*. AB returns in November and in October 1966. AB meets Liliana Macellari Johnson, born 25 September 1929 in Italy. Their affair begins in December; on 9 August 1964, their son Paolo Andrea is born. Later he takes the name Andrew Burgess Wilson.

1964   Heinemann and Norton bring out *Nothing Like the Sun: A Story of Shakespeare's Life* to commemorate the four hundredth anniversary of the poet's birth. In 1967 he writes the film script for a Hollywood musical called "The Bawdy Bard," which was never filmed. Jonathan Cape publishes AB's biography *Shakespeare* in 1970.

1965   *A Vision of Battlements*, the first novel of AB, finally appears, along with *Here Comes Everybody: An Introduction to James Joyce for the Ordinary Reader*, published by Faber and Faber in the U.K. and Norton in the U.S. as *ReJoyce*. AB continues his work on Joyce in 1973 with *Joysprick: An Introduction to the Language of James Joyce*, published in the U.K. by Deutsch and by Harcourt Brace Jovanovich in the U.S. two years later.

1966   AB publishes his thriller *Tremor of Intent* with Heinemann and Norton.

1968   Lynne dies 20 March. AB and Liliana marry on 9 September. They move to Malta in November.

1969   In January AB's agent Deborah Rogers informs him that two film producers have bought the rights to *A Clockwork Orange* and will pay him $25,000 to write the film script. The script is not used and disappears until it is discovered in the Burgess house in Bracciano, Italy, in 2004.

1970-71   AB, Liana (Liliana), and Paolo Andrea move to Bracciano, just north of Rome. There AB completes the manuscript of *MF*, after a lapse of three years while he was writing film scripts and other texts, rather than novels. In 1971 his work ranged from writing the music and libretto for a production of Joyce's *Ulysses* to completing a new translation of *Oedipus Rex*, commissioned by Michael Langham of the Tyrone Guthrie Theater in Minneapolis. Stanley Kubrick begins work on a film adaptation of *A Clockwork Orange*. AB's agent Deborah Rogers apprised him in a letter that Kubrick was aware of the two versions of the novel and was seeking the author's permission to use the American edition, omitting the last chapter. The Kubrick film opens in New York on 1 December 1971 to a storm of hostile response, of which AB was ultimately the object.

1972-73   AB and his family are in New York where he holds a one-year position at City College. Some of his experience provides material for *The Clockwork Testament; or, Enderby's End*, published by Hart-Davis, MacGibbon in London (1974) and Knopf in New York (1975).

1973   AB completes a new verse translation of Edmund Rostand's *Cyrano de Bergerac* for a theatrical production and a musical, both directed by

Michael Langham. Christopher Plummer wins a Tony for his performance as Cyrano.

1974   AB publishes *Napoleon Symphony* in London with Cape and in New York with Knopf. French and Italian translations follow soon after. AB and his family move to Monaco to avoid threats of Paolo Andrea's kidnapping and the burden of income taxes in both the U.K. and Italy.

1980   *Earthly Powers*, arguably his last and perhaps most important novel, is published by Simon & Schuster in New York and Hutchinson in London.

1984   *Enderby's Dark Lady; or, No End to Enderby*, the last novel of the Enderby quartet, is published in New York by McGraw-Hill, the next year in London by Abacus.

1985   *Flame into Being: The Life and Work of D. H. Lawrence* is brought out by Heinemann in London and Arbor House in New York.

1987   AB publishes the first volume of his memoirs, *Little Wilson and Big God: Being the First Part of the Confessions of Anthony Burgess* (Heinemann, London, and Weidenfeld & Nicholson, New York. The second volume, *You've Had Your Time: Being the Second Part of the Confessions of Anthony Burgess* (Heinemann, 1990, and Weidenfeld & Nicholson, 1991) follows. William Boyd considers them among the author's best works of fiction.

1992   On 8 October AB receives the report from Sloane-Kettering that he is suffering from lung cancer.

1993   On 22 November AB dies in London.

Conversations with Anthony Burgess

Going on Writing till Ninety or One Hundred

Thomas Churchill/1971

From the *Malahat Review* (January 1971). Reprinted by permission of Thomas Churchill.

Churchill: You've said you're leaving for Malta to start "a new life." Would you expand?

Burgess: It's a multiple thing, really; my wife died this year in March, and I'm married again and it seems, you know, that one had to break with the past pretty well, so I'm making the break pretty absolute. I've changed both of my publishers. I hope to have a new domestic language. I've a child now and I thought it best to have a new locale. But there are other factors as well; that is, the main factor is the position of authors financially in this country. There is the tax problem—authors don't have much, as you know, and occasionally they get a windfall, and I seem to be having such a windfall this year with a couple of film scripts. The money you get from this kind of break is regarded by the tax authorities as just an ordinary year's income and it's taxed accordingly, and you lose nearly all of it in surtax and the like. At the same time I've had to pay £7,000 in death duties on my wife's estate, and I find that the only way I can sort out the financial tangle and free myself from it is to work hard at journalism in order to pay taxes . . . then get out to a country where the tax situation is very favorable to expatriates. You see, preferably we'd go to Italy, but there are various problems there. One can't just export sterling so we thought we'd go to a half-way house, sterling area, Malta, Mediterranean climate, fifty minutes from Naples by air, breathe for a little while, write a bit, see how things go.

Churchill: When you say that journalism's getting you down, what do you mean exactly?

Burgess: It isn't that one *has* to do journalism, but if somebody rings up and says, "Look, will you review such and such a book for us," you want to see the book, so you say yes and you probably spend too much time writing about it for too little money and in consequence you're neglecting your own work. I think a good example is the *Times Literary Supplement*, which pays practically nothing. You can, in fact, spend a fortnight or even a month writing a learned article on linguistics, say, and get at the end of that something in the nature of £20. You don't like saying no, because you're friendly with the editor and you feel it's a duty to write for *TLS* and do the thing, but if you're away from the telephone, well, if you're away from London. . . . Anyway, you're not tempted quite as much to fritter time away by writing journalism, that's the real reason. Look, I enjoy journalism, anybody does; you see the results immediately, you've got an immediate audience instead of having to wait for your audience as you do if you're writing a book, and you get a bit of money coming in and you can see more clearly how you're paying the bills. But it's not a good position for the serious novelist to be in. One has to get away to a place where the tax situation is easier and you can regard novel writing as a primary job.

Churchill: But you do enjoy writing criticism.
Burgess: I do, I do, indeed, I enjoy it. That's part of the trouble.

Churchill: I wondered about that. I liked the book *The Novel Now*; in fact, I find it very useful.
Burgess: It's only meant to be a useful book; it's not a deep book. It's useful for students. It's got a very British bias, of course. I'll do a revised version of it I hope soon, you know, with extra chapters dealing more fully with some of our own people, like Margaret Drabble, then Barth and Styron, whom I haven't touched.

Churchill: I thought you had mentioned Styron.
Burgess: I mentioned Styron very briefly, but not in proportion to his obvious importance, at least to Americans. I don't think he goes down all that well here. I find it very hard to get on with him, but this is a failing in myself, not in him.

Churchill: The new book—*The Confessions of Nat Turner*—is getting very mixed reactions.
Burgess: Sold well, sold very well.

Churchill: Yes, it sold well, but the blacks, black reviewers and others as well, weren't all that satisfied with it.
Burgess: What were they objecting to—Uncle Tomism, that sort of thing?

Churchill: Yes. . . . You said something about Keith Waterhouse and Yorkshire before we went on tape, and your own country. I wanted to ask you if the sense of place is very important to you as a novelist.

Burgess: In a way it is. I was born in Manchester, brought up there. My back-ground is Lancashire Catholic, you see, but like many people I left my home town to join the Army when the war started, and after six years abroad you tend to lose your affiliation, lose your roots, and when I came back to England I tended to be nomadic and just get a job where I could. I went abroad to Malaya and came back and tended naturally to gravitate towards the south, I suppose, near London where things seemed to be going on; but I'm still a Lancashire man, and what I want to write someday is a novel about Manchester. Very much a regional novel. I don't see myself as a regional novelist now, but I could very quickly become that, given time. I like the idea of a regional novel if the tone of the novel breathes a kind of substitute for the metropolitan. The pride in the place as small and culture-less and dialect-speaking, I think, is misplaced. If you can present a town like Manchester or Leeds as being a sort of substitute for London where things go on and culture occurs, and the dialect is a living, intellectual force, then you've got something valuable. I don't think this has been done here yet. It was done only with one writer who's not highly regarded, that's Howard Spring. He wrote a book called *Shabby Tiger*, which was set in Manchester.

Churchill: Keith Waterhouse seemed very insistent that *Billy Liar* was a regional, not a "universal" novel.

Burgess: 'Tis a regional novel. It's typical of the young man brought up in the provinces, living in the provinces, that he should try and make a bigger man of himself than he is by indulging in fantasies and by lying.

The regional novel I want to write is really set in Manchester University on a particular day—not a *Ulysses* type novel but a novel called . . . "Rag Day." I sup-pose you have it in America, too. Once a year we used to—on Shrove Tuesday, in fact—we used to go out in the streets on wagons. Each wagon represented a tab-leau of some kind, comic tableau. We'd go around collecting money for the hos-pitals, before they were nationalized, and this was a very special day. The town and the gown got together, there was drunkenness and fornication, this, that and the other. Of course, the following day was Ash Wednesday—absolutely flat—and I wanted to get something of this in a novel if I could, a big comic novel about Manchester.

Churchill: Sounds good. OK, but as far as Malta being a region for exploration—you're going there strictly because you know it's going to work. That is, to allow you a kind of freedom you haven't had lately.

Burgess: Well, we're learning Maltese. It's possible something may emerge about the country. I hope so, anyway.

Churchill: Do you write with a specific genre in mind? Do you know you're writing a comic novel, a futuristic novel?
Burgess: Not normally. No, when I first began to write fiction I didn't think I was a comic writer, I thought I was a serious writer. I was surprised when the first novel I wrote was regarded as a funny novel. It came as quite a shock, and I had another look at it and I saw that it was in fact comic; and I've never deliberately sat down since to write a funny novel, but if I think of working on a plot seriously, comedy breaks in. I exploit coincidence and exaggeration and that sort of thing. This is not what I intended.

Churchill: So writing comedy must come very natural?
Burgess: That's obviously the way one *is*. You see it's as if the clown wanted to play Hamlet. I'm a natural clown, I suppose, in writing, and one has to accept that; I can't do anything about it. I have written one or two novels which are not specifically funny. I wrote a study of Shakespeare which was not intended to be funny, but some people regard it as such. Oh, Peter Hall, who runs the National Theatre—Shakespeare Theatre, anyway—he never laughed so much in his life. I was gratified, but this was not my intention.

Churchill: Is this the novel *Nothing Like the Sun*?
Burgess: Yes.

Churchill: I just read the novel. I like it very much. I wanted to ask you . . .
Burgess: It didn't make you laugh, though, did it? It was not intended to.

Churchill: Maybe not chuckle-ha-ha; of course, I have my own notion of what comedy should be. It's as much what makes you feel good as laugh.
Burgess: Yes, of course. Well, I don't mean essentially laugh, but I laugh at Evelyn Waugh, for instance; and I feel if one is going to write comic novels one should evoke some sort of physical response. I'm happy if people do laugh aloud. I'm very happy about it for a very childish reason—obviously they're happy. Laughter is obviously the indication of happiness. I've just received a letter from New York saying that somebody laughed at the new novel I've written. I'm very pleased, very pleased indeed. They obviously feel better; it's therapeutic.

Churchill: What is the newest novel?
Burgess: Well, it's called *Enderby*, it's a big novel. In America it's one book; this was always the intention, to make *Enderby Inside* and *Outside* a single book on the life of a poet—two angles—and I wanted this done in England, but for various reasons, mostly financial, I had to publish the first part as a single entity and wait

some years before publishing the second part. But now in the States I've got the thing in a single volume called *Enderby*, which is what I always wanted.

Churchill: This question grows out of the remark about genre. Did *A Clockwork Orange* begin as a futuristic novel or had you other purposes in mind?
Burgess: No, it didn't begin as a futuristic novel at all. It began as a novel about the present day. The first third of it—I've lost it somewhere, had it in typeset till recently—was written in British teenage slang of the present day. But while I was writing I began to feel, well, look, this slang is already getting out of date while I write it. Give it a year between now and publication and it will be totally out of date or a good deal of it will be.

Churchill: Like those dictionaries of slang.
Burgess: Yes, indeed. Well, while we're on that, I was commissioned by Penguin Books to write a dictionary of slang, but I've done A and B and find that a good deal of A and B is out of date or has to be added to, and I could envisage the future as being totally tied up with such a dictionary. So, I'm dropping the whole project. Leave it to Eric Partridge. Well, what happened was this, though, about *A Clockwork Orange*: I dropped it and then I went to Russia for a trip. I went to Leningrad and discovered that they had these *stiljagi* there, they had teenage riots and gangs, cult of violence, so it struck me that if I could combine East and West in a single teenage persona, it would be appropriate to use a composite dialect that is Russian and English. So I did this and very tentatively with some fear, knowing that at least it would not be out of date as it didn't exist, and then I found that people started using the dialect in this country anyway. Ah, you know, used various terms like "yarbels" or something. It's already out of date, so the novel must seem dated to many people by now.

Churchill: Why use Nadsat as a narrative vehicle?
Burgess: It could have been anything. I could have chosen Maltese, for that matter. What I tried to do was to present a state which, of course, had to become a future state because of the dialect, which was neither West nor East. I think it comes up mostly West.

Churchill: Did you have a sense that you were taking a risk in using a language that had to be glossed?
Burgess: No, I didn't think so. I've taught languages in the past, and I know one way of doing it is to frighten the reader at first with a spate of new words, but then gradually to break it down and introduce other new words, gradually, and I

don't think there was any need for a glossary. In America a glossary was provided, but I think it was misguided. A good deal of the glossary was wrong, anyway. I was not consulted.

Churchill: It looks like a kind of joke, like the notes at the end of *The Waste Land.*
Burgess: Yes, which are joking, really. I mean they're no use to anybody at all.

Churchill: Can we stay with *A Clockwork Orange* for awhile?
Burgess: Well, I've written other books. I've written twenty other books, and this was very much a *jeu de spleen* when I wrote it, at least it was intended to be. I had difficulty in publishing it at first. But the theme is true, the central theme is one that is very important, to me anyway. The idea of free will. This is not just half-baked existentialism, it's an old Catholic theme. Choice, choice is all that matters, and to impose the good is evil, to *act* evil is better than to have good imposed.

Churchill: You pick up that idea in *The Wanting Seed*, history broken down to gusphase, interphase, telephase and two primary "rhythms," the Augustinian and Pelagian.
Burgess: Yes, I do. Again it's a very important theme.

Churchill: I tend to think of those two novels as part of a similar creative design.
Burgess: Yes, well, they were written about the same time, I think. No, *Wanting Seed* was written in 1960 when I wrote five novels. That was the year I was supposed to be dying and I was trying to get as much done as I could before I passed out. But I didn't die, as you can see, and *Clockwork Orange* was written in 1961. And I forget what else I wrote in that year (came out in '62, that's right). There was a kind of log jam of novels. This explains why *Inside Mr. Enderby* was held back two years and then came out under a pseudonym, which was stupid, bad publishing, very bad publishing.

Churchill: Have you written many novels under a pseudonym?
Burgess: I only wrote two, I wrote two novels under the name of Joseph Kell; one has not appeared in the States yet, it's called *One Hand Clapping*, and I dare say it will. I want it published in a volume of something else. Yes, that's right, that came out in 1960 and *Inside Mr. Enderby* came out under Joseph Kell. It's stupid, you see, because if you invent a new author it means you have to start promoting a new author, instead of using an author you've already got, and this is bad publishing. The two Joseph Kell books didn't do too terribly well. They didn't get as many reviews as they should have got and so on, and now that the true identity of

the author comes out, it's too late to do anything with them, or with *One Hand Clapping*, anyway, which is not a bad book. It's a good book.

Churchill: You just said that *Enderby* is about the life of the poet. Do you mean this in a literal way?

Burgess: This, I think, is what life for a poet is probably like. Well, it's exaggerated, probably, but it's about the total devotion to craft and the tendency to shut yourself off, and even shut yourself in the smallest room in the house, which is also the remotest. The lavatory being a kind of symbol, not primarily a symbol of purgation, simply the smallest room. The smallest room you need, a room of one's own.

Churchill: It's a very compelling book. I remember laughing out loud, but at other times I was caught up in a much different way.

Burgess: It's a sad book, sad because the state takes over, regards poetry as a disease, in fact (though this hasn't happened, it might well happen), and the poet must be rehabilitated and made a useful citizen. What happens in the second part of the story is that the muse will not be put down. The muse comes back—

Churchill: Yes, and the muse is working counter to the woman, is that right?

Burgess: There's a lot in that, though it's dangerous to work up a symbolism too strictly. But the idea is that the muse isn't quite Graves's White Goddess; it is a *fe*male force, highly capricious. And may well be the inhibitor of normal sexual relations, which explains the irregularity of Enderby's sexual life; but in the film we're making, he achieves fruition. That's the idea—that he actually copulates. In the book he doesn't, he becomes a major poet.

Churchill: What do you think of the idea of making Enderby potent?

Burgess: The idea is all right. It's a good filming idea but goes against the true concept of the novel.

Churchill: Keith Waterhouse said something like that regarding his novel *Jubb*. The thing which distressed him about the anti-hero, as he's been done in the last ten or fifteen years, was that despite the fact that the character seemed to make a balls-up of most of his life, he always makes it in bed, which Waterhouse felt was all wrong.

Burgess: 'Tis wrong, totally wrong. Does he always make it in bed? Yes, he does. He's potent. Waterhouse is right, I think, and *Jubb*'s a very good novel. But authors for some reason are scared of presenting a character who's sexually impotent or sexually incompetent, because they always think it reflects on themselves. I've had this kind of response—"Naturally," I mean, you know, "this is obviously a portrait of Mr. Burgess. He's sexually incompetent, undoubtedly, or he's probably homosexual and won't admit it."

Churchill: This next question I had thought of keeping for the end, and I think it's pretty dodgy but still worth asking. That is, as long as we're on this subject, sex in the novel, there seems to be a curious kind of emphasis on sexual incompetence, particularly on masturbation, in recent fiction. Do you know Philip Roth's new series, "Whacking Off," "The Jewish Blues," and "Civilization and Its Discontents"? These are the first three parts of a new novel [*Portnoy's Complaint*].
Burgess: I met him the other day. I'd heard a lot of talk about this novel, but it hasn't appeared. There's trouble with it, isn't there? There's certainly trouble brewing with it here.

Churchill: You mean because of censorship?
Burgess: Well, it may be easier since *Last Exit to Brooklyn* was done. . . . Oh, Roth's a good writer, very good writer, good man, too. But tell me more about masturbation, what do you mean exactly?

Churchill: It's just that there seems to be a growing emphasis in fiction . . .
Burgess: Oh, in fiction generally. I think masturbation is probably very common among artists. I think that the mere fact of creative excitement tends to generate sexual excitement. It's got to be got out of the way quickly, almost. Almost like a pain.

Churchill: Henry Green has a remark in an interview with Terry Southern that his compulsion to write is sex.
Burgess: There's a whole lot of truth in that, I feel. I know that when I tried to write in a piece of fiction a description of the sexual act, or love-making generally, this excited me so much that I probably had to masturbate. Go to the bathroom, get it out of the way and get on with the job. Otherwise the whole tone of the. . . . This doesn't apply now. My life has changed, my life is different, but it became painful. I found it very hard to present the sexual act directly at all. In fiction I've always had to dress it up or do it symbolically, or intellectually, or anything rather than present the naked reality. People who do that strike me as being genuine exhibitionists. Those who can give you the whole lot—like, I think, Updike—this is genuine exhibitionism, the sort of wife-swapping type of person.

This is probably commoner in America than here. I don't know. . . . The need to demonstrate grows there. I mean, if we're effete, we're effete and to hell with it. But one mustn't do that in America.

Churchill: No, because we've still got that whole Western mystique going, which is a total lie, something we're just beginning to realize now that everyone's getting his head shot off.

Burgess: Well, I noticed this with an American friend of mine. He's a big man, and he's played with Burt Lancaster in films; he's a big fellow, and he had to demonstrate, you see, his potency. It became wearisome, night after night, much as I love the man (love the man dearly), but he had to go to night clubs and he had to pick up a woman, and he had to meet this woman the following night and be told how good he was in bed. And his main aim—I'd just become a widower at that time—was to get me laid, you know. He even paid a woman to do it. Of course, nothing's more off-putting than that, to know you've got a lay in the bank waiting for you. This struck me as very American. I didn't find it unpleasant; I mean, I found it rather charming in a way. It's very different from us here.

Churchill: Do you admire Evelyn Waugh?

Burgess: Greatly, yes, but with reservations. He had horrible areas of conservatism. He hated Joyce, he felt that Joyce went mad to please the Americans. He had these horrible ideas. He said that prose was only good when it could be translated into other languages. It's stupid. Prose is, I think, suspect when it translates too easily.

Churchill: What about Anthony Powell and his *Dance to the Music of Time*?

Burgess: Powell, well, I think there was a time when we'd get people like Lady Ottoline Morrell, who was keen on Lawrence, people who desert their aristocratic station and try to become bohemians. But I don't think that sort of confluence has had a great part to play in English life. Powell's a writer, he's an aristocrat, or he's married to an aristocratic family. Writing was just his means of getting the two worlds together, I think. It's very much a projection of himself. The whole sequence is interesting, the using of time as fluidity, but I worry very much about the ultimate importance of the book, and I must confess I'm probably blind to it. This applies to so many areas in contemporary fiction. This is very much an English sort of thing, the provincial, Catholic, red-brick man thing, which probably most of the writers you speak to will talk about. Probably Amis won't because he was an Oxford man and already had an entree to the world.

Churchill: He got turned off some place, got turned off at Cambridge, didn't he?

Burgess: Well, yes, he went as a director of studies, I think. But Kingsley is probably far less plebian than he pretends to be. You know, he pretends to like a pint of beer. Well, probably he does, but he goes to the pubs far less than he used to. He's been drawn into a very unreal sort of world, where you meet the best people, whoever those are.

Churchill: He's become something of a conservative.

Burgess: Oh, very much so. Big Tory, big Tory. I think this all too frequently happens to left-wing people who suddenly make money . . . happened to John Braine. You make money and, of course, you want to protect your money, and instead of being as I am—God knows what I am, politically—they become violently the other thing. So I've never been a man of the left, I've never been a labor supporter even in my university days. I never had any feeling toward the left. I never belonged to the Socialist party. I always tended toward a vague, vague Toryism, very vague Toryism. Some Jacobitism in it, Catholicism.

Churchill: Were you raised a Catholic?

Burgess: Yes, the whole family was Catholic, right from the beginning. You see, we never had the Reformation. We were cut off, we're what we call old Catholics, in fact.

Churchill: Are you cut off from it now?

Burgess: Yes, I proselytize, but I have to keep that quiet in various areas because— well, I'll tell you, we had a telephone call last night from the Archbishop of Birmingham, who's my cousin, and I have to pretend, you see. "You'll be delighted, George," I said, "that I'm marrying a Roman girl." And he said, "Glory be to God," and all that. I didn't tell him that Liliana is probably a communist, or certainly anti-Christian democrat. Well, a little lying all the time to certain people . . . apparently the lie is not too patent because what I write looks like Catholic writing. I will not allow Catholicism to go over to the converts and I will not allow the Protestants to attack it. That's what it really amounts to. I'm quite prepared to find arguments for the Pope's encyclical, if anybody wanted me to. If anybody said, "Look, could you please write 2,000 words defending the encyclical?" I'd probably do that fairly easily. My tongue would be in my cheek, but I know how to do it. Now people like Greene and Waugh are converts, they're not real Catholics. They're just using Catholicism to further private ends of their own. I think

Greene wanted this, but mainly he wanted evil, and Waugh did it because he wanted an endless aristocracy.

Churchill: He does go on about it. *Brideshead* seems all wrong to me because of it.
Burgess: I like *Brideshead*, it's one of my favorite books. I know I shouldn't like it, I know I should hate it, but tears always come to my eyes when I read the final bit about making the sign of the cross on his [Marchmain's] death bed. "Glory be to God," all that, "another soul is saved."

Liliana probably got it more than any of us being born Italian, being a daughter of the Church, but with me . . . I go mad at the various changes of the Church very much from the Catholic angle. I hate this ecumenical business and I hate the use of liturgical changes and the use of the vernacular. I loathe it but who am I to loathe it? I've no real stake in the Church at all now.

Churchill: Does Catholicism get into your novels?
Burgess: To some extent it does, because I'm pretty certain my cousin the Archbishop reads my novels and he still assumes I'm a good Catholic. The princes of the Church, they know when to shut their eyes.

Churchill: I suppose there's something of a Catholic argument going in *The Wanting Seed.*
Burgess: Well, yes, it's a very Catholic book. It's a total vindication of the encyclical. You know, of course, what the encyclical leaves out of account is the acceptance of natural checks, you know, is in fact Malthusianism. Malthus has always been condemned by the Church, yet the Church will now accept Malthusianism, at least tacitly. What's going to happen to our excess population? "Well, Nature will take care of it." As Malthus said, in other words, wars and pestilence, earthquakes.

Churchill: But that book must have been more consciously futuristic than say *Clockwork Orange.*
Burgess: I'd had it in mind for a long time. I've always wanted to write it, but it's a fantasy. What I really wanted to do was to present the English mind as tending to waver between Pelagianism and Augustinianism. The British mind being primarily Pelagian, accepting the notion that people are all right, really, you know, you needn't worry too much about things like grace, divine grace.

Things all work out pretty well. This gives you socialism, then you get some disappointments.

Churchill: What phase are they looking forward to at the end?
Burgess: At the end they're looking forward to a new Pelagianism. One doesn't know what it would be like. It may last a long time, there's no need to repress anymore. There's already a machine for a brain, handed over to a public corporation like the BBC.

I think in actual practice the thesis is a sound one. The thesis is a viable one, because it's viable in our own country. You know, the way we shift from Toryism to Socialism. What we don't get here, though, is an intermediate phase where disappointment takes the form of violent repression. We don't get that here but we could get it. That's why I fight with Socialism; it has a dynamic which leads to that sort of oppression. Of course now, this is all right, this is a very free state, but there's a good deal of repression. I mean, we can't send three dollars out of the country. In other words, I can't get married because I can't send three dollars out of the country, simple as that. I can't take my money abroad. Oh, it's not important, but the area of state control is steadily growing. This I don't like.

Churchill: Yet you don't have the kind of violent anti-English feeling that Sillitoe seems to have.
Burgess: Oh, well, Sillitoe's a rich man now, and I don't know what he's grousing about. He's reaping the rewards of free enterprise. He's very much a double-think character and he makes me very angry. I don't think he's very intelligent, for one thing. He wrote a book called *Key to the Door*, which was about his national service in Malaya and it totally misrepresented the case. I know this because I was there myself. He said what the Malays want is what the Chinese want, a Communist revolution. You see, this is what they all want, but the British are preventing it from happening. This is totally untrue. The Chinese and Malays didn't want a communist revolution because they had too much to lose. They are all capitalists, all businessmen. The Malays are not interested in politics. In any case, they're Moslems, and Communism would presumably fight against Islam. What all the Malayan people wanted was just to go on as they were with the British there in the background administering the war, building roads and doing the dirty work. But Sillitoe—so ideological in that way—totally misrepresented the entire picture. You see again, I get mad at the man who was so full of humility, *so* interested in the people. He never learned the bloody language even; he never *talked* with the Malays. He never knew what was going on in the Malay's mind. It was only the wicked capitalists who did all that. You know, he's always going on about the

sins of the past, what they did to my father, my grandfather. It isn't the fault of the present or of the past. Or a lad deserts from the army, and this is a good thing because, you know, he's showing his displeasure, revolting against the system. Well, anybody who deserted the army in the last war was a bloody traitor, because we were fighting an evil system. But, no, that's not it, you see. It's a very old-fashioned kind of socialism you get in Sillitoe. Yet he's a fine writer, he has tremendous gifts.

Churchill: You have to admire his kind of passion. I asked him about his book about Russia and he said the reviews were very bad.
Burgess: Yes, a silly book. *Road to Volgograd*—it was a silly, bloody book. It was all, well, very euphoric. Can you imagine him singing his way through Russia? He spells *Finnegans Wake* with an apostrophe *s*, too. Where is Sillitoe living now, anyway?

Churchill: He's been loaned a flat near Regents Park.
Burgess: Well, it's funny that Sillitoe's not living in the slums of Nottingham. Is he living on the right side of the park? Yes. Whereas I, the inveterate Tory, am living in a very slummy district. Correct? Not very good. Well, he lived for a time in Tangier, learned Spanish. He has a hell of a chip on his shoulder. I don't know what the hell's in him. I'm of course interested, that's all.

Churchill: But you think he's a good writer?
Burgess: I think he's potentially a very good writer, but I think his politics are vitiating his writing.

Churchill: I wanted to ask you about Sergeant Ennis and *Vision of Battlements.*
Burgess: Very much myself, very much a self-portrait.

Churchill: If the book had been published when you'd first written it, I understand that Ennis would have come out way ahead of Jimmy Porter and Lucky Jim. You might have been one of the leaders in the whole post-war movement, in a way.
Burgess: Oh, well, I can't prove it, except I can show you the date on the original typescript, which I think is in some American university right now. But when I wrote the novel, I wrote it to see if I could write a novel, and sent it to Heinemann. They said, "Oh, come along and see us," so I did, and they said, "We can't publish this as a first novel." I couldn't understand it. "Go home and write us a *first* novel," they said.

Churchill: What did they mean?

Burgess: I don't know what they meant by that at all. But I went home and wrote a first novel, which was heavy with Catholic guilt. I was going through a bad phase at the time. This they rejected totally, or one of the editors rejected it, so I said the hell with the lot of them and went back to writing music again. And I went to Malaya and found I had to write about it, and so I wrote the trilogy and that was published. But, the funny thing is, you see, I had a phone call from the man who rejected the first novel—only the other day—because this "first" novel is now coming out in the collected edition, and he liked it very much. He said he'd not read it before, and I said, "Well, you bloody fool, it's the novel you read many years ago and rejected." So I think it's a very good novel. You know, you can't win with these people. Well, if *Vision of Battlements* had come out at that time it would have fallen flat, probably. It was about the war, about war service, but it did anticipate to some extent this sort of figure, the anti-hero.

Churchill: Ennis wins that battle from Turner because Turner misses him and falls down the mountain.

Burgess: It follows the Virgilian ritual, Aeneas winning from Turnus in the twelfth book. The use of the frame was only just that, nothing like *Ulysses* meant. On the other hand, all the material in it is personal. You know, the failed musicianship, the conflict between two cultures, the Protestant wife and the dark-haired, dark-skinned European Catholic.

Churchill: Keeping the novel in a briefcase for sixteen years was not a matter of waiting for a change, just a matter of finding a publisher, then?

Burgess: I didn't try other publishers. When it was published, it was not published by Heinemann. They rejected it a second time, so I published it with another firm. I was told off, berated by Heinemann. I said, "Well, do you know what the hell goes on in your publishing house? One of your editors rejected it." So he said, "Well, you should have given it to me, dear boy." I said, "All right, why? Your editors are presumably filled with delegated responsibility and I'm not going to go crawling to you." This is one of the reasons I took the book to another firm. They've rejected too many books. I'll take them elsewhere.

Jonathan Cape's my publisher now. They haven't done anything of mine yet, but they will be doing a volume of essays in the autumn.

Churchill: In *A Vision of Battlements* there seems to be a crisis involved in Ennis's attempts at being a composer.

Burgess: Trying to be a composer and failing to. Well, failure hasn't really been proved yet, but it's been proved in myself, in my own mind. I don't think I'm a very good composer, but when I was asked to go over to Hollywood to discuss the writing of the script on Shakespeare's life—this was to be a musical, and as far as I know it still is to be a sort of musical, not like *Camelot*, but a film with music—and they said, "We'll get Lennon and McCartney to do the lyrics and music," and I said, "Well, this is not really a good idea." The music might be all right, but I don't think Lennon would do acceptable lyrics, and they said, "Why don't you do the lyrics yourself, John?"—John being my name—so I did. While I was writing the lyrics, I thought I might as well do the music, too, so I wrote the music to the lyrics. I went back to Hollywood in March this year, and of course they had the studio orchestra, the studio choir, everything on the job, and they said, "Listen to this, boy," and there was my music. So I'm getting music performed at last. Not quite in the genres I'd imagined, but getting some sort of music performed and possibly even used in the film. I hope they will. I admit in some ways I can't understand their doing it. I should not be disappointed if they don't because imagine, "Script by Anthony Burgess, music and lyrics by Anthony Burgess, based on a novel by Anthony Burgess."

Churchill: Sounds great.
Burgess: Sounds great to me, too.

Churchill: When were you there?
Burgess: I was there twice this year. In January and in March. They're very kind. They discovered somehow that my first wife had died and they rang me up and said, "Boy, you come over here." Very kind, American kindness, which is honest, and sincere, nothing can touch it. It was meant to be a good thing, but it wasn't a good thing because being away from home you still sort of imagine home is the same. So I went to a shop and bought a present for her, when she was dead, you know, that kind of business. But bringing me over was very kindly meant, it was well meant, and we got some more work done. Now the script is finished. The first draft's in script, and I suppose I'll go over there again this year to script conferences and complaints about lack of motivation. . . . "Lag of motavashun."

Churchill: Is this going to be based on *Nothing Like the Sun*?
Burgess: No, it's a very complicated business. But *Nothing Like the Sun* was bought by a New York man, or rather options were taken out on it. He wanted to make a stage musical from it. Well, he hasn't done this in four years. And Warner

Brothers wanted to buy it, but this man wouldn't release his option, so if Warner Brothers can't get it, it means a very difficult job for me. We have to have an absolutely parallel script. I mustn't plagiarize my own work. It is difficult, you see, isn't it? I think Warner Brothers probably will buy it. I hope so, anyway. That would ease the problem immensely. It would be a good film. If they use a bit of common sense, let Joe Mankiewicz have his own way with the direction, it could be a very good film. He knows all about Ben Jonson and these people. He's a bit of a scholar in his way.

Churchill: Does your musical ability and talent apply to novel writing—do the two interests combine? I'm thinking now of Joyce's "scrupulous language" and the emphasis upon tone and sound values in writing fiction.
Burgess: I think there's a tendency that way, though writing music is not scribbling on your knee. It's a very exact art. Even the writing we've done calls for scrupulous exactness. It's a bit of a simple piece for the film, you see, but you've got to be so exact in every detail. That's staccato and there's a crescendo, and it tends to make you feel that way about words, and you try to be similarly scrupulous. At the same time, to watch things like rhythm. You know, if possible to imitate musical effects. Of course, music's far righter because you've got many things going at the same time. Prose is sheer monody, but if you give the impression it's not monody, you achieve something. Joyce did this of course—in *Finnegans Wake* he goes beyond monody. Musical background does certainly affect the way one writes.

Churchill: This is hard to get at, but in all your novels the language seems absolutely reflective of what we are seeing, or of the times. How did you do this in *Nothing Like the Sun*? It rings "true," though no one's been back there.
Burgess: Well, it was a matter of learning the language. It was simply a matter of, well, we're going back to another country now so we'd better learn the language. The language is so appealing, very lush, who doesn't like it? . . . but the problem of actually writing in Elizabethan English or getting somewhere close to it was immense. So I began writing everything and even speaking in something approaching Elizabethan English . . . saying things like, "To take withal," you know.

Churchill: Affecting ruffs and codpieces.
Burgess: Not quite that, but, you see, the book itself is a fake in that it is enclosed in a lecture. There's a man giving—it's myself, in fact—giving a lecture to some Malayan students, and he is drinking three bottles of samsu rice spirit, because

it's his final lecture. And towards the end he gets drunk and he passes out, and his passing out is identified with Shakespeare's passing out. That means you get away with the charge of bad naturalism. Not many people noticed this, it doesn't matter. It is, in fact, a lecture, very eccentric lecture.

Churchill: Were there literally students at one time?
Burgess: I imagine some, I imagine a sort of cosmopolitan gang of students, whose names frequently even appear in the novel. But this is not essential, it just helped me a little, and it pointed to the fact that I was trying to bring in an Eastern woman and the East into a novel about Shakespeare. Trying to bring in an Eastern woman and possibly suggest that Shakespeare may have a son, that Shakespeare may go on elsewhere, which is a bit tendentious, I suppose. But the novel was so difficult to write anyway. It was so murderous that one was entitled to use any device that would ease the problem. Murderous, because of the language problem.

Churchill: WS comes on as very sympathetic.
Burgess: Very weak, very put-upon. The same way in the film. He must have been like that, really. Try as you will, you cannot get a very powerful image. He's somebody watching all the time . . . tremendous verbal gift.

Churchill: We went to New Place, or next door to it, while we were in Stratford.
Burgess: They pulled that down, stupidly. The mulberry tree, as well. I found Stratford a most ghastly place. The theater's good, except the audiences are lousy. The great difficulty in visiting the birthplace and of trying to put it in a film is that it must have been bigger than it looks, or they must have had next door as well to accommodate two whole families. Well, undoubtedly Hollywood will sort it out. No trouble at all.

Churchill: Is the idea for *Nothing Like the Sun* influenced by the discussion of *Hamlet* in the library scene in *Ulysses*?
Burgess: Oh, totally. Well, the notion of Ann's adultery with the brother is very close to what Stephen gives us. They use it in the film, too. As to whether they want to keep it in, I don't know. But I have a scene in which they've just done *Richard III* and Burbage is saying, "By God, Will, there seems to be a lot of personal feeling in that." You know, the business of a limping Richard courting a simpering Ann. Suddenly you get a shot in which Richard the brother is limping towards Ann the wife . . . backing into the tavern scene. Useful motivation, and in the film it explains Ann's tirade against Will as being the father of all sin. It's her own guilt as well as his.

Churchill: Talking about biography or approximate biography, and Joyce's library scene, makes me think of Richard Ellmann's book. I was wondering if there weren't material there for a novel about the creative man. I mean, think of the wonderfully careful way Ellmann treats James and Nora's relationship.

Burgess: I think there's a novel in Joyce's life, and I think Ellmann's biography is superb, it's sheer pleasure. I've read it about ten times, I suppose. There's boundless material for a novel there, and I'm fascinated by the idea of writing fiction about an artist. But it's not quite what I'd want to do. I'd like to use up some of my wasted, useful knowledge and ability. Do something on the life of a composer. Do a whole study of someone, maybe like Debussy, still essentially the life of an artist. Probably present it as biography with photographs, faked photographs, bits of music-type illustrations so people aren't quite sure whether they're reading a novel or reading a real story.

Churchill: How about bringing tapes into it?

Burgess: Yes, the later part might give opportunity for that sort of experimentation. Use letters in it as well as straightforward *récit.* I want to bring Mahler in, and Puccini, and Debussy, the first night of *Le Sacre*—that would be about 1913—all these various things into it. The Rise of Jazz, everything. Make it a general panorama of European life. Because music does lend itself to the international approach, you see. Music transcends national lines, but it has to be a British composer, I feel. A British composer, not Italian, or French. I mean, it has to be ultimately comic, has to be full of many comedy amours, opera singers, a lot of temperament. But it ought to be a genuine picture, made genuine by the fact that you show some examples of what our composer wrote. You discuss a symphony. Not as something very vague but as something definite, which has something happening in it, and which goes like this. Sort of ultra-naturalism, in a sense.

Churchill: Not to change the subject, but something you said reminded me of the American writer Ken Kesey. Do you know *One Flew Over the Cuckoo's Nest*?

Burgess: Oh, I know that one, yes. I read that. Liked it very much. Oh, yes, admire that.

Churchill: He's got a new idea now. He served a jail sentence, six months voluntary for possession of marijuana, and he did a journal, including drawings. Now his idea is to try something like a novel in which he includes drawings and tapes and sounds—everything. I don't know how it would work.

Burgess: You don't buy the tape with the novel, do you? Play it yourself? Of course, that is coming. A record inserted in the dust jacket. Well, with *Time* and *Life*, I and various other people did an edition of the "Ancient Mariner" with Doré's illustrations. A nice little record of Ralph Richardson reading the poem, you know, inset. That seemed to work easily enough. You could do that with the novel, too. I think the time certainly is coming for fiction totally recorded. This is *it*. This is what the people sound like, this is how it was conceived. Here's someone speaking for the first time, his novel, you're hearing a novel. Could be done.

Churchill: I wanted to ask you a general question about American writers.
Burgess: I think very highly of American writers. Think more highly of them than the British. I think Nabokov is probably very important, very important indeed. I do greatly like Bellow. I think Barth is a very promising novelist. I think he shot his bolt a little too early. I think *The Sot-Weed Factor* is a very important novel. Don't think *Giles Goat-Boy* is. It's fake; its allegory is too easy. The whole symbolism shells out much too easily.

Churchill: It seems to give support to the idea that the American university is the most important place one can be.
Burgess: It's bound to appear so to him, I suppose. He's hardly been off the campus.

Churchill: No. Now he's at Buffalo.
Burgess: Oh, Buffalo. I thought of going there—workload was tempting. But he plays the drums, doesn't he? I could play the piano, get a band going.

Churchill: Everything seems to be happening at Buffalo.
Burgess: Well, yes. There's a lot of Joyce stuff going on there. It's very tempting. But I think we'll just have to go to Malta and write these books, you know, which have to be written and then, after a couple of years, see how things are. There shouldn't be any difficulty in selling the house.

Churchill: Is the novel on the life of the composer one of the books you plan?
Burgess: It's not one of the three. What I want to do is a life of Shakespeare. It's about time we had a new popular life of Shakespeare with a lot of illustrations . . . musically produced book. You know, a humorous, accurate account of Shakespeare's background for the ordinary reader. And I want to write a structuralist novel. The first of the structuralist novels, I hope, based on the Lévi-Strauss theater of the correlation between language and social forms. So that I want to exploit the Algonquin legend, the boy who was bound to commit incest because

he could answer all the riddles correctly, which is a direct tie-up with Oedipus. This I have worked out. It has to be written. I want to write a novel in the form of a segment of an encyclopedia (this sounds very French) in which you present our world, but it's subtly different. There are entries which you wouldn't get in normal encyclopedia. People you've never heard of—great writers, greater than Shakespeare, great politicians; so the reader is all the time trying to piece together a world which is a parallel world to our own but not another planet. This has to be worked out in detail.

Churchill: You're obviously not worried about the future of the novel.
Burgess: Well, not about the future of myself as a novelist. I have the time to write, thank God for that. I started late, but I can go on writing till ninety or one hundred without any trouble at all.

Churchill: That's a question I wanted to ask, How the hell do you do it? How do you write so much?
Burgess: Well, in quantity, yes. I'm very lazy by nature. I'm not a great worker at all. Remember this, when I first began to write professionally I was living in the tropics and doing a full-time job, but at the same time working on a novel. The heat is a tremendous stimulus. I can work in the heat. I can't work in this light—totally impossible. With sharp lights I can work like a Trojan the whole time. I cannot work in English light. I can probably write an article, but I find it extremely hard to write a novel. It's easier in the house we have in the country, where the light is rather better. You know, I have a big study with a south window. The light is clearer there, anyway.

I give people the impression of overworking, because when I came back from the Far East in 1959, I was supposed to have a tumor on the brain, and they couldn't locate the tumor. All the symptoms pointed to a tumor; they said the tumor was probably hiding behind some tissue. They couldn't get it, and they said, You've probably got a year to live. It was all a whirl, you know. Well, I wrote five novels in that year. Seemed to do me a lot of good. I was all right after that.

Churchill: When you're working and conditions are right, do you work pretty fast?
Burgess: No, I'm not a fast writer. I'm a very slow writer. I have a lot of energy, I'm fairly strong, I can stay at the table for a long stretch, smoking a lot. Get a fair amount done that way. I get a thousand words a day down, you see, in good conditions. Which is all right. Ideally you get an 80,000-word book done in eighty

days, two and a half months, about three months. I have written a novel in four weeks.

Churchill: When you're working at that rate, do you work every day or do you take time off?
Burgess: No, I work every day, including weekends. Having started to write very late, I feel guilty about wasting any time, even socially. Going out to dinner, you know, I feel very guilty about it.

Cynical about the Great Words
G. Riemer/1971

From *National Elementary Principal* (May 1971). Reprinted by permission. Copyright 1971 National Association of Elementary School Principals. All rights reserved.

Riemer: Let's think of your son, Andrea, six and a half years old. What do you expect his education to be? Here he is facing seven or eight years of elementary school.

Burgess: Well, he's not facing it here in the United States. Thank God for that! I suppose we have learned a lot about American elementary education by having Andrea here. And I'm grateful for that. But the more we work with him here at home, reading and so forth, the less concerned I am about what is happening at school.

I hate to say this, because I try to be a good guest, but America is totally dishonest. Even Russia is more honest than America. Going through America, one is aware that its citizens are free; yet they behave as it is assumed people behave in Soviet Russia. Russian people assume they are not in a free country, but they behave as if they have a great deal of freedom. In the United States, it's the opposite way around.

I like authority, because children can rebel against authority. It's much more difficult to rebel against red tape. What makes it difficult to understand the conformist attitudes in the United States is that they do not proceed from a totalitarian system. They proceed from a free-trade system.

They are part of the pattern in a free society. In an unfree society like Russia, this doesn't apply. It is as though the Russians themselves—the people, not the state—are so fluid and so individual that they need state imposition from above to survive.

Riemer: How does America's dishonesty show itself in education?

Burgess: America says one thing and means another. It doesn't want the free, individualistic person it pretends to value—the Patrick Henry type—coming along.

24

It doesn't want the great genius emerging from the masses; its system of education is mechanized. It's automated. I don't know if I'm any good or not, but I couldn't have learned anything from these readers they give Andrea. I should do more with Andrea to help him with them, but I can't. I get so bored, frankly, by this rubbish. It's not only important for the child to be stimulated by the materials, but the teacher ought to be stimulated, too. Of course, I recognize that some learning must be mechanical—the elements of practice, of instant recognition, such things. But there is something decidedly antihumanistic, I think, about education levels, about your whole grading system, your controlled vocabulary, and so forth.

Riemer: Are you aware that the textbook publishing industry does a three-billion-dollar annual business?
Burgess: Well, you've got a timocracy here. That's your whole trouble. Of course, it enables our novels to get published, but this is what is wrong with the United States. It's money, money, money, all the time. A true timocracy. You can't become a representative of the people unless you have property.

I cannot trust an American radio announcer or an American TV announcer. I know that behind all the hot words, all the persuasive language, there is a sell. Someone is trying to sell something all the time.

Riemer: Are you saying that English television supports education but American television does not?
Burgess: American television undermines education. In every single country in the world, including Japan, television is a medium for education. This is true no matter how poor the country. It is true in Italy, where there are only two channels; in England, where there are only three. Kids can be educated through television. I don't mean just programs like *Sesame Street* for pre-readers but rather genuine adult school programs that go on during vacations, programs where you have experts—Sir Trevor-Roper, the historian, or whomever you like—on the job.

The job of television is partly a conservatory job, I think. Television should preserve and disseminate the culture of the past. And this is what American television does not do. We have only one educational channel, NET, here in Princeton, and that uses programs mostly from England. Its programs very rarely originate from here. It has no money, or at least very little money, and the other networks, of course, support only pablum.

It worries me a great deal that children are cut off from the actual historical stream of culture. They are not aware of history. Everything is *now*. In Europe, we don't have this. We are not a *now* continent; we are very much a *past* continent. All we have is the past. What more does anybody really need?

Riemer: The past is what educates.
Burgess: Exactly.

Riemer: A Czech artist told me that in New York he is always going to museums, but that in Prague, one doesn't have to go to a storage place to see the past. The past is everywhere. In New York, you need to save what you can before it is covered by concrete or torn down to make space for a parking lot.
Burgess: Nowadays, you never see mad people. You never see the insane. They are always tucked away in asylums. Whereas there is a long, ancient tradition in Europe that the mad and the sick are among you all the time. It is an aspect of life, the other side of life. Just as old churches are another side of life. America wants only the sane, the modern, the clean. It wants to expunge the dirty and the old and the insane. But we've got to have insanity, and we've got to have conflict between the past and the present. We've got to have this sense of dynamic tension. It is not there, really, in American history.

Riemer: Do you think these tensions are about in England?
Burgess: England has been very influenced by America. The sense of the past in England is dying very quickly. It's a great shame. If it dies in Italy, I don't know what we shall do.

Riemer: Have television advertisements had much effect on Andrea?
Burgess: Oh, yes. Very powerfully so. He's indoctrinated with them. He knows all the ads: "My legs ache, my nose is stuffed up, my head hurts, and I need some rest. I don't know what I would do without you, Mabel." He does the whole thing. I don't think this is bad. But, you know, he will ask, "Is that kitchen roll 'Bounty'?" And it is obvious that he is judging things by the commercial.

Riemer: How about advertisements aimed directly at him?
Burgess: He tends to ignore those, for the most part. I think he was disgusted—and so was I, heartedly disgusted—on Easter Sunday, when they put on a marvelous film about the Gospel according to St. Matthew. The thing was billed as a great, great movie. But it was consistently interrupted by commercials, usually very tasteless. In fact, it was even interrupted at the point of the Last Supper. Yet they promise Doris Day's *April in Paris* will "not be interrupted by commercials."

Riemer: I remember a documentary TV show of the Nuremberg trials. When film showing how the Jews were killed in gas ovens was run, the word *gas* was blipped. You didn't hear it. There was just a little blank space and you heard ovens. The word *gas* was cut out because the sponsor for the show was the American Gas Company. You would think that listeners would become desensitized by this indifference.

Burgess: I remember during the Easter Sunday film I just mentioned, there was a commercial on behalf of the Cancer Society, in which John Wayne was telling me that he had found a spot on his lung, and said, "I was cured and life is good," and all of this just before the Crucifixion of Christ. This is blasphemous.

Riemer: You've written twenty novels, two books on James Joyce, a book on Shakespeare, a book on the novel. You compose music. Such varied achievements suggest a good education. About your schooling, then, what was it like?

Burgess: I went to Catholic primary schools and to Xaverian College in Manchester. After leaving college, I spent a couple of years trying to get into the Customs and Excise Department, but this required a competitive exam, and I didn't get very far with it. I did some work, saved a bit of money, and later than most went to Manchester University.

Riemer: Did you become interested in teaching while you were at Manchester University?

Burgess: Never. Never. I got into teaching during the war when there was a great need for instructors. When the war was over, I taught at an army college a number of years and then went into a training college, teaching drama. I did a fair amount of acting at the university and also a bit of directing at the training college. I had the job of lecturing in speech and drama, and I produced plays there. I was able to combine both talents, such as they were.

Riemer: Were you teaching English in the army?

Burgess: Oh no, far from it. I taught map reading and military things. I taught a kind of minimal language, minimal German and that sort of stuff, you know. I taught educational courses to regular soldiers who had to take exams to get promotions. I taught current affairs a great deal. I taught practically everything except my own subject.

Riemer: You learn languages, do you, along a musical route? Do you learn them aurally, or do you learn them intellectually, that is, by grammar?

Burgess: I learn them intellectually, I suppose. I'm very bad at picking up languages by just listening. I have to see what they look like written down. I don't know whether this is a personal trait or a national trait. But I have to see the thing on paper. I have to see music on paper, too. The sound itself is not enough.

Riemer: Music is evident in your writing, in your language, rhythms, and choice of words, and even in your forms. You also write music. How did you ever get started in music? What were your influences?

Burgess: My family influenced me very strongly. My mother had been on the stage, and my father was a pianist in the cinema theater. He played the background music for silent films. It used to be a good job in the old days, a highly regarded job. I love that sort of work myself.

Riemer: Did you sing?

Burgess: I was no good. I was tested for choir but couldn't make it. I was never a performer. I began to teach myself music when I was about fifteen. I took music in the higher S.C. (School Certificate) exam which gave me the equivalent of an intermediate B.A.

Riemer: You've just completed the incidental music for your own translation of *Cyrano de Bergerac*, and you're now working on a musical based on Joyce's *Ulysses*. Do you keep a kind of notebook of themes that come to you?

Burgess: I am sometimes afraid of forgetting a theme. Of course, a theme is only a couple of bars, and it doesn't take long to note it down. You have to get it down. I do keep a notebook and just today added some things to *Ulysses*.

Riemer: Do you use a musical form or outline when you speak to new audiences?

Burgess: I never know what I'm going to say until I face the audience. You get a strange kind of feeling that you can say something to one audience that you can't say to another. I sense this from the very beginning. It comes from experience. I got it teaching in the army, and army audiences are the most difficult in the world. When they are forced to sit in a room and listen to a lecture, you have to use all sorts of devices to keep them interested. Then too they are such a mixed bag, usually with no academic background. They are just not used to sitting and listening to a lecture. But in the army, of course, there is a great deal of lecturing, a great deal of teaching. I learned more from the army about teaching, I think, than anywhere else.

Riemer: In *A Clockwork Orange*, I was impressed by the way you used the phrase, "O my brothers." It provides a musical line that runs throughout the entire book.

Burgess: It is to engage the reader. It almost makes him an accomplice.

Riemer: But, because of the changing context in which it is set, it has different tonal and emotional effects. In the beginning, it is quite sarcastic, rather cold, but at the end it grows deeply pathetic and cello-like, very touching.

Burgess: It's a kind of leitmotif. Similarly, there is a line used at the opening and throughout the book: "Well, what's it going to be, then? Eh?" That is meant for the reader. It means *are you going to use free will, or are you not?* It's a colloquial way of posing a traditional problem.

Riemer: It's a problem apparent today in the case of Lt. Calley. Many people would like to take his freedom of choice away from him, and President Nixon seems willing to help.

Burgess: Oh yes. All the way. Well, Calley must abide by his choice. They are saying now that it was a collective choice, that he was a mere instrument, and that we are all guilty. This is not so. *He* was guilty. And *he* has to face up to that as a human individual.

Riemer: Do the English believe in collective guilt?

Burgess: I think the big difference between America and the Old World is that America has only recently discovered collective guilt. America was founded on Freedom, wasn't it? All the guilt was left back there in the Old World. Now it is being discovered for the first time that America, as much as any other nation, can engage in evil. It was astonishing to find this in a *Time* essay on the My Lai case. The point was put across about the Pelagians and the Augustinians. I never expected to see this in a popular news magazine. But there it was: the American nation would have to face up to an evil situation for the first time. Evil had always before been back there in the Old World. The people who want to absolve Calley want to reject original sin. Calley was impelled by a good, solid dose of original sin. Not anybody's collective guilt, not the guilt of his officers, his superiors, not the guilt of the nation, but his own bloody guilt.

I tried for many years to write a kind of allegory—a retelling of the story of the Minotaur. The Minotaur in my work would stand for original sin, and he would be imprisoned in a labyrinth, but the labyrinth itself would represent human achievement, represent art, a future art gallery. The Minotaur is killed by Theseus, who is American and comes from across the sea. When the Minotaur is killed, the whole labyrinth falls down. So the killing of the idea of original sin also kills culture, a sense of human responsibility, and everything else. Kill the Minotaur, which has got to live, which has got to be there roving around the labyrinth, and you kill civilization.

I've often called Pelagianism, "Americanism." I'm using "Americanism" in the widest possible sense. I use it to imply a culture totally disjunct from the Augustine sin-based culture.

Pelagius was a British monk, so I've always thought of Pelagianism as the British heresy, and I've tried to distinguish it from the heresy called *Americanism*. But I am not a theologian.

Riemer: Pelagius rejected the idea of original sin.
Burgess: I think the time has probably come to write a play about Pelagius. Pelagius said that man was not born in original sin. Augustine said that he was.

Riemer: On the other hand, in the case of Charles Manson, there doesn't seem to be any popular rush to be involved with his guilt.
Burgess: That's because he couldn't be identified with national purpose or ideology or anything like that. Manson was working in a private sector, in a very perverted way. I don't think the public knows exactly what he did. I think some of the things he did were very terrible, too terrible to get into the newspapers. The public has a sense of something very evil that cannot be mitigated by a sense of mission or purpose, and it doesn't want anything to do with it. Yet, Calley and Manson are guilty of the same sort of thing.

Riemer: Manson came from a broken home, was brought up in orphanages and institutions, and lived much of his life in prison. Some people will say that society formed Manson by neglecting him.
Burgess: I don't think society should feel guilty about that. All through history, people have labored under difficulties. It's a very modern heresy of a stupid society that tries to impose individual guilt on us all. People are always looking for mitigating circumstances.

Riemer: The terrible thing is that in doing so, they destroy what beauty and dignity the person may have.
Burgess: The dignity of human choice, "If you do good, that is your own. If you do evil, that belongs to the collective body"—a lot of false thinking there.

Riemer: Have you seen evidence of such thinking in other matters, outside the Calley and Manson cases?
Burgess: I've not, really. I've been lecturing in a very limited area, the literary area. But generally I detect a new kind of masochism in America that I don't like very much. I mean, one can go to a party and start berating America, and people will say, "Oh, yes, yes. That's true. Whip me again." I find this disgusting.

Riemer: It is part of that collective guilt, though. If you whip me, of course, I'll be less guilty. I also involve you in my guilt for punishing me.
Burgess: Yes, that's right. Yes.

Riemer: Besides Princeton and Columbia, where you gave your writing courses, which other schools did you visit over here?
Burgess: Oh, I've been through a great number in America, although there are certain areas of the country I don't know.

I've had a fair experience in American universities, mostly state universities, and I admire them, for the most part. I admire them far more than the Ivy League schools. I think Ivy League and Oxford and Cambridge days are over. I think the new vitality resides in the new institutions, those that scorn traditions.

Riemer: What do you think of what is called the Youth Movement?
Burgess: It's all right. It's in order. But there's a terrible danger that it will be used by highly sophisticated elements who will just harness the youth's enthusiasm to their own ends. I see this as a very great danger. What the kids themselves don't seem to realize is that enthusiasm is not enough and good intentions are not enough. They must have knowledge. And they haven't got enough knowledge. They disdain knowledge. All knowledge comes from a segment of society that they now reject.

This is caricatured in the attitude of black youth. At various universities, I've seen black men who are treated very indulgently, overindulgently. They are allowed to do what they want, take what they want, drop what they want. I met one young man in Philadelphia, a young black, who wanted to learn music. But he wouldn't learn music from whites because it was "tainted" music. Well, this is bloody ridiculous. A piano is a neutral instrument. It is not tainted by the whites. Musical notation is not specifically white, any more than mathematical symbols are white. In any case, mathematical symbols are Arab. So the black man thought it might be good to study mathematics because it was not a white man's sign.

You see this same kind of thing among white students, rejecting the culture and art of the old man. The counter-culture is producing a vacuum into which anybody can march. This man Herbert Marcuse, for example, is marching in there, and that is most disturbing to me.

The significant thing is that the technologists and scientists and doctors and engineers are not part of the counter-culture. They are getting on with the job of taking over the state. I think the youngsters who are in the vague disciplines like social science, English literature, and history ought to learn to fight the system with its own weapons. But they are not prepared to learn anything. They think the state of primal innocence is enough. In a technological society, this is ridiculous. You just can't do it at all.

I think also that these prelapsarian youngsters who are trying to get back to a kind of Adamic state are doing great evil to the earth in setting up their communes. They don't even know how to look after their pigs, cows, and hens. I'm serious about this. They will not learn how to sow seeds. You've developed some very good strains of barley and wheat out West. They allow these to be cross-pollinated through sheer ignorance. They won't protect their growing, they have no notion of how to treat the soil, and they won't learn these things because these are the preserves of the reactionary culture. It's stupid.

Riemer: Have you visited the communes?
Burgess: I've seen several of them, yes. In California. They are rather pathetic in some ways. This desire to be innocent again—it won't work.

I think this fusion of ideas and ignorance is dangerous. Out of it, you can get a genuine Fascism. It worries me a great deal that these kids are not sophisticated. They must learn and then reject. But they mustn't reject without learning. First learn, and then they can reject if they really want to.

Riemer: If you were in a university or high school where violent students have taken over a building, would you call in the police?
Burgess: I think as far as possible it should be handled internally. If the governing body of the university is properly in authority, it should be able to do so. But it plays into the hands of the militants to have armed police on the campus in the first place. There should be no police on campus. I shiver when I remember in North Carolina having to give a lecture on *Paradise Lost*, very appropriately, with a squad of police outside the window. This is mad, and I protested it. But I was told, "Universities have to enter the modern world." I really object to that kind of modern world entering into the university. If these events cannot be controlled from within, then the governing body should resign. They should never call in outside police.

Riemer: How about hair?
Burgess: I don't think it matters very much. Again, it is rather pathetic. I have these rich children in class who wear jeans with holes in them. They pretend to be poor. But this is mockery. I always think of the American hippies in Majorca, with their long hair and their dirty, torn clothes, living among people who dress like that only because they can't afford to dress any other way.

Riemer: You've said students in New Zealand are more involved with drugs than students in any other part of the world. What do you think can be done about drugs in schools?

Burgess: If they are already there, I don't see how you are going to extirpate them. I don't object to certain drugs; pot, for instance. I object very strongly to mainline drugs. Heroin is a totally destructive drug. I object to drugs as a way to attain instant ecstasy. Ecstasy has to be worked for.

Riemer: Yes, like peace.

Burgess: Exactly. If you get this instant sense of fulfillment, of course its quality diminishes. There is not a sufficient involvement of human will or human choice. I don't like being thrown into a state of ecstasy without having any control over it. I don't like its just taking me over, as LSD does for example. I think we have to find some kind of philosophical, counteractive device or devices. It has to be argued out. I'm doing that frequently with the students.

Riemer: I refuse to experience LSD because I'm afraid it may hurt my mind. I can break a leg and still work. I can hurt any part of my body and continue to write, but I won't risk losing my mind.

Burgess: Of course. This is the natural sense of responsibility you have to your art, your craft.

Riemer: Do you see a connection between violence and the impatient wanting for instant achievement? Some people go on one demonstration march and then quit the peace movement because the war hasn't stopped.

Burgess: This, again, is terribly naive. Some people think that because the students staged a revolution in Europe and it worked, they can make a revolution work here. They can't. The circumstances are not the same. The government is not sufficiently unstable. In Italy, where governments are always changing, the students can turn the balance. Not here. Not yet. If they're going to start changing America, they've got to start with political science. They've got to start looking at the Constitution again.

Riemer: You've lowered the voting age in England. Will eighteen-year-old voters change America?

Burgess: The Labour government lowered the vote and thought this would result in a large victory for Labour, because youth is supposed to be revolutionary and on the side of labor. It had the opposite effect. Young people voted for the Conservative Party. I don't think it really matters what age you introduce the franchise.

There are plenty of stupid, bloody stevedores and taxi drivers who are sixty-five who don't vote any better than a child of fourteen would vote.

What is not done in America, and ought to be done, is to reconsider the whole basis of the American political structure. Is the country too big? Is the Constitution an anachronism, or is it not? Should the presidential system be changed? These things ought to be discussed, but they are not. Instead, the kids are trying to cause a revolution even though they don't know what the hell they are revolting against except in terms of big abstractions. Change requires a lot of preparation, a lot of study. They are not prepared to go in for that at all.

Riemer: There is a drama professor at Yale, a Pole, who recently came back from a tour of universities around the country. He said that he found the students could only pay attention to him for fifteen minutes before he began to feel that he was losing them. He blamed this on television and the interruptions of commercials.
Burgess: I think he must be bad speaker. I've never had much difficulty, I'll tell you that. I don't think it is a fault of the students. I think it is a fault of himself.

I think kids are better now at listening and hearing things than they used to be. It may be something to do with rock festivals, I don't know—the willingness to sit and listen to music. And they are used to listening to these harangues from the political leaders. They're very keen on listening to poetry recitals. It's a very remarkable thing about America. In the old days in London, you couldn't get anybody to listen to a poetry recital. You can now. They actually go to them and listen to them. I think this Polish professor is totally wrong. The auditory sense in America is very developed.

Riemer: According to your program, you gave your classes a lot of speech work? How did you prepare them for speaking?
Burgess: What I did twice a week with most classes was to read to them as well as I could, dramatically differentiating the roles in the dialogue, and so forth. Odd words and concepts would come up, and one could write these concepts on the board and discuss them and then go back to the reading. The kids would get enthusiastic about things. And they would talk about them. This was all based on listening to literature returned to the spoken word and as material for oral discussions.

Riemer: Would you comment on their own accents, their intonations, and so on?
Burgess: Well, it was always a problem. In England we are such a class-ridden so-

ciety that speech becomes an index of attainment, of class status, often an index of education. If a man has been to Eton or Harrow, it is supposed, rightly I think, that he has certain abilities that will be useful in the state or in the foreign office. He is tactful, he is courteous, and the like. One has to equip children in England with the knowledge of how to speak R.P., or as we call it, "The Queen's English," as well as their native dialect.

Riemer: R.P.? Real proper?
Burgess: It means "received pronunciation." It is the dialect of Oxford, London, Cambridge, Eton, and Harrow. It's a metropolitan, educated sort of dialect. It has the status we seek, which of course the Lancashire or the Northumbrian or the Yorkshire dialect doesn't have. These other dialects still have overtones of provinciality. They indicate lack of education.

Now, in a certain sense, this is not as stupid as it seems. Polite converse, educated converse, does tend to draw unto itself a special kind of speech—a mode of speech that irons out dialectal differences, that is fairly subtle, that is varied. You see, I was brought up on Lancashire dialect. I can still use this if I want to. But it is useless in the bigger world. One must not use it in the bigger society to which one aspires. The result is that one has to be equipped in England with some notion of how to use another language. This is not done in America, where there is no received pronunciation, except perhaps with news commentators on television and radio.

Riemer: Is R.P. founded on wealth, property, and title?
Burgess: It is class, but it is not class in the narrow sense. It isn't class in terms of money. In England today, probably the most polite people in the old sense, the people with the highest and the best social graces and education, are not the ruling class any longer. The money is not with the aristocracy. The aristocracy still does provide a kind of pattern, a sort of life-style that is useful to pattern one's own life on.

Riemer: This reminds me of the Jesuit drama schools that taught language, poise, and movement all at once. That was how Molière and Voltaire learned, in Jesuit theater schools. Do English schools teach movement?
Burgess: Yes, gymnastics is very important. Games are exceptionally important. Dancing is quite important. And, of course, there's the well-known interest in drama.

Riemer: I believe that confidence in one's speech and movements should underlie writing development. You taught writing by asking your students to do an interior monologue in the style of James Joyce. What would that do for them?

Burgess: It would teach them to write fluently without having to consider formal structure too much. This was highly successful. I would read, at a fairly low level, at say Form 2 (the kids would be twelve or thirteen years old), passages from *Ulysses*, and say, "Now, this is what is going on inside the man's mind. It's happening at the preverbal level, he is not saying this aloud. He is not bothering about grammar. Try now, take yourself, or take an imaginary character, and do this." They would turn out reams of interior monologue, a lot of it extremely interesting, interesting psychoanalytically. But I found it also as a way into contemporary literature. It was the most natural thing in the world. One could start a course in modern literature using that kind of thing. To hell with formal design.

Of course, I have been talking about what we call the A and B streams—the more intelligent children. There is less you can do with C stream children; on the other hand, one has a greater freedom with the C stream because one is not so tied to an examination system. One can have a free study of literature without reliance on any syllabus. You are handicapped by being up against a lack of quickness, a lack of the quick ear and the quick brain. There is no good in pretending.

Riemer: Do you think egalitarian aims hurt or help education?

Burgess: I think once you introduce an egalitarian principle into education, you debase it for those at the top.

Riemer: Also for those at the bottom?

Burgess: Yes. Definitely. You assume they can do less than they can. This is now happening in England, I fear. Kingsley Amis has been saying, "More means worse." And he is right. More education means worse education.

I think what is needed for education is a very lively value of reading. This depends a great deal on the personality of the teacher. We need more mad eccentrics in school—people who are so keen on reading and learning that some of it will rub off on the kids. Most teachers are just technicians, as far as I can see. They don't give a damn about reading. Children are not in school primarily to learn tricks. Granted, they are there to learn techniques, to learn crafts. But they're there primarily to learn about what a human personality should be like. The kind of teacher who is madly interested in things—who is prepared to break off from a mechanical, specialist exposition and launch off into a tremendous enthusiasm that is quite irrelevant—does more than the average teacher to open the children's eyes to the sense of diversity of life. I've learned more—and I think most people learn more—from the eccentric teacher, the teacher who gives us a fascinating divagation, breaking away from the subject totally. Such a teacher often will teach less of a subject but will give far more than could be learned from a cold, crop-haired specialist.

Riemer: Did you have one of those frenzies, a teacher who influenced you and stays with you in memory?
Burgess: Oh yes, indeed. Brother Campion at Xavieran. He taught French, but he would break away and talk about French cuisine. I probably learned more French from his excited exposition of how to cook a particular dish and what the various items were called than from anything else. He was connecting language with the palate, with something very immediate.

Riemer: The tongue and the palate. That *is* immediate.
Burgess: I remember he would also break off and talk about English literature—some aspect of it we were studying—and it would tie in with French culture at some point. As a result, one got a good sense of European literature. He would bring in Dante or Goethe or someone like that, and then it would be back to grammar again.

I also had an enthusiastic English teacher who would always go on from the text to the circumstances that produced it. I learned more about social history and biography from this man than I learned about literary criticism. He led into dress and music, work, travel. He had this wonderful holistic approach, which is what the eccentric teacher can give. He didn't give a damn about the narrow boundaries of the subject.

I think educational theory in England has often held that you will learn more from the digressions than from the subject that you've "contracted" to learn. I know when I was teaching in the Far East, teaching in colleges there, I would take, say, a news item about Elvis Presley. This would start a discussion about popular music, about American culture, about the cult of pop heroes. There is no room for these topics in a normal curriculum. They've got to spring out of a piece of chance reading.

There are some things that kids are very interested in that are never taught. Some kids are interested in ornithology—bird watching. Ornithology is never taught in school. I knew one youngster in England who taught himself Hebrew because he became fascinated by the way the Hebrews wrote. This type of thing is desperately important. The teacher must be *aware*, and he must be a very, very open person. To be closed into a narrow conclusion is to be anti-educational.

Riemer: Your school system in England allows digressive education?
Burgess: It does less than it did. The Labor government was very cold-blooded and mechanistic and materialistic. It represented an ideology of that kind anyway. It wanted to get rid of the big public schools, the ancient, the endowed schools, and this would mean getting rid of the "useless" education. It wanted to get rid of a lot of Latin, Roman, and Greek literature and get down to political economy and sociology, the "important" subjects.

This policy kills the richness of life. It's in the English public schools that teachers are allowed free rein. It's there that the best education goes on. The important subjects, one finds, are not included in the curriculum. The areas where customs meet, where literatures meet, where languages meet, these are not taught in segmented education. I learned everything on the side at school, very little directly.

Riemer: Fortunately you did have some mad teachers.
Burgess: I've had mad teachers all my life. I'm a mad teacher myself. Very mad.

I used to teach my students a little Chinese. This was totally heretical. I also taught them a little about Arabic writing. It gave them a sense of the problems involved in writing down speech, the conventional nature of the alphabet. I've never worried too much about bad spelling.

Riemer: You released them from the feeling that English spelling was the only spelling in the world?
Burgess: That I did. I'd say, "Let's try to write this word down in Arabic." After trying Arabic for a while, they went back all the more happily to writing English. The most successful ventures I've ever had in teaching usually have come from total lack of preparation. This is probably the best way to approach teaching.

I always felt that the children in grammar school, especially those in the A stream, were never stretched enough. And generally this is true of the whole educational system. I always felt that what the child was given was somewhat inside the child's capabilities. I deplore this. I met great opposition all the time. I meet it here, too.

As an example, let me describe the year's work, or term's work shall we say, that I did for a 3A form in an English school. The kids were thirteen, going on fourteen. I'm going back now to 1950.

I taught them how to use the International Phonetic Alphabet, how to read sounds, how to interpret symbols of all languages, how to read a foreign language, how to read the various dialects of their own language, how to distinguish between the ghost of authority and the reality of speech. This was done in relation to what we called "speech training." There was also some speech work done. Then there was "composition," which normally centered on contemporary literature. They learned how to do an interior monologue in the style of James Joyce, learned how to write free verse in the style of T. S. Eliot. They learned how to act poetic drama, even write a little of it themselves. In a single year, we did, either in copies that I gave out or that I read in class, these books:

First, H. G. Wells's *The Invisible Man*, for pleasure and also for stimulating the imagination, for dealing with the vocabulary, the scientific background, the ethical implications of this kind of situation, et cetera, et cetera. The next book was what you call here *The Martian Chronicles*, by Ray Bradbury, and what we call *The Silver Locust*. After that came George Orwell's *1984*, which in 1950 had only recently come out; Evelyn Waugh's *Decline and Fall*; and Jerome K. Jerome's *Three Men in a Boat*. These books were dealt with in two sessions a week. In addition, I used to have excerpts from the *Times*, from *Life*, from *Time* magazine, odd things, for appreciation, comprehension, vocabulary expansion, and I used to have various general knowledge items that usually related to literature, in which the students were taught about the great world.

This, I thought, was a very adequate English course. At the end of the year, they knew something. They were interested in literature. Books were no longer things like *Black Beauty*. Books were about the real adult world. The students were building up a modern vocabulary. They were learning how to read newspapers. They were learning to be interested in speech as a phenomenon, as a language phenomenon. Now I doubt you could do that here.

Riemer: I'm quite sure you couldn't. Not in our sixth grades. You'd find yourself backing up to give them skills and crafts they failed to learn in their earlier grades. There's another reason: English schools can teach for excellence because they are selective. American schools have the ideal of teaching everyone.
Burgess: It is an inevitable consequence of the totally egalitarian theory of education that everybody goes to a university. Now so long as you have, beyond these universities, another kind of university that is like the old universities, then it becomes just a matter of nomenclature. I don't think the American universities are essentially what universities were intended to be; that is, for the equipment of

people with strong, very powerful intellectual abilities. American universities are just places where people go because they have a right to go there. I think this is going to happen in England, too.

Riemer: I think some schools are consumer-training pens. We have to keep students there to keep them out of the labor market.
Burgess: That is true of the modern secondary school in England. The kids just go there and hang around until they are fifteen. Then, under law, they can leave and get a job. But while they are there, why can't we teach them something? Teach them to read and write a little if they can't already. Teach them how to apply for a job, or how to conduct themselves during an interview. Teach them a little arithmetic. But from what I've seen, they are merely marking time. They are not really doing anything.
    The big thing is to get them to want to read. This is what education is based on. Reading makes them want to write.

Riemer: How can a book teach someone to talk or write?
Burgess: Reading a book will provide materials. You see, reading is only a kind of phatic communication. It is the most wonderful thing in the world, for example, to be able to get in touch with Socrates's mind.

Riemer: But children who don't learn that writing is an extension of their talk will not realize that reading Socrates is a way of listening to him. I believe a child learning to write has to have the experience of someone reading what he writes just as his earliest listeners taught and encouraged him to learn to speak. If I were teaching primary grades, I would try to move children through gesture, motion, and dance, to talking and drawing and then finally writing. All of this before I ever introduced books. Children ought to learn to understand and communicate with each other before exotic materials are brought in to them.
Burgess: But historically reading precedes writing, doesn't it? I mean, for the masses, you see. Writing was a hieratic thing. I know this is directly opposite to what you are saying. But you learn how to write from seeing things written down. You learn how to imitate them.

Riemer: No, not entirely.
Burgess: But somebody has to do it.

Riemer: But the writer had to come before the reader, or the reader would have nothing to read. I agree that we need to imitate words we see before we can write them, but this is only true of English, which spells out so badly that we can't spell a single English word and be sure we are spelling it correctly unless we first see it spelled for us.

Burgess: Spelling is not so difficult. The very design of English spelling is made for reading.

Riemer: All spelling is made for reading. The symbols are supposed to stand for sounds of speech. We have only twenty-six symbols to stand for almost fifty basic sounds. English has to be hard to spell.

Burgess: But we can't do anything about it. We can't reform spelling.

Riemer: I agree we will never reform spelling, nor should we waste time trying. But I think it's possible to give children some temporary learning alphabet so they won't have to struggle with the inconsistencies of our spelling during their earliest years in school. The Japanese have such a system for their children, and it's quite successful. It's because of spelling that we have the Dick and Jane system in America.

Burgess: Spelling doesn't have to be taught mechanically. For example, why do we spell *light*, l-i-g-h-t? What is the "gh" doing in there? I think it is easy to appeal to the child's natural curiosity. Andrea is quite willing to listen to an account of what the word once sounded like. You say: "Well now look, if you go to Germany you'll hear them say licht." A thousand years ago, we used a word like that in England. Today we say "light," but we've kept the "gh" because we're too bloody lazy to throw it out. Similarly, the old word in Anglo-Saxon for lamb was "lambu." We got rid of the "u" but we were too lazy and forgot to get rid of the "b."

Riemer: Don't you think children learn by doing? They will learn to write by writing, to talk by talking.

Burgess: They do, indeed. Reading a book that is officially beyond their powers is in itself an act. They have to learn to grapple with a series of situations.

Riemer: Maybe they do, maybe they don't. We can't know, can we, since the grappling is in the mind?

Burgess: Well, this is where your testing comes in again, doesn't it?

Riemer: Right. Do you know there are some sixty different ways of testing reading ability and only one highly limited test for writing? Yet, a written composition can be handed about by psychologists, measured if need be, weighed. When the testers can show us a test for visible writing, I'll be more open to believe they can test invisible reading.

Burgess: I agree testing is dishonest. When I was working in the teachers' training college, it was decided to hold an education test that involved the use of matrix with the usual black/white, and so forth. One particular problem was: "Divide the following words into two columns." It was supposed to be evident to the average mind how the words could be divided. These words meant "gay" and these words meant "sad," something like that. One very, very bright boy made a "wrong" division, and the automatic system of marking failed him. What he had done was divide the words according to their Greek or Latin derivation.

Well, I had to save him. He was going to be graded down. Possibly, even rejected from the college. He had failed on what was supposed to be a very simple test. The point was, it was too simple. He thought there must be something else more difficult in the test. I think there must be other kids who are similarly affected by tests. They become petrified because they think, Well, what I have in mind doesn't fit in here. They are in such a dither about it that it becomes most destructive.

We can't talk about the American state, the American community, the spirit of America, within the context of education and arrive at any specific conclusions. But a good question is: What does America want from its education? Is its approach to education mainly a vocational one? Is its concern mainly with turning out people who can do particular jobs? Is it preparing people to attend the universities?

Frankly, I'm a bit cynical about the great words, the great mystical view of education, as being the means of elevating the soul and that kind of thing. I think kids need to be equipped with only one or two techniques. I think the major technique is the ability to read, and once they can read they *will* read. They will read books that introduce them to various things. The whole thing should be based on reading and writing ability and on an oral ability, with odd indications as to where knowledge lies. I think arithmetic is possibly of some value. But more and more, the kids are taught to compute. They aren't taught arithmetic any more. Books exist. Read books. To have, say, geography or history and that kind of thing, I believe, is unnecessary. I don't remember anything I was taught in geography or history.

Riemer: Robert Benchley wrote an article in which he listed everything he remembered from each of his four years in college. It's unfair to rate our schooling according to what facts we remember having learned.
Burgess: The present is going to become the past soon enough. That's mere quibble.

But there's a vast body of knowledge that is the result of trial and error in the past. There is also a great deal of rubbish in the past, of error. We've got to sift through this for the value. It is the job of the teacher, it is the job of the writer, the educationalists in general to decide what is valuable out of the past and to communicate this through media that are primarily and essentially verbal. Education is concerned with using words, either spoken or written or read, for the purpose of transmitting past culture to the present or to the future. This is all it can do. It hasn't any further value. It can't turn people into good citizens or induce them into being better human beings. It is not concerned with ethics. But it *is* concerned with sifting the past. This is the only thing that education can do. The rest is up to the child.

Riemer: I call acquiring these values of the past, learning. Education is different. Education is personal development through improved judgments and decisions. I think of reading and listening as the skills needed for learning. I see speaking and writing as essential for education.

An ex-Jesuit I know, a brilliant philosopher, told me that all his life he had gotten A in every class he had ever attended. He had received a law degree before entering the Society. He had gotten A in every class, and he said now at fifty, after all those years of learning, he realized he was not educated.

Burgess: At fifty-four I feel the same. I know nothing. I know all scraps of things.

Riemer: I feel there are natural times when you are just right for reading a certain kind of thing. I've owned your book, *A Clockwork Orange*, for six years now, and I've just read it in the past few months.

Burgess: I'm a very bad reader. I get bored quickly. I find it hard to read *The Brothers Karamazov* or to re-read *Crime and Punishment* or something like that. I understand the difficulties of kids who are faced with reading a big block of words. I no longer pretend. I know I am not a good reader. I read what I want to read. Also as an author I am impatient with other people's books.

Riemer: But you can communicate. And you have found yourself, and you can communicate who you are. This, I think, is all one needs.

Burgess: But you see the example of William Shakespeare whom the Baconians get wrong. They think that this man who shows such learning must have had general learning behind it. This is not so. Shakespeare had the most desirable education for a writer; namely, he had odd scraps of information. If he wanted to create a lawyer or a sailor, he could put the right words into the lawyer's or sailor's mouth. But it didn't mean he knew law or knew sailing.

Riemer: He had a good ear.

Burgess: This has got a lot to do with normal social intercourse, as you know. If you are in contact with a barrister, you may bring up something you have in common; you may learn from him by pretending you know a little about it. This is the way we learn throughout our lives. We don't learn a lot. We just learn enough material to be able to seize some kind of social communion.

Riemer: You've just finished a long article on the novel for *Encyclopedia Britannica*. Did you write it without using references?

Burgess: I didn't use any references except a dictionary of biographies to get dates of various people. No, I wrote it all out of my own existing knowledge.

Riemer: Did some of your ideas come alive as you were writing?

Burgess: Some did. I thought of things I hadn't thought of before.

Riemer: What I'm getting at is that the work of communicating clearly is educative.

Burgess: Yes, to some extent, but in simplifying for the sake of communicating, there is a danger of oversimplifying for yourself. It is very hard to put into words an extremely complex situation or an extremely complex body of knowledge. Yet the complexity and the hidden contradictions are of the very essence of all our learning. Once we start putting all these things into words, we inevitably tend to oversimplify. So when I talk about social communion, I don't mean this kind of thing. I mean there is only one purpose in any social communion, and that's learning about the other person.

Riemer: And getting him to learn about you.

Burgess: Yes. The really important things in life are people getting together, meeting, talking, praying.

Riemer: Deciding . . .

Burgess: Possibly deciding, possibly reaching decisions.

Riemer: . . . about whether to marry, to sleep, or to work.

Burgess: So they can live with someone with whom they're going to have phatic communion. If we are concerned with building a state, we're going to have to get more satisfactory phatic communion.

Riemer: Right.

Burgess: There is nothing else to learn. There is nothing more to learn. Illiterate

Negroes in the South have been better educated than the moneyed, the white children.

Riemer: Until they came to school.
Burgess: Yes. Because the folk tradition, the songs, the tales, all these gave them the experience of phatic communion. Can you think of anything else in life? All right, we make love, we beget children, we cook food, we eat food, but is there anything more important than people talking together? I can't think of anything.

Riemer: Then why shouldn't it be taught? It should be the primary objective of schools.
Burgess: Well, of course, it *should* be taught.

Dealing with the Hinterland of the Consciousness

John Cullinan/1972

From *The Paris Review* (Spring 1973). © 1973 by The Paris Review, permission of The Wylie Agency.

The following conversation appeared in the Spring 1973 issue of *Paris Review* and was reprinted in *Writers at Work: The Paris Review Interviews* (Viking, 1976). Much of the interview was conducted through an exchange of letters from June 1971 until the summer of 1972. On 2 December 1972, a portion of the interview was taped at the Center of Twentieth Century Studies of the University of Wisconsin. Burgess's schedule during his two-day visit had been backbreaking; there was scarcely a break in the round of class visits, Joyce readings, and interviews. Tired as he appeared after that routine, Burgess showed no tendency to curb the flow of his responses; and his spoken portions, when spliced with the previous exchanges, seem as polished as a written draft.

Cullinan: Are you at all bothered by the charges that you are too prolific or that your novels are too allusive?

Burgess: It has been a sin to be prolific only since the Bloomsbury group—particularly Forster—made it a point of good manners to produce, as it were, costively. I've been annoyed less by sneers at my alleged overproduction than by the imputation that to write much means to write badly. I've always written with great care and even some slowness. I've just put in rather more hours a day at the task than some writers seem to be able to. As for allusiveness—meaning, I suppose, literary allusiveness—that's surely in the tradition. Any book has behind it all the other books that have been written. The author's aware of them; the reader ought to be aware, too.

Cullinan: At what time of day do you usually work?

Burgess: I don't think it matters much; I work in the morning, but I think the afternoon is a good time to work. Most people sleep in the afternoon. I've always found it a good time, especially if one doesn't have much lunch. It's a quiet time.

It's a time when one's body is not at its sharpest, not at its most receptive—the body is quiescent, somnolent; but the brain can be quite sharp. I think also at the same time that the unconscious mind has a habit of asserting itself in the afternoon. The morning is the conscious time, but the afternoon is a time in which we should deal much more with the hinterland of the consciousness.

Cullinan: That's very interesting. Thomas Mann, on the other hand, wrote religiously virtually every day from nine to one, as though he were punching a time clock.

Burgess: Yes. One can work from nine to one, I think it's ideal; but I find that the afternoon has always been a good time for me. I think it began in Malaya when I was writing. I was working all morning. Most of us slept in the afternoon; it was very quiet. Even the servants were sleeping, even the dogs were asleep. One could work quietly away under the sun until dusk fell, and one was ready for the events of the evening. I do most of my work in the afternoon.

Cullinan: Do you imagine an ideal reader for your books?

Burgess: The ideal reader of my novels is a lapsed Catholic and failed musician, short-sighted, color-blind, auditorily biased, who has read the books that I have read. He should also be about my age.

Cullinan: A very special reader indeed. Are you writing, then, for a limited, highly educated audience?

Burgess: Where would Shakespeare have got if he had thought only of a specialized audience? What he did was to attempt to appeal on all levels, with something for the most rarefied intellectuals (who had read Montaigne) and very much more for those who could appreciate only sex and blood. I like to devise a plot that can have a moderately wide appeal. But take Eliot's *The Waste Land*, very erudite, which, probably through its more popular elements and its basic rhetorical appeal, appealed to those who did not at first understand it but made themselves understand it: The poem, a terminus of Eliot's polymathic travels, became a starting point for other people's erudition. I think every author wants to *make* his audience. But it's in his own image, and his primary audience is a mirror.

Cullinan: Do you care about what the critics think?

Burgess: I get angry at the stupidity of critics who willfully refuse to see what my books are really about. I'm aware of malevolence, especially in England. A bad review by a man I admire hurts terribly.

Cullinan: Would you ever change the drift of a book—or any literary project—because of a critic's comments?

Burgess: I don't think—with the exception of the excision of that whole final chapter of *A Clockwork Orange*—I've ever been asked to make any changes in what I've written. I do feel that the author has to know best about what he's writing—from the viewpoint of structure, intention, and so on. The critic has the job of explaining deep-level elements which the author couldn't know about. As for saying where—technically, in matters of taste and so on—a writer is going wrong, the critic rarely says what the author doesn't know already.

Cullinan: You've mentioned the possibility of working with Stanley Kubrick on a film version of Napoleon's life. Can you remain completely independent in devising the novel you're currently writing about Napoleon?

Burgess: The Napoleon project, which began with Kubrick, has now got beyond Kubrick. I found myself interested in the subject in a way that didn't suggest a film adaptation and am now working on something Kubrick couldn't use. It's a pity about the money and so on, but otherwise I'm glad to feel free, nobody looking over my shoulder.

Cullinan: Has working as a professional reviewer either helped or hindered the writing of your novels?

Burgess: It did no harm. It didn't stop me writing novels. It gave facility. It forced me into areas that I wouldn't have voluntarily entered. It paid the bills, which novels rarely do.

Cullinan: Did it bring you involuntarily to any new subjects or books that have become important to you?

Burgess: It's good for a writer to review books he is not supposed to know anything about or be interested in. Doing reviewing for magazines like *Country Life* (which smells more of horses than of calfskin bindings) means doing a fine heterogeneous batch which often does open up areas of some value in one's creative work. For instance, I had to review books on stable management, embroidery, car engines—very useful solid stuff, the very stuff of novels. Reviewing Lévi-Strauss's little lecture on anthropology (which nobody else wanted to review) was the beginning of the process which led me to write the novel *MF*.

Cullinan: You've stressed the importance of punctuality to a good reviewer. Do you find that a creative writer needs to stick to a strict work schedule, too?

Burgess: The practice of being on time with commissioned work is an aspect of politeness. I don't like being late for appointments; I don't like craving indulgence from editors in the matter of missed deadlines. Good journalistic manners tend to lead to a kind of self-discipline in creative work. It's important that a novel be approached with some urgency. Spend too long on it, or have great gaps between writing sessions, and the unity of the work tends to be lost. This is one of the troubles with *Ulysses*. The ending is different from the beginning. Technique changes halfway through. Joyce spent too long on the book.

Cullinan: Are you suggesting that Molly Bloom's soliloquy is an inappropriate ending because it's technically different from the opening chapters devoted to Stephen Dedalus?

Burgess: I don't mean the very end of *Ulysses*. I mean that from the Cyclops episode on, Joyce decides to lengthen his chapters to make the reading time correspond with the imagined time of enactment. In that sense the book is technically not so much a unity as people like to think. Compare the Aeolus episode with the Oxen of the Sun and you'll see what I mean.

Cullinan: Considering the length of time that Proust spent on his novel and that Mann devoted to *Joseph and His Brothers*, is seven years really so long for a work as great as *Ulysses*? What, then, about the seventeen years Joyce frittered away on *Finnegans Wake*?

Burgess: Time spent on a book is perhaps no concern of the reader's, really. (*Madame Bovary*, a comparatively short book, took longer to write, surely, than the *Joseph* sequence.) The whole question is whether the writer can be the same person, with the same aims and approach to technique, over a long stretch of time. *Ulysses*, being innovative, had to go on being more and more innovative as it was written, and this makes it a sort of disunity. *Finnegans Wake*, though it took much longer, got its essential technique established pretty early.

Cullinan: Your new book, *Joysprick*, is coming out soon, I understand. How does it differ in emphasis from *Re Joyce*?

Burgess: It covers a little of the same ground but not very much. It's an attempt to examine the nature of Joyce's language, not from a strictly linguistic point of view but from a point of view which may be said to be exactly halfway between literary criticism and linguistics; it doesn't use many technical terms. It makes a phonetic analysis of Joyce's language; there aren't many linguists who can do this nowadays. Phonetics is rather old hat. But it does examine dialects of *Ulysses*, the importance of establishing a pronunciation in *Finnegans Wake*, an analysis of the way Joyce constructs a sentence. It is not a profound book; it is meant to be a beginner's guide to the language of Joyce, and the real work of probing into Joyce's linguistic method must be left to a more scholarly person than myself.

Cullinan: You say that you are taking what you call an old-fashioned phonetic approach to Joyce's language; and yet in *MF* you make use of Lévi-Strauss's structuralism. Are you at all interested in considering Joyce from the point of view of structural linguistics?

Burgess: I don't think that's my line; I think this has to be left to a scholar. I think somebody has to be in a university, has to be not engaged as I am in the production of books and teaching and lecturing and living a pretty varied "show-biz" life; this is a job for a cool scholar. I don't think I qualify to do it. I'm interested in what sounds Joyce is hearing when he is writing down the speech of Molly Bloom and Leopold Bloom and the minor characters. It's a matter of great literary import, I would suggest, because the final monologue of Molly Bloom inclines a particular way of speech which is not consonant with her declared background. Here in Joyce there is something very implausible about the fact that Molly Bloom is the daughter of a major, brought up in the Gibraltar garrison, coming to Dublin speaking and thinking like any low Dublin fishwife. This seems to be totally inconsistent, and the point has not even been made before. I know Gibraltar better than Joyce did and better than most Joyce scholars. I'm trying to examine this.

Cullinan: If Molly's monologue is too elegant, isn't it one of Joyce's points to have the poetic emerge from the demotic?

Burgess: It's not elegant enough. I mean, the fact that she uses Irish locutions like "Pshaw." She would not use any such term, she would not.

Cullinan: There's a geographical thing.

Burgess: There's a pattern implied. There's a social thing. In a very small garrison town like Gibraltar with this man, Major Tweedy, whose previous wife is Spanish, his half-Spanish daughter would speak either Spanish as a first language (and not with the usual grammar) or English as a first language—but certainly both languages: in the first instance in an Andalusian way, and in the second instance, in a totally class-conscious, pseudo-patrician way. She would not come back to Dublin and suddenly start speaking like a Dublin fishwife.

Cullinan: So Molly's language is probably closer in terms of social background to that of Nora Barnacle.

Burgess: It is indeed; this final image is an image of Nora Barnacle and not of Molly at all. And as we know from Nora's letters, Joyce must have studied the letters and learned from them how to set down this warm, womanly pattern of speech. Nora wrote the letters totally without punctuation, and sometimes it is hard to distinguish between a chunk of one of Nora's letters and a chunk of Molly's final monologue.

Cullinan: I'm looking forward to this book. Have you thought of writing a long, expansive novel?
Burgess: I have in mind two long novels—one on a theatrical family from the Middle Ages till today, the other on a great British composer. The projects are so big that I'm scared of starting on them.

Cullinan: Could you begin with a few excerpts in the form of short stories?
Burgess: I can't write short stories, not easily, anyway, and I'd rather keep my novel dark until it's ready for the light. I made the mistake once of publishing a chapter of an emergent novel in the *Transatlantic Review* and the sight of the extract in cold print turned me against the project. This is my one unfinished novel.

Cullinan: Do you still hope to write a novel about Theseus's encounter with the Minotaur, or has Rawcliffe's scenario in *Enderby* disposed of that project?
Burgess: As for the Minotaur idea, I have thought of publishing a volume of all Enderby's poems, and they would include *The Pet Beast* (which has become, incidentally, the title of the Italian version of *Enderby—La Dolce Bestia*). I can see the sense of pretending that someone else has written your book for you, especially your book of poems. It frees you of responsibility—"Look, I know this is bad, but I didn't write it—one of my characters wrote it." *Don Quixote, Lolita, Ada*—it's an old and still lively tradition. I don't get writing blocks except from the stationer, but I do feel so sickened by what I write that I don't want to go on.

Cullinan: Do you write the big scenes first, as Joyce Cary did?
Burgess: I start at the beginning, go on to the end, then stop.

Cullinan: Is each book charted completely in advance?
Burgess: I chart a little first—list of names, rough synopsis of chapters, and so on. But one daren't overplan; so many things are generated by the sheer act of writing.

Cullinan: Do you write nonfiction any differently?
Burgess: The process is the same.

Cullinan: Is the finished product much influenced by the fact that you do the first draft on the typewriter?
Burgess: I don't write drafts; I do page one many, many times and move on to page two. I pile up sheet after sheet, each in its final state, and at length I have a novel that doesn't—in my view—need any revision.

Cullinan: Then you don't revise at all?
Burgess: Revising, as I said, is done with each page, not with each chapter or the whole book. Rewriting a whole book would bore me.

Cullinan: Why did you decide to continue *Inside Mr. Enderby*, the first half of *Enderby*, after several years?
Burgess: I planned the work as the long book that came out in America, but—since I was approaching the end of the one year that the doctors had given me to live—I was not able to do more than the first half in 1959–60. Unwillingness of the publishers to publish *Inside Mr. Enderby*—as Part I was called in England—made me delay the writing of Part II. But I had it all in my mind right at the start.

Cullinan: After the doctors had diagnosed a brain tumor following your collapse in a Brunei classroom, why did you choose to write during that "terminal year" rather than travel, say? Were you confined in semi-invalid status?
Burgess: I was no semi-invalid. I was very fit and active. (This made me doubt the truth of the diagnosis.) But to travel the world one needs money, and this I didn't have. It's only in fiction that "terminal year" men have something tucked away. The fact is that my wife and I needed to eat, and so on, and the only job I could do (who would employ me?) was writing. I wrote much because I was paid little. I had no great desire to leave a literary name behind me.

Cullinan: Did your style change at all during that year, possibly as a result of your feeling under sentence?
Burgess: I don't think so. I was old enough to have established some kind of narrative style; but the real business of working on style, of course, came later. The novels written in this so-called quasi-terminal year—pseudo-terminal year—were not written with, you know, excessive speed; it was just a matter of working hard every day, working very hard every day—and *all* day—including the evenings. A good deal of care went into the works and what people look for in what seems an excessive amount of production is evidence of carelessness. There may be a little of that; but it's not because of the speed or apparent speed but because of flaws in my own makeup. I don't think it is possible to say that a particular work is ob-

viously written during the terminal year. I don't think there is any qualitative difference between the various novels; and certainly I was not aware of any influence on style, on way of writing, caused by this knowledge.

Cullinan: Several of your novels contain poetry written by various characters. Have you thought of writing poetry again seriously?

Burgess: I've seen produced my version of *Cyrano de Bergerac*. This is in rhyme, and it worked well, as I expected it to. But I don't plan volumes of verse—too naked, too personal. I plan further stage translations—*Peer Gynt*, Chekhov's *Chaika*—and I'm working on a musical of *Ulysses*. I'm much more likely to return to music. I've been asked to write a clarinet concerto, and my music to *Cyrano* has gone down well enough.

Cullinan: Do you ever use musical forms in designing your novels?

Burgess: Ah yes, one can learn a lot from musical forms. I'm planning a novel in the style of a classical symphony—minuet and all. The motivations will be purely formal, so that a development section in which sexual fantasies are enacted can follow a realistic exposition with neither explanation nor transitional device, returning to it (now as recapitulation) with a similar lack of psychological justification or formal trickery.

Cullinan: Composers traffic heavily in transitions. Isn't this particular instance of literary composition by musical analogy an example of "formal trickery," best understood by the reader who is at least an amateur musician?

Burgess: I think that music does teach practitioners in other arts useful formal devices, but the reader doesn't have to know their provenance. Here's an example. A composer modulates from one key to another by the use of the "punning" chord, the augmented sixth (punning because it is also a dominant seventh). You can change, in a novel, from one scene to another by using a phrase or statement common to both—this is quite common. If the phrase or statement means different things in the different contexts, so much the more musical.

Cullinan: One notices that the form of *A Vision of Battlements* is meant to be similar to that of Ennis's passacaglia, but can any but the most tenuously analogous relation be established between literature and music generally?

Burgess: I agree that the musico-literary analogies can be pretty tenuous, but in the widest possible formal sense—sonata form, opera, and so on—we've hardly begun to explore the possibilities. The Napoleon novel I'm writing apes the *Eroica* formally—irritable, quick, swiftly transitional in the first movement (up to

Napoleon's coronation); slow, very leisurely, with a binding beat, suggesting a funeral march for the second. This isn't pure fancy: It's an attempt to unify a mass of historical material in the comparatively brief space of about 150,000 words. As for the reader having to know about music—it doesn't really matter much. In one novel I wrote, "The orchestra lunged into a loud chord of twelve notes, all of them different." Musicians hear the discord, non-musicians don't, but there's nothing there to baffle them and prevent them reading on. I don't understand baseball terms, but I can still enjoy Malamud's *The Natural.* I don't play bridge, but I find the bridge game in Fleming's *Moonraker* absorbing—it's the emotions conveyed that matter, not what the players are doing with their hands.

Cullinan: What about film technique as an influence on your writing?
Burgess: I've been much more influenced by the stage than by the film. I write in scenes too long for unbroken cinematic representation. But I like to run a scene through in my mind before writing it down, seeing everything happen, hearing some of the dialogue. I've written for both television and cinema, but not very successfully. Too literary, or something. I get called in by makers of historical films to revise the dialogue, which they then restore to its original form.

Cullinan: What happened to the proposed film versions of *Enderby* and *Nothing Like the Sun*?
Burgess: The filming of *Enderby* fell through because the producer dropped dead at the Cannes film festival. The Shakespeare project came almost when Warner Brothers was being sold, and all existing enterprises were scrapped when the new regime started. It may, however, yet be fulfilled. Film people are very conservative about dialogue: They honestly believe that the immediate grasp of lexical meaning is more important than the impact of rhythm and emotionally charged sound. It's regarded as cleverer to pretend that the people of the past would have spoken like us if they'd been lucky enough to know how to do so, delighted with the opportunity to view themselves and their times from our angle. *The Lion in Winter* is thought to be a triumphant solution of the medieval dialogue problem, but of course it's just cheap.

Cullinan: Does your novel in progress pose any special linguistic problems that may create obstacles for Stanley Kubrick as well?
Burgess: The Napoleon novel is difficult from the dialogue angle, but my instinct tells me to use rhythms and vocabulary not much different from our own. After

all, Byron's *Don Juan* could almost have been written today. I imagine the soldiers speaking as today's soldiers speak.

They're speaking in French, anyway. As for the Napoleon film, Kubrick must go his own way, and he'll find it a difficult way.

Cullinan: Do you expect to write any more historical novels?
Burgess: I'm working on a novel intended to express the feel of England in Edward III's time, using Dos Passos's devices. I believe there's great scope in the historical novel, so long as it isn't by Mary Renault or Georgette Heyer. The four-teenth century of my novel will be mainly evoked in terms of smell and visceral feelings, and it will carry an undertone of general disgust rather than hey-nonny nostalgia.

Cullinan: Which of Dos Passos's techniques will you use?
Burgess: The novel I have in mind, and for which I've done a ninety-page plan, is about the Black Prince. I thought it might be amusing blatantly to steal the Camera Eye and the Newsreel devices from Dos Passos just to see how they might work, especially with the Black Death and Crécy and the Spanish campaign. The effect might be of the fourteenth century going on in another galaxy where lan-guage and literature had somehow got themselves into the twentieth century. The technique might make the historical characters look remote and rather comic—which is what I want.

Cullinan: Are Mary Renault's retellings of Greek myths as bad as all that?
Burgess: Oh, they're not unsatisfactory, far from it. Rattling good reads if you like that sort of thing. They just don't excite me, that's all. It's undoubtedly my fault.

Cullinan: Do you expect to write another novel of the future, like *A Clockwork Orange* or *The Wanting Seed*?
Burgess: I don't plan a novel about the future except for a mad novella in which England has become a mere showplace run by America.

Cullinan: Is England going to become simply an oversized tourist boutique—or the fifty-first state?
Burgess: I used to think that England might become just a place that liked to be visited—like that island in J. M. Barrie's *Mary Rose*—but now I see that so many of the things worth seeing—old things—are disappearing so that England can

become a huge Los Angeles, all motorways, getting about more important than actually getting anywhere. England is now going into Europe, not—as I had once expected and even hoped—America, and I think it will now have Europe's faults without its virtues. The decimal coinage is a monstrosity, and soon there'll be liters of beer, as in *Nineteen Eighty-Four*, and no cheap wine or caporal tobacco. Absorption, anyway, since England either has to absorb or be absorbed. Napoleon has won.

Cullinan: You mentioned that *A Clockwork Orange* has a concluding chapter in the British edition that isn't available in the American ones. Does this bother you?
Burgess: Yes, I hate having two different versions of the same book. The U.S. edition has a chapter short, and hence the arithmological plan is messed up. Also the implied view of juvenile violence as something to go through and then grow out of is missing in the American edition; and this reduces the book to a mere parable, whereas it was intended to be a novel.

Cullinan: What happens in that twenty-first chapter?
Burgess: In Chapter 21 Alex grows up and realizes that ultraviolence is a bit of a bore, and it's time he had a wife and a malenky googoogooing malchickiwick to call him dadada. This was meant to be a mature conclusion, but nobody in America has ever liked the idea.

Cullinan: Did Stanley Kubrick consider filming the Heinemann version?
Burgess: Kubrick discovered the existence of this final chapter when he was halfway through the film, but it was too late to think of altering the concept. Anyway, he, too, an American, thought it too milk-and-watery. I don't know what to think now. After all, it's twelve years since I wrote the thing.

Cullinan: Did you attempt to get the complete novel published here?
Burgess: Yes—well, I was very dubious about the book itself. When I wrote the book, my agent was not willing to present it to a publisher, which is rather unusual; and the sort of publishers in England were very dubious about the book. So when the American publisher made this objection to the final chapter, I didn't feel myself to be in a very strong position. I was a little hesitant to judge the book; I was a little too close to it. I thought: Well, they may be right. Because authors do tend to be (especially after the completion of a book) very uncertain about the value of the book; and perhaps I gave in a little too weakly, but my concern was partly a financial one. I wanted it to be published in America, and I wanted some money out of it. So I said, "Yes." Whether I'd say "Yes" now, I don't know; but I've

been persuaded by so many critics that the book is better in its American form that I say, "All right, they know best."

Cullinan: Would it be possible for an American press to put out a limited, hard-bound edition which includes the excluded chapter as a sort of appendix?
Burgess: I think this should be possible. The best way of doing it is to bring out an annotated edition of the book with this final chapter—an idea which is being resisted by my publishers for some reason, I don't know why. I would be very interested in the comments of the average, say, American student on the differences between the two versions. Because I'm not able to judge myself very clearly now as to whether I was right or wrong. What is *your* opinion, what do you feel about that?

Cullinan: I find the last chapter problematical in that while it creates an entirely different context for the work, it seems anticlimactic after the neat resurrection of the old Alex in the twentieth chapter.
Burgess: Yes.

Cullinan: Still it should remain, because your meaning is altered by the cutting off of the context.
Burgess: Well, the worst example I know of unjustified translation is to be found in Ford Madox Ford's *Parade's End*, where the British edition, under the imprint of Bodley Head, Graham Greene has taken upon himself to present *Parade's End* as a trilogy, saying he doesn't think the final novel, *The Last Post*, works, and he feels perhaps Ford would have agreed with him; and therefore he has taken the liberty of getting rid of the final book. I think Greene is wrong; I think that whatever Ford said, the work is a tetralogy, and the thing is severely maimed with the loss of his final book. An author is not to be trusted in his judgment of this sort of thing. Authors very frequently try to be indifferent to their books. Certainly they are so sick of their books that they don't want to make any serious judgment on them. The problem comes up, you see, when one reads Evelyn Waugh's *A Handful of Dust*, because this frightful ending (where Tony Last spends all his time reading Dickens to this half-breed in the jungle), appeared previously as a short story; and knowing the short story one has a strange attitude to the book. Which makes us feel that here is a deliberate pasting together, where this giant figure at the end that turns up does not spring automatically out of the book but is just taken arbitrarily from another work. Perhaps one shouldn't know too much about these things. Of course, one can't avoid it. These two versions of Samuel

Butler's *Way of All Flesh*—this raises the problem. Which version would we like better, which is the right version? It's better to know only one thing, to be fairly ignorant of what was going on. You know, behind the version we know.

Cullinan: Isn't this an argument against publishing a complete *A Clockwork Orange*, since a twenty-chapter version is embedded in everyone's mind?
Burgess: I don't know; they're both relevant. They seem to me to express in a sense the difference between the British approach to life and the American approach to life. There may be something very profound to say about this difference in these different presentations of the novel. I don't know; I'm not able to judge.

Cullinan: In *A Clockwork Orange* and *Enderby* especially there's a persistent strain of mockery toward youth culture and its music. Is there anything good about them?
Burgess: I despise whatever is obviously ephemeral and yet is shown as possessing some kind of ultimate value. The Beatles, for instance. Most youth culture, especially music, is based on so little knowledge of tradition, and it often elevates ignorance into a virtue. Think of the musically illiterate who set themselves up as "arrangers." And youth is so conformist, so little concerned with maverick values, so proud of being rather than making, so bloody sure that it and it alone *knows*.

Cullinan: You used to play in a jazz band. Is there any hope that their interest in rock music may lead youth to jazz—or even to classical music?
Burgess: I still play jazz, chiefly on a four-octave electric organ, and I prefer this to listening to it. I don't think jazz is for listening but for playing. I'd like to write a novel about a jazz pianist, or, better, about a pub pianist—which I once was, like my father before me. I don't think rock leads on to a liking for jazz. The kids are depressingly static in their tastes. They do so want *words*, and jazz gets along very nicely without words.

Cullinan: In two of your novels the wordsmiths Shakespeare and Enderby are inspired by the Muse. But you've said as well that you like to regard your books as "works of craftsmanship for sale."
Burgess: The Muse in *Nothing Like the Sun* was not a real muse—only syphilis. The girl in *Enderby* is really sex, which, like syphilis, has something to do with the creative process. I mean, you can't be a genius and sexually impotent. I still think that inspiration comes out of the act of making an artifact, a work of craft.

Cullinan: Are works of art the products of strong libido?

Burgess: Yes, I think art is sublimated libido. You can't be a eunuch priest, and you can't be a eunuch artist. I became interested in syphilis when I worked for a time at a mental hospital full of GPI cases. I discovered there was a correlation between the spirochete and mad talent. The tubercle also produces a lyrical drive. Keats had both.

Cullinan: Has your interest in Mann's *Doctor Faustus* influenced the use of syphilis and other diseases in your own work?

Burgess: I've been much influenced by the thesis of Mann's *Doctor Faustus*, but I wouldn't want to have syphilis myself in order to be Wagner or Shakespeare or Henry VIII. Some prices are too high to pay. Oh, you'll want examples of these GPI talents. There was one man who'd turned himself into a kind of Scriabin, another who could give you the day of the week for any date in history, another who wrote poems like Christopher Smart. Many patients were orators or grandiose liars. It was like being imprisoned in a history of European art. Politics as well.

Cullinan: Have you used in your novels any of the GPI cases that you encountered?

Burgess: I did have the intention at one time of writing a long novel—a kind of *Magic Mountain*, I suppose—about life in a mental hospital; and perhaps I may yet get down to it. Of course, the trouble is it would take on a kind of political significance. People might think of works like *Cancer Ward*; it might be thought as presenting a clearly marked division between the patients and the hospital staff. One would be trading in a sort of political allegory; it's so easy to do that. Yet what interests me about a mental hospital that specializes in General Paralysis of the Insane is this relationship between disease and talent. Some of the tremendous skills that these patients show—these tremendous, mad abilities—all stem out of the spirochete. I have pursued this in a couple of novels (or at least in one novel), but to do it on a larger scale would require a kind of rationale which I haven't yet worked out. I don't think it should be done purely as a documentary novel, as a naturalistic presentation of what life is like in such hospitals; but it does suggest to me that it's tied up with symbols of some kind—tied up with an interior, deeper meaning. Of course one never knows what this meaning will be, but *The Magic Mountain* has its deeper meanings beneath the naturalistic surface. I wouldn't want to imitate that. One has to wait, I'm afraid—a long time sometimes—for the experience one's had to present itself in workable form, as a form that can be shaped into something like a work of art.

Cullinan: Do you see any contradiction in choosing a craftsman like Joyce as one of your literary models while classifying yourself as a "Grub Street writer" at the same time?
Burgess: Why contradiction? But I've never really regarded Joyce as a literary model. Joyce can't be imitated, and there's no imitation Joyce in my work. All you can learn from Joyce is the exact use of language. "Grub Street writer" means Dr. Johnson as well as our wretched columnists, and Johnson was an exact user of language.

Cullinan: You've certainly studied Joyce very thoroughly. Does knowing what he has done open more doors than it closes?
Burgess: Joyce opened doors only to his own narrow world; his experiments were for himself only. But all novels are experimental, and *Finnegans Wake* is no more spectacular an experiment than, say, *Prancing Nigger* or *His Monkey Wife*. It looks spectacular because of the language. *MF*, believe it or not, is a completely original experiment.

Cullinan: Isn't Joyce's attempt to devote virtually an entire novel to the unconscious more than a purely linguistic experiment?
Burgess: Yes, of course. The wakeworld is only narrow in that it's asleep, fixed on one set of impulses only, has too few characters.

Cullinan: Can't contemporary writers use some of Joyce's techniques without being mere imitators?
Burgess: You can't use Joyce's techniques without being Joyce. Technique and material are one. You can't write like Beethoven without writing Beethoven, unless you're Beethoven.

Cullinan: Has Nabokov influenced your work at all? You've praised *Lolita* highly.
Burgess: Reading *Lolita* meant that I enjoyed using lists of things in *The Right to an Answer*. I've not been much influenced by Nabokov, nor do I intend to be. I was writing the way I write before I knew he existed. But I've not been impressed so much by another writer in the last decade or so.

Cullinan: Yet you've been called an "English Nabokov," probably because of the cosmopolitan strain and verbal ingenuity in your writing.

Burgess: No influence. He's a Russian, I'm English. I meet him halfway in certain temperamental endowments. He's very artificial, though.

Cullinan: In what way?

Burgess: Nabokov is a natural dandy on the grand international scale. I'm still a provincial boy, scared of being too nattily dressed. All writing is artificial, and Nabokov's artifacts are only contrived in the *récit* part. His dialogue is always natural and masterly (when he wants it to be). *Pale Fire* is only termed a novel because there's no other term for it. It's a masterly literary artifact, which is poem, commentary, casebook, allegory, sheer structure. But I note that most people go back to reading the poem, not what surrounds the poem. It's a fine poem, of course. Where Nabokov goes wrong, I think, is in sometimes *sounding* old-fashioned—a matter of rhythm, as though Huysmans is to him a sound and modern writer whose tradition is worthy to be worked in. John Updike sounds old-fashioned sometimes in the same way—glorious vocabulary and imagery but a lack of muscle in the rhythm.

Cullinan: Does Nabokov rank at the top with Joyce?

Burgess: He won't go down in history as one of the greatest names. He's unworthy to unlatch Joyce's shoe.

Cullinan: Have any new writers appeared of late that you think are destined for greatness?

Burgess: I can't think of any in England. The trouble with American writers is that they die before becoming great—Nathanael West, Scott Fitzgerald, etc. Mailer will become a great autobiographer. Ellison will be great if only he'll write more. Too many *homines unius libri* like Heller.

Cullinan: American writers certainly tend to burn themselves out early, at least. Do you think it takes more than one book for a writer to earn the label "great"?

Burgess: A man can write one book that can be great, but this doesn't make him a great writer—just the writer of a great book. Samuel Butler's *Way of All Flesh* is a great novel, but nobody calls Butler a great novelist. I think a writer has to extend very widely, as well as plunge very deep, to be a great novelist.

Cullinan: Did Fitzgerald write a great novel?

Burgess: I don't think Fitzgerald's books great—style too derivatively romantic, far less of that curious freshness of vision than you find in Hemingway—Hemingway is a great novelist, I think, but he never wrote a great novel (a novella, yes). I think America likes its artists to die young, in atonement for materialistic

America's sins. The English leave the dying young to Celts like Dylan Thomas and Behan. But I can't understand the American literary block—as in Ellison or Salinger—unless it means that the blocked man isn't forced economically to write (as the English writer, lacking campuses and grants, usually is) and hence can afford the luxury of fearing the critics' pounce on a new work not as good as the last (or the first). American writers drink a lot when they're "blocked" and drunkenness—being a kind of substitute for art—makes the block worse. I've found it best, especially since my first wife, who drank less than I, died of cirrhosis, to drink little. But I smoke much, and that's probably worse than five martinis a day.

Cullinan: You've spoken highly of Defoe as a novelist and practical journalist, and you also admire Sterne as a writer. What special appeal do these eighteenth-century writers have for you?

Burgess: I admire Defoe because he worked hard. I admire Sterne because he did everything the French are trying so unhandily to do now. Eighteenth-century prose has a tremendous vitality and scope. Not Fielding, though. Sentimental, too much given to contrivances. Sterne and Swift (who, Joyce said, should have exchanged names) are men one can learn technically from all the time.

Cullinan: Speaking of the French—your playful novels of ideas tend to be more in the French literary tradition, perhaps, than any other. Has this kept them from becoming better known in England and America?

Burgess: The novels I've written are really medieval Catholic in their thinking, and people don't want that today. God forbid they should be "French." If they're not read, it's because the vocabulary is too big, and people don't like using dictionaries when they're reading mere novels. I don't give a damn, anyway.

Cullinan: This Catholic emphasis accounts in part for the frequent comparisons made between your novels and Evelyn Waugh's, and yet you've said you don't find Waugh's aristocratic idea of Catholicism attractive. What do you like about his work?

Burgess: Waugh is funny, Waugh is elegant, Waugh is economical. His Catholicism, which I despise as all cradle Catholics despise converts, is the thing in him which means least to me. Indeed, it injures his *Sword of Honor*.

Cullinan: This charge has often been made—along with that of sentimentality—against *Brideshead Revisited*, but *Sword of Honor* is often called the best novel in English about World War II. How does Waugh's (or Guy Crouchback's) Catholicism weaken it?

Burgess: Crouchback's Catholicism weakens *Sword of Honor* in the sense that it sectarianizes the book—I mean, we have Crouchback's moral view of the war, and this is not enough: We need something that lies beneath religion. In our age it's a weakness to make Catholic theology the basis of a novel since it means everything's cut and dried and the author doesn't have to rethink things out. The weakness of Greene's *Heart of the Matter* is derived from its author's fascination with theology: The sufferings of the hero are theological sufferings, invalid outside the narrow field of Catholicism. When I taught Waugh and Greene to Muslim students in Malaya, they used to laugh. Why can't this man have two wives if he wants them, they would say. What's wrong with eating the bit of bread the priest gives you when you've been sleeping with a woman not your wife, and so on. They never laughed at the tragic heroes of the Greeks and Elizabethans.

Cullinan: Does the difference between cradle and convert Catholicism influence an author's work in such an essential way that you tend to prefer a novelist like François Mauriac to Graham Greene?
Burgess: English converts to Catholicism tend to be bemused by its glamor and even look for more glamor in it than is actually there—like Waugh, dreaming of an old English Catholic aristocracy, or Greene, fascinated by sin in a very cold-blooded way. I wished I liked Mauriac more as a writer. The fact is that I prefer the converted Catholics because they happen to be better novelists. I do try to forget that Greene is a Catholic when I read him. He, too, is now, I think, trying to forget. *The Comedians* was a kind of philosophical turning point. *Travels with My Aunt* is deliciously free of morality of any kind, except a very delightful kind of inverted morality.

Cullinan: In an essay on Waugh you mentioned "the Puritan that lurks in every English Catholic." Do you see this residue of Puritanism lurking in your own writing at all?
Burgess: Of course it's in me. We English take our Catholicism seriously, which the Italians and French don't, and that makes us earnest and obsessed about sin. We really absorbed hell—perhaps a very Nordic notion—and think about it when committing adultery. I'm so Puritanical that I can't describe a kiss without blushing.

Cullinan: Are there any limits that you think an author should observe in the language he uses to present controversial subject matter?
Burgess: My aversion to describing amorous details in my work is probably that I treasure physical love so highly I don't want to let strangers in on it. For, after all,

when we describe copulation we're describing our own experiences. I like privacy. I think that other writers should do what they can do, and if they can spend— as one of my American girl students did—ten pages on the act of fellatio without embarrassing themselves, very good luck to them. But I think there's more artistic pleasure to be gained from the ingenious circumvention of a taboo than from what is called total permissiveness. When I wrote my first Enderby novel, I had to make my hero say "For cough," since "Fuck off" was not then acceptable. With the second book the climate had changed, and Enderby was at liberty to say "Fuck off." I wasn't happy. It was too easy. He still said "For cough," while others responded with "Fuck off." A compromise. Literature, however, thrives on taboos, just as all art thrives on technical difficulties.

Cullinan: Several years ago you wrote, "I believe the wrong God is temporarily ruling the world and that the true God has gone under," and added that the novelist's vocation predisposes him to this Manichaean view. Do you still believe this?
Burgess: I still hold this belief.

Cullinan: Why do you think that the novelist is predisposed to regard the world in terms of "essential opposition"? Unlike the Manichaeans you seem to maintain a traditional Christian belief in original sin.
Burgess: Novels are about conflicts. The novelist's world is one of essential oppositions of character, aspiration, and so on. I'm only a Manichee in the widest sense of believing that duality is the ultimate reality; the original-sin bit is not really a contradiction, though it does lead one on to depressingly French heresies, like Graham Greene's own Jansenism, as well as Albigensianism (Joan of Arc's religion), Catharism, and so on. I'm entitled to an eclectic theology as a novelist, if not as a human being.

Cullinan: In planning your novels, have you ever considered separating them, as Simenon does, into "commercial" and "uncommercial" works or, like Greene, into "novels" and "entertainments"?
Burgess: All my novels belong to the one category—intended to be, as it were, serious entertainment, no moral aim, no solemnity. I want to please.

Cullinan: Aren't you divorcing morality from aesthetics? This view is certainly consistent with your dismissal in *Shakespeare* of the Anglo-Saxon notion that a great artist must have a great moral sensibility.
Burgess: I don't divorce morals and aesthetics. I merely believe that a man's literary greatness is no index of his personal ethics. I don't, true, think that the job of

literature is to teach us how to behave, but I think it can make clearer the whole business of moral choice by showing what the nature of life's problems is. It's after truth, which is not goodness.

Cullinan: You've said that the novel gets an implied set of values derived from religion, but that other arts, such as music and architecture, are, unlike fiction, "neutral." Does this make them more or less attractive at this point?

Burgess: I enjoy writing music precisely because one is divorced from "human" considerations like belief, conduct. Pure form, nothing more. But then I tend to despise music just because it is so *mindless.* I've been writing a string quartet based on a musical theme that Shakespeare throws at us, in sol-fa notation, in *Love's Labour's Lost* (the theme is CDGAEF), and it's been pure bliss. I've been thoroughly absorbed by it, on planes, in hotel bedrooms, anywhere where I had nothing else to do and there was no bloody muzak playing. (Don't the muzak purveyors ever think of the people who actually have to write music?) Now I'm a little ashamed that the music engages nothing but purely formal problems. So I oscillate between a hankering after pure form and a realization that literature is probably valuable because it *says things.*

Cullinan: How does political neutrality figure in all this? In your novels the neutrals, such as Mr. Theodorescu in *Tremor of Intent,* are usually villains.

Burgess: If art should be neutral, if it can, life should be committed, if it can. There's no connection between political and religious neutrality and that blessed, *achieved* neutrality of, say, music. Art is, so to speak, the Church triumphant, but the rest of life is in the Church militant. I believe that good and evil exist, though they have nothing to do with art, and that evil has to be resisted. There's no inconsistency in holding an aesthetic so different from such an ethic.

Cullinan: Several of your recent novels have exotic foreign settings, even though you remarked a few years ago that the artist should exhaust the resources of the "here and now" as a true test of his art. Have you changed your mind?

Burgess: Yes, I changed my mind. I'm limited by temperament, I now discover, to being moved or excited by any place in the world so long as it's not England. This means that all my settings must be "exotic."

Cullinan: Why do you consider England so dull a subject?

Burgess: Dull for me, if not for others. I like societies where there's a dynamism of conflict. In other words, I think novels should be about the whole of a society— by implication if nothing else—and not just a little pocket inside. English fiction tends to be about these pockets—love affairs in Hampstead, Powell's bohemian aristocracy, Snow's men of power. Dickens gave you the lot, like Balzac. Much modern American fiction gives you the lot. You could reconstruct the whole of modern America from even a little mad fantasy like Phil Roth's *The Breast*. But I may have a personal thing about England—a sense of exclusion, and so on. It may even be so simple a matter as liking extreme climates, fights in bars, exotic waterfronts, fish soup, a lot of garlic. I find it easier to imagine a surrealistic version of New Jersey than of old England, though I could see some American genius making a whole strange world of Mr. Heath's inheritance. Probably (as Thomas Pynchon never went to Valletta or Kafka to America) it's best to imagine your own foreign country. I wrote a very good account of Paris before I ever went there. Better than the real thing.

Cullinan: Was this in *The Worm and the Ring*?
Burgess: Yes. Paris was a town I always tried to avoid. But I've been more and more in it recently and find that the account of Paris I wrote (although it smells of maps and tourist guides) is not unlike the reality. This is true also with Joyce's Gibraltar in *Ulysses*; one has no need to visit the country to write about the country.

Cullinan: And yet you draw a good picture of Leningrad in *Honey for the Bears*.
Burgess: Oh, I knew Leningrad. Yes, that's right. But not too well; for if one gets to know a town too well, then the sharpness of the impression is blunted, and one is not interested in writing about it. Anyway, the interesting point is that one first meets a town through its smells; this is especially true in Europe. Leningrad has a peculiar smell of its own, and you become habituated to these smells in time, and you forget what they are; and you're not able to approach it in those highly sensuous terms when writing about it if you know a place too well. If you're in a town for about a month somewhere, you can't retain a sensuous impression. As with Paris, you smell the Gauloise when you arrive; but you cease to smell the Gauloise in time. You get so used to it.

Cullinan: You've said that Leningrad resembles Manchester. How are they alike?
Burgess: I think it was just the sense of the architecture, the rather broken-down architecture of Leningrad, the sense of large numbers of the working class, rather shabbily dressed. And I suppose in some ways the *smell* of Manchester—I always associated Manchester with the smell of tanneries, very pungent smells, as you know. I got this same smell out of Leningrad. It's a small thing, but these small

things have a curious habit of becoming important. You try to fix a place in your mind. I don't know what the smell of Milwaukee is, I don't think the American cities have any smell. That's probably why they are rather unmemorable. Smell is the most elusive of the senses. To a novelist it is somehow the most important of the senses.

Cullinan: You've also said that the serious novelist should be prepared to stay in one place and really get to know it. Do you hope to do this with Italy now?
Burgess: Again, I seem to have changed my mind. I think I shall want to invent places more than merely reproduce them, and don't please put this down to the influence of *Ada*. The next four novels will be set, respectively, in medieval England, modern New Jersey, Italy in the last fifty years, Jane Austen's England.

Cullinan: Have your travels given you a special sense of the variety of human types, such as Forster's Professor Godbole?
Burgess: Fundamentally people are all the same, and I've lived among enough different races long enough to be dogmatic about this. Godbole in *A Passage to India* is an eccentric mystic of the type that any culture can throw up.

Cullinan: At this point do you regard yourself as an expatriate Englishman or as an exile?
Burgess: A verbal quibble. I've voluntarily exiled myself, but not forever. Nevertheless, I can't think of any good reason for going back to England except on a holiday. But one is, as Simone Weil said, faithful to the cuisine one was brought up on, and that probably constitutes patriotism. I am sometimes mentally and physically ill for Lancashire food—hot pot, lobscowse, and so on—and I have to have these things. I'm loyal to Lancashire, I suppose, but not strongly enough to wish to go back and live there.

Cullinan: What are "hot pot" and "lobscowse"?
Burgess: Hot pot, or Lancashire hot pot, is made in this way. An earthenware dish, a layer of trimmed lamb chops, a layer of sliced onions, a layer of sliced potatoes, then continue the layers till you reach the top. Add seasoned stock. On top put mushrooms or more potato slices to brown. Add oysters or kidneys as well if you wish. Bake in a moderate oven for a long time. Eat with pickled cabbage. Lobscowse is a sailor's dish from Liverpool (Liverpudlians are called "scousers" or "scowsers") and is very simple. Dice potatoes and onions and cook in a pan of seasoned water. When they're nearly done, get rid of excess liquid and add a can or two of cubed (or diced) corned beef. Heat gently. Eat with mixed pickles. I love

cooking these dishes, and, once known, everybody loves them. They're honest and simple. Lancashire has a great cuisine, including a notable shop cuisine—meaning you can buy great delicacies in shops. Lancashire women traditionally work in the cotton mills and cook dinner only at weekends. Hence the things you can get in cooked food shops—fish and chips, Bury puddings, Eccles cakes, tripe, cowheel, meat pies (hot, with gravy poured into a hole from a jug), and so on. Fish and chips is now, I think, internationally accepted. Meat and potato pie is perhaps the greatest of the Lancashire dishes—a "drier" hot pot with a fine flaky crust.

Cullinan: I'm tempted to visit Manchester. Lawrence Durrell, another expatriate English writer, has said that since America and Russia are going to determine our future, one is obliged to stop traveling and start thinking when one is in either country. It's different, he says, from going to Italy—a pure pleasure. Do you agree?
Burgess: Durrell has never yet said anything I could agree with. He reminds me of that TV show woman in America, Virginia Graham. I just don't know what the hell he can mean by that. In America and Russia I meet people, get drunk, eat, just as I do in Italy. I see no signs of purely metaphysical import. Those are left to governments, and governments are what I try to ignore. All governments are evil, including that of Italy.

Cullinan: That sounds vaguely anarchic, or at least un-American. Did you have an undergraduate Marxist period, like Victor Crabbe in *The Long Day Wanes*?
Burgess: I was never a Marxist, though I was always, even as an undergraduate, ready to play the Marxist game—analyzing Shakespeare in Marxist terms, and so on. I always loved dialectical materialism. But it was structuralist love from the start. To take socialism seriously, as opposed to minimal socialization (what America needs so desperately), is ridiculous.

Cullinan: Doesn't "minimal socialization" require an increase in the size and power of central government? Only the American federal government can fund the equivalent of the English or Scandinavian health plans; the need for inexpensive medical treatment is acute here.
Burgess: I loathe the State but concede that socialized medicine is a priority in any civilized country today. In England it saved me from bankruptcy during my wife's final illness (though perhaps a private insurance policy might have taken care of it. You can't opt out of the state scheme, however). Socialized medicine—which in England was a liberal idea, anyway—doesn't have to mean out-and-out socialism with everything nationalized. If America gets it, it will be only the doc-

tors and dentists who will try not to make it work, but, as in England, there's no reason why a private practice shouldn't coexist with a national health one. You go to a dentist in England, and he says "Private or National Health?" The difference in treatment is hardly noticeable, but the State materials (tooth fillings, spectacles, and so on) are inferior to what you buy as a private patient.

Cullinan: Do these views make you a political conservative, then? You've said you would reluctantly vote conservative in England.
Burgess: I think I'm a Jacobite, meaning that I'm traditionally Catholic, support the Stuart monarchy and want to see it restored, and distrust imposed change even when it seems to be for the better. I honestly believe that America should become monarchist (preferably Stuart) because with a limited monarchy you have no president, and a president is one more corruptible element in government. I hate all republics. I suppose my conservatism, since the ideal of a Catholic Jacobite imperial monarch isn't practicable, is really a kind of anarchism.

Cullinan: Many Americans believe their presidency has evolved into a form of monarchy, with unhappy results. Do you see anarchy as a viable political alternative?
Burgess: The U.S. presidency is a Tudor monarch plus telephones. Your alternative is either a return to the limited monarchy of the British Commonwealth—a constitutional monarch is at least out of politics and can't get dirty or corrupt—or devolution into unfederated states with a loose cooperative framework for large development schemes. Anarchy is a man's own thing, and I think it's too late in the day to think of it as a viable system or non-system in a country as large as America. It was all right for Blake or for Thoreau, both of whom I admire immensely, but we'll never get it so full-blooded again. All we can do is keep pricking our government all the time, disobeying all we dare (after all, we have livings to earn), asking why, maintaining a habit of distrust.

Cullinan: You've urged fellow artists to seek depth by "digging for the mythical." Are you more interested in creating new myths or in re-examining old ones, as you did with the *Aeneid* in *A Vision of Battlements*?
Burgess: At present I'm interested in what structuralism can teach us about myth. I don't think I can invent my own myths, and I still think there's a great deal of fictional revivification possible with regard to such myths as the Jason/Golden Fleece one (on which I plan a novel, incidentally). Existing myths carry useful depth, a profundity of meaning which saves the novelist a lot of inventive trouble.

Cullinan: How does Jason's pursuit of the Golden Fleece apply to our time?

Burgess: My Jason novel, if I ever write it, will just use the Argonaut story as a framework for picaresque adventures. No deeper significance.

Cullinan: Have you considered basing a novel on myths associated with Oriental religions, as Mann did in *The Transposed Heads*?

Burgess: Strangely, I've been contemplating making a musical play out of Mann's *The Transposed Heads*—very charming, but only a game despite the claims of psychological profundity sometimes made for it. I've six years in the East but am not greatly drawn to Eastern myths, except that of the endless Javanese shadow-play, which is like *Finnegans Wake*, anyway. But I've thought of a novel based on Munshi Abdullah's *Hikayat*. That German hunger for the East—Hesse as well as Mann—is very curious. They might not have seen it as so romantic if they'd been colonial officers. Perhaps that's what they really wanted to be.

Cullinan: Structuralism plays a big part in *MF*. How important is it to you as a novelist of ideas?

Burgess: Structuralism is the scientific confirmation of a certain theological conviction—that life is binary, that this is a duo-verse and so on. What I mean is that the notion of essential opposition—not God/Devil but just x/y—is the fundamental one, and this is a kind of purely structuralist view. We end up with form as more important than content, with speech and art as phatic processes, with the big moral imponderables as mere hot air. Marshall McLuhan has been limping along this track independently of Lévi-Strauss. How marvelous that the essential bifurcation which is man is expressed in trousers that carry Lévi-Strauss's name.

Cullinan: Along with establishing a firm connection between language and myth, you've also indicated about the future of the novel that "only through the exploration of language can the personality be coaxed into yielding a few more of its secrets." Would you expand on that?

Burgess: By extension of vocabulary, by careful distortion of syntax, by exploitation of various prosodic devices traditionally monopolized by poetry, surely certain indefinite or complex areas of the mind can more competently be rendered than in the style of, say, Irving Stone or Wallace.

Cullinan: Are you ever tempted to lavish complex prose on a simple protagonist, as Flaubert did in *A Simple Heart*?

Burgess: Try and make your language fit your concept of the subject more than the subject itself. "Here's this stupid man who's written a most highly wrought work about a housemaid called Félicité." But Flaubert was concerned, surely, with the nobility of that heart and lavished his prose riches upon it. Style is less a preoccupation than a perennial problem. Finding the right style for the subject, I mean. This must mean that the subject comes first and the style after.

Cullinan: You've referred to yourself as a "serious novelist who is attempting to extend the range of subject matter available to fiction." How have you tried to do this?
Burgess: I've written about the dying British empire, lavatories, structuralism, and so on, but I don't really think that that kind of subject matter is what I had in mind when I made that statement. I meant the modification of the sensibility of the British novel, which I may have achieved a little, a very little. The new areas are more technical than thematic.

Cullinan: In *The Novel Now* you said that the novel is the only important literary form we have left. Why do you think this is true?
Burgess: Yes, the novel is the only *big* literary form we have left. It is capable of enclosing the other, lesser, literary forms, from the play to the lyric poem. Poets are doing well enough, especially in America, but they can't achieve the architectonic skill which once lay behind the epic (for which the novel is now a substitute). The short, sharp burst—in music as well as poetry—is not enough. The novel has the monopoly of *form* today.

Cullinan: Granted this limited primacy of the novel, it's disturbing that novel sales in general are declining and that public attention is focused more on nonfiction. Are you tempted to turn more to biography, for example, in the future?
Burgess: I shall carry on with novelizing and hope for some little reward on the side. Biography is very hard work, no room for invention. But if I were a young man now, I wouldn't dream of trying to become a professional novelist. But some day, perhaps soon, the old realization will come back—that reading about imaginary characters and their adventures is the greatest pleasure in the world. Or the second greatest.

Cullinan: What is the first?
Burgess: That depends upon your own tastes.

Cullinan: Why do you regret becoming a professional novelist?
Burgess: I think that the mental strain, the worry, you know, the self-doubt, are

hardly worth the candle; the agonies of creation and the sense of responsibility to one's muse—all these various things become more than one can live with.

Cullinan: Are the odds much longer today against anyone's sustaining himself by quality fiction writing?

Burgess: I don't know. I know that the older I get the more I want to live and the less opportunity I have. I don't think I wanted to become chained to an art form; establishing one's identity through an art form, one is a kind of Frankenstein creating a monster, so to speak. I wish I could live easier; I wish I didn't have the sense of responsibility to the arts. More than anything, I wish I didn't have the prospect of having to write certain novels, which must be written because nobody else will write them. I wish I were freer, I like freedom; and I think I would have been much happier living as a colonial officer writing the odd novel in my spare time. Then I would have been happier than as a sort of professional man of letters, making a living out of words.

Cullinan: Do film versions help or hinder novels?

Burgess: Films help the novels they're based on, which I both resent and am grateful for. My *Clockwork Orange* paperback has sold over a million in America, thanks to dear Stanley. But I don't like being beholden to a mere film maker. I want to prevail through pure literature. Impossible, of course.

Cullinan: You've referred to *A Vision of Battlements*, your first novel, "like all my stories since, as a slow and cruel stripping off of illusion," yet you are often called a comic writer. Is comedy by nature so cruel, or do you consider yourself more as a satirist?

Burgess: Comedy is concerned with truth quite as much as tragedy; and the two, as Plato recognized, have something fundamental in common. They're both stripping processes; they both tear off externals and show man as a poor, forked animal. Satire is a *particular* kind of comedy, limiting itself to particular areas of behavior, not to the general human condition. I don't think I'm a satirist.

Cullinan: Are you a black humorist as well—or are all these categories too confining?

Burgess: I think I'm a comic writer, *malgré moi*. My Napoleon is turning out comic, and I certainly didn't intend that. I don't think I know what black humor is. Satirist? Satire is a difficult medium, ephemeral unless there's tremendous vitality in the form itself—like *Absalom and Achitophel*, *Tale of a Tub*, *Animal Farm*: I mean, the work has to subsist as story or poetry even when the objects of the satire are forgotten. Satire is now an element in some other form, not a form in itself. I like to be called just a novelist.

Cullinan: About ten years ago you wrote that you considered yourself a pessimist but believed that "the world has much solace to offer—love, food, music, the immense variety of race and language, literature, the pleasure of artistic creation." Would you make up the same list of saving graces today?
Burgess: Yes, no change.

Cullinan: Georges Simenon, another professional, has said that "writing is not a profession but a vocation of unhappiness. I don't think an artist can ever be happy." Do you think this is true?
Burgess: Yes, Simenon's right. My eight-year-old son said the other day: "Dad, why don't you write for *fun*?" Even he divined that the process as I practice it is prone to irritability and despair. I suppose, apart from my marriage, I was happiest when I was doing a teaching job and had nothing much to think about in the vacations. The anxiety involved is intolerable. And—I differ here from Simenon—the financial rewards just don't make up for the expenditure of energy, the damage to health caused by stimulants and narcotics, the fear that one's work isn't good enough. I think, if I had enough money, I'd give up writing tomorrow.

Dressing for Dinner in the Jungle

Charles T. Bunting/1973

Studies in the Novel, v. 5, no. 4, Winter 1973. Copyright © 1973 by North Texas State University. Reprinted by permission of the publisher.

Bunting: Would you explain the subject matter of your new book, *The Clockwork Condition*, that is scheduled to be published this May?

Burgess: Is it? That's news to me. It hasn't been written yet. I don't see any likelihood of its being published for quite a time. What happened was that I was asked to write a book with that title and the content was left to myself. But it was meant to be a kind of nonfiction, a socio-theological work, and I thought about it and found myself totally unequipped to do it. I'm not a thinker; I try not to be a thinker. I was persuaded by someone to write the book, and I will write *a* book, probably not with that title, but a small book just to give the man his money's worth, but I don't think it can be written for a long, long time, not until I get back to Italy, because the time's not propitious for writing a book at all.

Bunting: Do you find it difficult to write while you're teaching here?

Burgess: I find it virtually impossible to do any serious writing because I think that teaching is a full-time job—marking and so on—and you can't just grab odd hours. You've got to feel that you have an unlimited swath of time ahead of you before you can start writing seriously. I have been writing, of course. I have been writing articles. I've also been rewriting and rewriting and rewriting again the script for this musical *Cyrano*, which is playing in Toronto and is soon to be playing in Boston and then in New York. So my writing has been mostly in the fields of lines for actors and also lyrics for songs. That's the kind of work I've been mainly doing and also planning other musicals, writing outlines. The only thing at the moment I'm seriously, solidly writing is a television series on the life of Moses for Italian television. This is not what I really feel I should be doing. I feel I should be getting on with a novel I've already started, half done, and haven't touched since last August. It's bad.

Bunting: What novel is that, Mr. Burgess?

Burgess: This is a novel called *Napoleon Symphony*, which is based on the life of Napoleon, but the life is so organized that it fits into a symphonic pattern, so that you don't worry too much about chronology. You worry more about themes and trying to contrive an allegro movement, a slow movement, a scherzo, and a set of variations for a finale. In other words, following exactly—well, when I say "exactly," I suppose I mean that—following the pattern of Beethoven's *Eroica*, what I have in front of me when I'm working is the score of the *Eroica*. I will make the various sections of the novel correspond to the various sections of the symphony, so that if I take, say, eight bars of Beethoven, it's roughly equivalent to three pages of my own work. I try to be consistent with that correspondence. It's interesting. It's very difficult, though, very difficult. It's not really a historical novel at all. It's an experiment in form.

Bunting: What will the subject matter be?

Burgess: Oh, this is just Napoleon as a figure, as a great demonic force, and essentially as a very modern man, really a very contemporary man, because he—well, can I say that even?- -he's half-animal and half-computer. It's only possible to think in those terms in the modern age. His head was a computer. His body was the body of an ape. His chest was preternaturally big. His lungs were preternaturally large. And he was over-oxygenated, so the rest of his contemporaries, who were under-oxygenated, I suppose, are seen as physically insufficient beings, whereas Napoleon was over-energetic, even sexually so. His excessive sexual energy, of course, explains why he had so little success with women. And he was also a very obscene man, which never comes out in the official biographies or romantic novels about him. This is a very obscene novel. It's full of soldiers' language. We have records of the fact that Napoleon would piss his trousers with rage and hit his generals in the face and then scream the foulest obscenities at them. Well, these obscenities are there in the novel. The novel is, in fact, a product of our own age, a permissive age, and it's possible to set down with great exactitude the kind of language, the kind of habits he had, and the kind of sexual mores he practiced.

Bunting: What have been your chief sources of information? Have you had to do much research?

Burgess: I've had to do far too much research, but, for the most part, I've relied on secondary sources. Living in Rome, of course, I have access to the Napoleon Bonaparte Museum, which has strange things, odd objects, including a sculpture of Napoleon's sister's left breast, and odd drawings, portfolios of drawings, and odd works in Italian. I've been reading a lot of works in Italian, but also certain standard works like the big book on Napoleon's campaigns. I've had to spend a lot of time sorting out the campaigns, seeing how they work out on paper, on the table, and setting them down in the book in various ways, setting them down in geometrical patterns or, as in one instance, a battle is set out in the form of a poem of notes, so the poem represents the terrain, and the position of the figures referring to footnotes is not numerical; it varies according to position so that you can tell by reading the poem, by moving around, exactly where they are and when they're conducting the battle. That sort of thing. It's full of odd little bits of experimentalism. It's full of verse, heroic couplets, and Byronic verse. Of course, verse is a great speeder-upper of things. You can speed up the transitional passages by using verse. How it will go down I don't know. It will probably enrage the French. But they shouldn't really be enraged because he does turn out, I think, to be a highly human individual.

Bunting: You seem to have had a fascination for Napoleon for some time now. In your first novel, *A Vision of Battlements*, Richard Ennis talks to a group about Beethoven and Napoleon.

Burgess: Oh, yes. But I've never really known much about Napoleon. Being an Englishman, I've never been attracted to Napoleon because, after all, he was the enemy. This is what I was brought up to believe, but having done some research and having seen it from my wife's point of view—my wife's an Italian—I see now that he was not really the enemy; he was only the enemy of the ruling class in Britain, and, of course, he was very popular with the lower class. And in my own town of Manchester when the Peterloo Massacre took place, the working people were animated by Napoleonic principles. They were more on the side of the Revolution, and Napoleon seemed to them to embody the ideas of the Revolution. They were not on the side of the ruling class, and I see now that it's possible to be an Englishman and a Bonapartist. I see also that Napoleon has fulfilled posthumously his intention of bringing England into Europe. It's been done by peaceful means, but the great dream of a united Europe with England as part of it has been fulfilled with the Common Market. So Napoleon is still a living force.

Bunting: You have done a translation of *Cyrano de Bergerac*. Were you dissatisfied with the translation that we read here?

Burgess: Well, the translation you have here in America is totally appalling. It's written in rather weary blank verse, and, of course, the original play by Rostand has heroic couplets, or Alexandrines. And these are essential. You've got to have rhyme because the things that the actors say are epigrammatic, and they depend on the quick snap or rhyme, so my version is a rhyme version. It was very successful. This is not a boast because it's just a matter of box office returns. The thing was rather successful in Minneapolis, and it was determined then to make a musical out of it. I think this was a bad idea because the success of the play was a verbal success, a success of rhetoric, and the first thing you do in a musical is to get rid of the rhetoric and substitute song for it, so the problems I'm having at the moment stem from an initial misconception. The thing will work, but it will work with difficulty.

Bunting: Are you exhilarated to be writing music again?

Burgess: I'm not writing music, unfortunately; I'm writing lyrics. Another man is doing the music, and I find this very constricting because the composer is a Welshman who writes very fine, simple, melodic lines, but he has no notion of English prosody. No Welshman ever has because their own language is an unstressed language, and so I couldn't allow him to set lyrics. I had to ask him to write me a tune and let me put lyrics to the tune, but this is very limiting. It means you cannot indulge in a verbal rodomontade. You're always kept down to what the tune is telling you to do. And the lyrics aren't as good as I'd like them to be. They're good within their limits, but the limits are pretty killing at times. It's very hard, for instance, if you're given a tune, which is full of minims, I think which here you call what? Not fourth notes. Second notes, or something like that. But you can't write a passage of verse, which sounds like speech. It's too slow. Speech is what we call a quaver movement. Like a trip. That's the way we speak. But his tunes, of course, derive from a totally different way of looking at things, which is the Welsh way, and, of course, deriving also from a long tradition of hymn writing, and are not quite what I wanted. Still, there it is. I've done the job, such as it is, and look forward to doing rather different jobs in the musical field.

Bunting: Would a reader who is coming to the works of Anthony Burgess for the first time do well to brush up his musical background? Would that be a help?

Burgess: I think it's sometimes a help. I don't think it's essential, but I've never written a novel yet whose appreciation depends on the knowledge of musical notation or harmony or orchestration. But the time is coming when I shall have to write a rather long novel about a composer. This will have to look at the composer very much from inside the process of making music, and it may be essential then for the reader to know something about it. I think all readers should anyway. It's

a sister art to literature, and not to know the simplest musical terms is really a terrible ignorance. People always know the general terminology of the motor car, but
music is supposed to be outside their field; music is something for the specialist. I
don't think that Shakespeare would have looked at it that way. If you take a line in
Macbeth: "Screw your courage to the sticking place, / And we'll not fail." You can't
understand that line unless you understand the guitar or the lute, and Shakespeare obviously understood it. He'd seen lutes tuned; he may have tuned the lute
himself, and this business of screwing it up to the stick, to the place where you
could make it stick, is definitely a musical image. Of course, Shakespeare had to
be a musician because he was an actor, and all actors were musicians then, but
nowadays there's a fissure between music and literature, and this is disturbing. It
is not there in the works of Thomas Pynchon, who is perhaps America's best living novelist. In his new novel there's a great deal of musical theory behind his
whole concept of human nature and human history. But people still are not willing to take the trouble to understand, say, what the term "dodecaphonic" really
means or what a dominant seventh is. People ought to know these things.

Bunting: In your book, *Shakespeare*, you surmise that when Shakespeare retired
from the London theater, he devoted more time to his musical interests.
Burgess: Again, it's only a pure fancy, but I can't help feeling that with that particular combination around, I should feel that he himself may have been a tenor
or a baritone of some kind. His son may have been a bass or a tenor—his son-in-
law, I mean, Hall—one of his daughters, a soprano; his wife, a contralto. There
was a combination of voices there, and probably what could they do in Stratford
after dinner but say, "Why don't we sit down to some music and sing a madrigal?"
He might even have taught them to sing a madrigal, I don't know, but you cannot exclude that possibility that as a gentleman he would regard it as obligatory
of him to have a little music after dinner and to take part in it himself. Certainly
he wrote a musical theme, as I point out in my book. In *Love's Labour's Lost* he
makes Holofernes come out with a musical theme: six notes, which, I think, are an
original composition by William Shakespeare. But nobody gives a damn. Again,
scholars aren't interested.

Bunting: In your preface to *Shakespeare* you mention that you would be grateful
for even the least bit of minutiae that would lend some credence to his biography.
How does the recent "discovery" of A. L. Rowse regarding the identity of the Dark
Lady set with you?
Burgess: I don't trust Rowse at all. I never have trusted him. I think he's a bigot

and pigheaded and, of course, violently Protestant, violently anti-Catholic. I took an instant dislike to his book on Marlowe, which I thought was a bad book, and the work that he did on Shakespeare in that year, the quatercentenary, I thought didn't give us anything new. There's far more novelty in the work of Leslie Hotson about the identity of Mr. W. H., but Rowse comes forward with these rather well-worn, rather trite ideas, and indulges in ballyhoo, and people believe that he's made a new discovery. I don't know what his grounds are for supposing that the Dark Lady was an Italian or French woman, but I'm not at the moment prepared to accept it because I don't trust Rowse. I cling to my contention that the Dark Lady was probably genuinely a dark-skinned woman. I don't see why not. Nothing, no reference in the sonnets, kills that assumption, and the fact that there were black women in the Clerkenwell brothels, where Shakespeare was living—Clerkenwell—seems to intrigue us with the fact that he had contact with dark women. I don't see why not.

Bunting: W. H., in your opinion, still remains Henry Wriothesly, the Earl of Southampton?
Burgess: Oh, I don't know. I don't think it has anything to do with Shakespeare anyway. The dedication of the sonnets was done by Thomas Thorpe, and this could have been to William Harvey or the Earl of Pembroke, who was a man of immense influence, of course, with whom Shakespeare had come into contact in his later life. But, oh, I played around with the idea in the novel. I wrote that— oh, you know, let's try this idea: say, your family must come first, not Mr. H. W., but Mr. W. H. But that's only a little quip, a little joke, and it doesn't really mean very much.

Bunting: I assume that the greatest difficulty in writing *Nothing Like the Sun* was not with the identification of the people, but rather with the language.
Burgess: The language was extremely difficult to manage because we have a long tradition in England and America of trying to write mock Elizabethan, and it always turns out to be Wardour Street English. What I had to do was to try and teach myself the language and make it sound as though people meant it. It meant for a long time I was thinking in Elizabethan, using it in the shops and in the home, and looking for a means of eventually seeing how far I could sit down and write it naturally. After a long labor I was able to do this, I think, to some extent, although it is not completely Elizabethan English; it's rather Joycean. Yet it is not modern English; that's the important thing. I think it's a terrible confession of weakness when you have to write a historical novel and use the language of today.

A terrible weakness. It's not your job. One of your jobs is not only to make these past people come back to life, but also to make their language come back to life.

Bunting: A preoccupation with the past and its effect upon the present seems to be a constant motif in your fiction, Mr. Burgess.

Burgess: Yes, well, of course, this probably is a very English thing. I don't know. We're so aware of the past as coexisting with the present; you can't avoid it, especially if you're living in provincial England, in the country. For instance, I lived in a village of Oxfordshire, where there was nothing but the past. There was no building younger than, say, about 1600, and you were surrounded by the objects of the past. Moreover, you were surrounded by the timelessness of the inhabitants, who, I remember, when I was living in Adderbury, which is a village in Oxfordshire, not too far from Banbury, not too far from Oxford. This was the place where John Wilmot lived, the Earl of Rochester, and some of the people there would talk about him as though he lived, you know, in their great-grandfather's time or even their grandfather's time. "There were rare goings-on when the old Earl were alive here. He would do this, that, and the other, and all his women there, you know." And it was all right. It was all true. The image they got of Wilmot was a true image. It confirmed about what we know about him, and they tell stories about his dressing up as a tinker and going around and collecting people's pots and pans and then flogging them for booze. And this again turns out to be true. The same way they would talk about Shakespeare, and the stories that have been handed down, and I don't see why I shouldn't believe these at least as much as, you know, the supposition of scholars. This is folk history, folk mythology, and it's very much a part of English life. You can't avoid it. It's not contrived. It's natural. Things don't change very rapidly there. So you're always aware of the past in England and probably far more so than in America, although in parts of America you're aware of the past: New England and so on.

Again, one takes the simple thesis that the future does not exist and the present is only an infinitesimal line between the past and the future, and the past alone exists. If we're going to know what's going to happen in the future, if we're going to build up an art of exact prediction, we can only do it by a close study of the past, and the discovery of patterns emerge, perpetually emerging patterns, repeated patterns. This is what Joyce was doing in *Finnegans Wake:* trying to show how the past and the present do coexist because of the patterns that they have in common. This is very reasonable.

Bunting: In both *A Clockwork Orange* and *The Wanting Seed*, we have visions of the future. In writing these two novels in what way did the past influence you? Or was it more an influence of the present; that is, taking stock of the present and looking toward the future?

Burgess: Well, I don't think any writer is wise to attempt to predict the future. When I wrote *A Clockwork Orange*, which was back in 1959, 1960, 1961—I forget, now—I was really writing about the present, but I was mythicizing it a little. I was freeing myself from the historical facts, but I didn't envisage a future. In any case, you see, that present has already become the past. People who saw the film said, "Ah, a vision of the future," but if I'd said, in writing it in 1960, I was envisaging 1972, that would still be making it a sort of futuristic novel. These things don't really matter. What matters is the continuation of the particular sort of human conduct and the perpetual conflict between authority and the individual.

George Orwell's *Nineteen Eighty-Four* was regarded as a—still is regarded in America, I think—as a prophecy, but it's not a prophecy. The original title was *Nineteen Forty-Eight*, and it was an attempt to show what life would be like in London, what life really was like, in a sense, in London in the imaginations of the readers of *The New Statesman*. This is what the left-wing intelligentsia wanted to make of England. This is in a sense what they're already making of England. The picture of London he gives you is very much the London one remembered after the Second World War with bomb craters and rationing and nothing to smoke, nothing to drink. Even the main buildings in his image of London were already there. For instance, the BBC Broadcasting House was the Ministry of Truth, and the room where Winston Smith is tortured, Room 101, was the room where Orwell did his broadcasts. And The Chestnut Tree, you know, the place where doomed men go and drink, is around the corner again, a pub called The Blue Pot. And it's all there. Everything's there in it. There's no need, really, to write about the future. You just look at the present and extend into a minimal world of fantasy the tendencies of the present and you get a so-called futuristic novel.

Bunting: Were you bothered by the inevitable comparisons between *A Clockwork Orange*, Huxley's *Brave New World*, and Orwell's *Nineteen Eighty-Four*?

Burgess: Oh, that's always a cheap thing to do. Critics automatically do that. I was not trying to do the same thing at all. I was merely trying to point out the very real danger, an imminent danger, that is, that the State is taking on more and more control, a tentative try on the part of the State in Britain to intrude into all regions of the individual life. They even talk about nobody having wages but everybody's just drawing from the State; getting what we want from the State; the reorganization of education in terms of total democratization; the lack of an elitist system; the assumption that the State had a right to control your entire life. This was already emerging in England at the time. The idea that criminality should be expunged through modern techniques. A very socialist idea. It was already going around so I had to write about these things.

Bunting: In her book *The Origins of Totalitarianism*, Hannah Arendt remarks: "Once public affairs are regulated by the state under the guise of necessity, the social or public careers of the competitors come under the sway of chance. In a society of individuals, all equipped by nature with equal capacity for power and equally protected from one another by the state, only chance can decide who will succeed." Are you inclined to agree with Ms. Arendt's statement?
Burgess: The chance business. I think, on the whole, I would agree with that. Yes, she certainly has been well aware of the dangers. The danger, I think, is stronger here in America at the present time. The dangers have always been implicit, and they're there in the American Constitution, which is a very dangerous document, a very dangerous system. A written Constitution itself is a bad thing, but to base the Constitution on a misconception is now showing its dangers. The misconception, of course, is Montesquieu's misconception of the British settlement. To have an Executive, a head of the Executive, who is totally free, although in theory there is supposed to be a system of checks and balances, is dangerous. You have an absolutist kind of monarch who could suspend the Constitution.

Bunting: In a footnote to her remark, Ms. Arendt adds a comment about literature in which she states that "the drama became meaningless in a world without action, while the novel could deal adequately with destinies of human beings who were either the victims of necessity or the favorites of luck." Do you hold the same contention about the novel?
Burgess: I don't know. When you say *the* novel, what novel do you mean?

Bunting: The novel as a *genre*.
Burgess: As a *genre*. That is very hard to say. I have never had any clear idea in my mind as to what a novel is. I studied the history of the novel and even taught it, but don't know what its purpose was. I don't think it has ever had really a social purpose. If there's been a social purpose there, it's been on the margin or by accident. The novel is primarily a mode of entertainment. It is an invention. It

is a godlike creation of new human beings and a manipulation of them. If one finds social significance in novels, it is probably because of the assumptions that the novelist makes. To set out to use the novel as a means of portraying a period, portraying the society of the times, I think, is never a good thing. It was done by George Eliot to some extent. It was certainly done by Zola. But I don't think this is what the novel is about. I think the novel is essentially a free form in which you don't have the necessity of depicting society as it really is; in fact, you're wiser not to do this. To invent a society turns the novel into a kind of science fiction. But the term "novel" covers so much today. It covers anything in prose that contains dialogue, anything that does not merely purvey fact. It doesn't try to teach. It has become so loose a form that one is rather losing faith in it. What I want to make is not novels so much as prose structures of some kind or another in which human beings shall figure, but in which there shall be no genuine purpose—no moral, perhaps, no real plot even—in which the laws of probability can be suspended and in which you end up with a structure: something which you weigh in your hand and look at as you look at a Tiffany jewel, which gives pleasure as an artifact. This is the kind of thing I want to do, I'm trying to do.

Bunting: Your greatest lament, I believe, is that modern novelists fail to experiment with form.

Burgess: Well, not many of us do experiment all that much, and the fact is if you are earning your living as a novelist, as I am—not at the moment, admittedly—then you have to think of what your readers can take. It's no good blaming readers if they reject your book as unintelligible. We have a young man in England called B. S. Johnson. I rather admire his work, but he has been pretty boldly experimental. By that I mean he has gone back to *Tristram Shandy,* which is about the most experimental novel there is, although it was very popular at the time, and he published a novel in which all the pages, or rather all the chapters, were separate fascicles. You bought them in a box, not between covers, and you shuffled them in an aleatory way, and you got what pattern you wished. Well, this, I think, is an excellent idea, but it didn't sell. Nobody wanted to buy it, and, as a consequence, he had great difficulty in placing his next novel.

Now, one has to temper one's idealism to economic circumstance, and I have not experimented as I would have liked to have done because I have the necessity to pay the rent. Now, there is no shame in this; there's no shame at all in producing works that may bring in a little money and help you to stay alive. But when people deliberately turn their backs on experimentation, then they are violating the essential principle of the novel, i.e., that it is novel; it is something new. The idea of experimentation is, of course, as old as the first novel, as old as the *Satyricon*. Certainly an eighteenth-century notion of the epistolary novel is a very astonishing form. It is a very highly experimental form. *Tristram Shandy* is, of course, still the most experimental novel that there has ever been.

It is the women novelists of England and the women novelists of America who are scared to experiment. They are so concerned with the importance of the content they can't be bothered with the form. This is what is wrong with a lot of them, I think.

Bunting: You mention in *The Novel Now*: "It is dangerous to move the novel too far out of the sphere of enjoyment: any work of art must be a compromise between what the writer can give and what the reader can take."
Burgess: I think that is true.

Bunting: Do you feel you have had to compromise too much yourself?
Burgess: I have compromised a great deal, but, on the other hand, I have compromised within myself because I do recognize the pleasure one gains from a well-plotted story. When people turn against plot, I suspect they do this because they can't create plots. They make a virtue out of necessity. I think this is true of the French *anti-romancier*. I think that Michel Butor rejects plot because he can't write plots. I think Nathalie Sarraute rejects characters because she can't create characters. But I do maintain that is why—I may be contradicting myself now, but never mind—that one essential thing in the novel is to have at least one character who is totally seductive and to present him doing things. This is where you begin with a novel. Or by her doing things, less frequently. This explains why *Finnegans Wake* can be read because it is about a man, whereas if Nathalie Sarraute had written it, it would be totally unreadable because it would be about formless essences and not human beings at all.

Bunting: Your novel *One Hand Clapping* is told from the point of view of a female protagonist, Janet Shirley.
Burgess: That is right. I wrote that a long time ago; I wrote that in 1960. It's been quite a time ago. It only came out here last year, I think. I don't know why it was held back. Yes, I tried that. I tried becoming a woman. It is not too difficult, really.

Bunting: I was wondering if you had any difficulty with that particular point of view.
Burgess: No, it's not difficult. Women are rather like men but with certain de-

lightful differences. A man enjoys the working of a woman's mind. That is why these women's lib people are so dull because they try to make their minds work like men's minds. Women can't do it. Why the hell should they do it? Women can't do certain things that men can do. They can't drink as much as men without suffering for it. They cannot, on the whole, think logically. They have something far better than logic. They have intuition. They genuinely have that. I admire this fact in a woman. They also are very much on the side of life, which they cease to be when they become politically minded. They become a side of destruction. They want to destroy men. These are the faculties I try to get into this rather silly little novel. I try to get a rather lower middle-class woman's point of view, living in a changing Britain, in which the old values are dying. She stands for life, and her husband obviously stands for death. He wants to die.

Bunting: Her husband, Howard, is quite caught up with the past, of course. He says, "Aaaaah, it must have been a damned sight better to live in those days than in these." But back again to *Nothing Like the Sun* and your book *Shakespeare*, those good old days meant quartering and disembowelment.
Burgess: Yes, indeed.

Bunting: Then the historical past as being a time of peace and contentment is really a myth.
Burgess: Yes, it is an aspect of the romantic fallacy, I agree: the past is always better. In some ways, of course, the past was better. We cannot deny, let's say, the vitality of the eighteenth century. London, Dr. Johnson's London, must have been a terrible place to live, because there was this pollution. On the other hand again, there was organic food where there was nothing else. People managed to put up with the diet of the times. There was a lot of talk. I don't know, it was a brutal period, but in a way people were less frightened than they are now. There were fewer of them. Perhaps the State wasn't all-powerful. It was more human. We have learned the techniques of dehumanization which they hadn't yet learned. I think I would be quite happy to go back to Elizabethan England or to Johnson's England. I'd be quite happy to go back. I think, I think, I think.

But one automatically misses things. Now, you see this very clearly when you get a gang of young Americans to a very primitive region. I was working in Majorca some years ago with some graduates. I was interested to see what they would think of it. Of course, they were all against the establishment, mechanization, and the cult of the internal combustion engine, etc. When they got into this small village of Majorca, Deya, they had precisely what they wanted. They had organic food. They had fish. They had rice. They had peppers. And that was about all. They had cheap, red Spanish wine. They had fiery brandy. They had no refrigeration. They had no cokes. They had no cars. They had no television. They didn't have very much radio, either. They had no drainage. They had no sanitation. They should have been happy, but, no, they were ill, for the most part. And they were screaming to get back to a Howard Johnson's.

I could sympathize. I was dying myself at one point for a chunk of ice and a lavatory that worked, but, you see, they themselves came very romantically to Deya. Europeans tend not to become quite so romantic because we've had to put up with a life that did not have many labor-saving or hygienic devices. We are less hygienic in Europe than you are here, and, as a consequence, we may be fitter because we have more antibodies. I know a lot of soldiers coming over to Europe find this out. They are very ill frequently because they haven't got the antibodies.

Bunting: In your recent *New York Times* article about Manchester and Lancashire, there seems a kind of nostalgia for the place where "the women are lovely but fierce."
Burgess: Oh, yes. This is true. This is true. Lovely but fierce.

Bunting: You may have exhausted this topic elsewhere, but I assume there is no desire to return to England.
Burgess: Not a great deal. If I were going back to England, I would prefer to return to the North than to the South, but, of course, I might get very fed up with the North. No, the fact is that there is a very close similarity between southern Europe and northern England which is what people do not normally realize. Again, if you want to take America, the South of England is the North of America; the South of America is the North of England. It's a kind of chiasmus, and this is economically so. We up in the North, in Manchester and Lancashire, generally have, strangely enough, a kind of tropical climate. You don't expect this. You expect it to be cold, but it is not cold. The Gulf Stream is flowing up there. The atmosphere is humid. There are tremendous spells of tropical heat. It is never very cold, and, of course, this is why we spin cotton there, the cotton we got from Alabama. We're closely tied up with the South.

The temperament of the people there is much more like a Sicilian temperament. There is none of this stiff upper lip business that you get in the South, a kind of Norman imposition, a Norman upper-class imposition, and most Italians I have spoken to married Northern women from England. All say that they're

"*Come Siciliani*," just like Sicilian. This is true. So temperamentally, you see, a
Northerner like myself finds himself much more at home in the Mediterranean
than he does in the South of England. So leaving England really means leaving
London.

Bunting: Do you now make your home on the island of Malta?
Burgess: No, not at all. I have a house in Malta, but I've not been in Malta now
for three years. I'm going back to the house to see how it is getting on, but I may
be put in jail as soon as I arrive for evasion of taxes. I have a house in Bracciano,
which is about twenty miles north of Rome, and a flat in Rome. That suits me
well enough.

Bunting: You are a well-traveled man, Mr. Burgess. Have you found a place that
you find most agreeable to your temperament?
Burgess: I find New York most agreeable in some ways to my temperament: the
sense of everybody being displaced, everybody being a little neurotic, commu-
nicative, garrulous. New York is a kind of Europe. Well, I could live in New York
forever and ever, but there are very few places on the surface of the globe where
one could really be happy. I always imagined I could be happy, let's say, in Penang,
in Venice, in San Francisco, but the place where you are the happiest is the place
where you have to be, and this is probably the trouble with most writers, that
they don't have to be anywhere. If you have to go to a place like Minneapolis or
Columbus, Ohio, you have to live there. You have to do a job there. If you'd leave
there, you'd lose your job, so you make the best of it. You start things. If there is
no good restaurant, you agitate until you get a good restaurant. If there are no
avant-garde films, you make sure you get them. And this is, I suppose, what life
really was: the building of communities and not just the going to communities
already built, which pleased you. But writers are in this unfortunate position of
being nomadic, of being restless because they know they can go anywhere they
want to. All they need is the typewriter and some paper. And so I have been pretty
restless and pretty dissatisfied.

Bunting: I assume that you do find the literary climate, that is, as far as working
and writing, more agreeable in America than in England.
Burgess: I think that is true on the whole, although I don't meet many writers.
I don't particularly want to. Why should one meet writers? What does one talk
about? They only talk about money. I try to keep out of the way of writers and literary cocktail parties, but, on the other hand, I think writing is taken fairly seri-

ously in America. Some writers get vast financial rewards from writing. Writers like Mailer seem to have a part to play in public life, whereas in England unless a writer is also a friend of the Royal Family, like Sir John Betjeman, or a scientist like Lord Snow, he is pretty well cut off. If you live in a village as I did, you have no place in the stratification. You are not a retired admiral. You are not a stockbroker. You are not a farmer. You are not a shopkeeper. What the hell are you? You are not the vicar, the rector. You're just somebody there that is a writer. Consequently, you have no real place in the community.

Bunting: In a recent issue of *The Spectator* (13 January 1973) David F. Holbrook comments on a situation which is similar to your present one. He remarks: "For the first time in my life, I have found myself at odds with students. If I were asked what my feelings are after just a year roughly attached to a College of Art, as 'writer in residence' my answer would be, like Cordelia's, 'Nothing!' My inquirer might reply, like King Lear, 'Nothing will come of nothing.' And that is exactly my point." His views seem to parallel your own about the academic situation today.

Burgess: Yes, I think I'd accept this to a great extent. Yes, he's come to this conclusion rather late, I would say. I've always felt this.

The problem in America of coping with the youth should not really be a problem at all, but I think, on the whole, it is their fault. If one can't achieve any rapprochement, I think it is their fault. A person in my position has no stake in the establishment. I read widely. I am curious as to what people write, and I am prepared to be sympathetic to students whose velleities I understand for the most part, but they don't make any effort to meet me. They won't read the books that I've read, although I read the books that they've read. They will not bring to a course I give the requisite background. They don't think it is necessary. They don't think any preparation is necessary. They will not read the books of the past. You must read them before you reject them. You must know what you are rejecting.

And I think they have very silly little *schwärmer*. They talk about a drug culture, which, of course, is an absurdity. They are in love with Hesse; they are in love with Vonnegut and Tolkien. All these idols disappear. They look for the wrong things in a book. They look for content rather than form, and they honestly believe that the world can be changed. Of course, this is rather a fine and admirable thing, but not changed to their pattern. They do not realize the evolutionary process is the way the world is changed. They are ill-equipped to start a revolution. Very ill-equipped. They're all impotent. They're a rather impotent, flaccid lot—which is a pity. They shouldn't be like that. They should be vigorous; they are not vigorous even in their demeanors. They sit in the classroom, not with the intention of learning, not with that rather uptight, tense posture. They relax. You cannot learn relaxed. You cannot play music relaxed, but, you know, the virtues of relaxation have been promoted so much in this country that it is about time people began to think seriously about what the virtue is. Why should we?

You know, I always associate America with: you pull off your tie as soon as you get into a room; you slouch; you take of your jacket. The British view has always been different. You regard dress or deportment as an aspect to action. When the Americans laugh at the British for having dressed for dinner in the jungle, the British were perfectly right to dress for dinner. If they did not dress for dinner in the jungle, they would just wear the same clothes they were wearing all day long: sweaty, dirty clothes that they would probably put back on again in the morning. They would relax. Everything would relax. Law would relax. Discipline would relax. The jungle would creep back again. So they deliberately did this. It was not foolishness. It was a deliberate technique for maintaining self-discipline. There is not enough self-discipline. This may be a very English thing to say, I don't know.

Bunting: By the way, may I ask if you gave the title to your *Malayan Trilogy*, which was retitled *The Long Day Wanes* in this country?

Burgess: Yes, I called it that here. It was my title.

Bunting: The American title comes from Tennyson, I believe.

Burgess: Yes, from a poem called "Ulysses":

> The long day wanes: the slow moon climbs: the deep
> Moans round with many voices. Come, my friends,
> 'Tis not too late to seek a newer world.

Bunting: This was your first published work?

Burgess: Yes, my first published prose work. I published poetry before I published prose, but it was my first published prose work; it was my first published novel. Of course, that goes back a long way now. It goes back to the 1950s. It won't be long before it's twenty years since the first novel in the series was published. It was a bit late coming to America because it was assumed that Americans wouldn't understand it or wouldn't really be interested in the Far East, but, of course, Americans have had to become interested in the Far East. Our war in Malaya was just a prelude to your war in Vietnam. The war, incidentally, the Malayan War, was a war which the Americans would not learn from. It's a bit curious.

Bunting: We refused to learn from the Korean War.

Burgess: No, it's a bit strange there. But we did win our war which was a nasty war. It was a nasty guerrilla war, and we won it by not using Pentagonal methods, but by offering regular amnesties, regular generous amnesties, free passages to China, and, of course, not using too much force, just cutting off food supplies. This is one way of doing it. The best way of doing it, really, is just to flush them out of the jungle. They come to search for food, and then you capture them.

Bunting: The novel is, I assume, a *roman à clef* and characters such as the Abang and Mr. Raj are based upon people whom you knew here.

Burgess: Oh, yes, I think practically every character in that book is based on a real person. It would be stupid to invent in an area like that. Oh, I don't know. The character Crabbe is an invention. It's not myself. His wife is an invention, but the rest are based on people I knew. I think the idea of Abang—*abang* means "big brother"—I think that was something of an invention, perhaps. But you can take it from me that life was like that in Malaya, and life is probably still like that. I was back in Singapore two years ago, and life is still a bit like that.

Bunting: In your first novel, *A Vision of Battlements*, Richard Ennis is wrestling with the problems of the Manichaean duality. I would appreciate a statement regarding your Manichaean view of the universe as it affects the techniques of your novel writing.

Burgess: Ah, yes. I will say this first of all: I heard a lecture on this novel given a number of years ago by a young professor, and he said that the name Richard Ennis, R. Ennis, was "sinner" spelled backwards, which, of course, is perfectly true, but I didn't intend this. I'd better get this out of the way now in case you start finding it. No, this was really a kind of structural novel in a way. It was an attempt to define life as subsisting in a duoverse in which we maintain our stability by learning to cope with these great opposites. But in the army one felt this much more strongly, almost in a cartoon way, because there was the army, the great symbol of authority, and it was bound to suggest the church, and in Gibraltar it was symbolized in the rock, this great, big crouching lion of a rock, which was God and authority, and one saw this authority of the rock as twofold: it seemed to stand for an ancient civilization to which the hero is drawn, and at the same time it stands for imposition of the army, the cold, abstract discipline, dehumanized, which is imposed upon him. That's where it came from and through sheer contemplation of the rock itself. But I suppose it was a kind of fairly jejune theological statement or philosophical or metaphysical statement, I don't know what. I don't think it has to be taken too seriously. It's just the position that I've always found myself in, being strongly aware of this duality and not knowing which side to take. Always taking the wrong side, whatever happens, the right side being by definition the other side.

Bunting: Would you state something of the theological ramifications of your novel writing?

Burgess: There's not a great deal of theology in them. It's just that I think that every piece of fiction—every work of literature—has to have some kind of philosophical groundwork, and in our civilization it tends to be religious. I happened to have been brought up a Catholic, and I find certain propositions of Catholicism rather useful, and I also think that a lot of them make a great deal of sense. I think that the notion of the eternal dichotomy of good and evil is a reasonable one. The idea of original sin is a reasonable proposition, and I think even some of the sacramental aspects of Catholic Christianity have a great symbolic value; you know, the Eucharist, for instance, the oil of Extreme Unction. All these things are fundamental and real and true, and bread and wine and oil are fundamental Mediterranean properties. They're life. This is what life is about. I think the use of theological properties in the novel is primarily a means of bringing me down to my roots and the human roots generally. You can't get too far away too long from things like bread and wine and oil and good and evil and original sin.

Bunting: Have you resolved the problem of free will which many of your characters wrestle with?

Burgess: Well, no, I haven't resolved it. I still maintain, more than ever I did, that it's the only thing we have, that this capacity to choose is the big human attribute, which, along with the power of articulate speech, we have to hang onto, and the pressures to believe that it's not essentially a good thing are, of course, increasing.

I think one of the most dangerous books ever written is the book of Professor Skinner, *Beyond Freedom and Dignity*, which seems to miss the whole point of human life. He's saying, in effect, that we only revolt against the idea of being controlled because we've always thought of control in terms of negative reinforcements, pain and deprivation, whereas if we think in terms of positive reinforcements, pleasure and advantage, then we'll be willing to take control. But this is not the point at all. I think a lot of us would still prefer to carry on fighting for the desire to make our own choices against every possible opposition, however pleasant it were made for us to yield to the conditioning process, yield to the corporate will. I still think we'd be cussed enough to wish to hang on to our individual freedom.

There's a good book, which is much neglected, about this, a novel written by an American called David Karp. The novel is called *One*, and this is set in the future in which a man is cussed enough, under all circumstances, even when he's brainwashed, to hang on to this spark of opposition to the corporate, to the imposed, against all odds, and they try to knock this out, of course. It's always there. Whatever happens, it's always there, and it just has to be eliminated. This seems to be a pretty fair statement of the human position: the desire to make one's choice, not because the choice is necessarily good, but because it's one's own choice. It's something you have to reckon with, and it's one of the most human, one of the most essentially human things, and our rulers will have to realize this. They have to realize that people start revolutions, not necessarily because they think that they're going to produce a better system, but because it is in the nature of man to wish to start revolutions because a revolution is just a kind of emanation of his own will, of his own cussed, dogged will. This is to be prized. I prize this above everything.

Bunting: Concerning some of your religious figures, I wonder if there is a kind of repressed hostility that emerges when you sketch in the character of your priests? In an early novel, *The Enemy in the Blanket* (from *The Long Day Wanes*), Father Laforgue is a comic figure. The chaplain in *A Clockwork Orange* is an alcoholic. In *Tremor of Intent*, it is slightly incredulous that the spy, Denis Hillier, becomes a priest at the novel's end. Most recently, in *MF*, Father Costello is literally a clown named Pongo.

Burgess: Yes, that's right. Well, this is a typical Catholic viewpoint. You'll find it in Graham Greene. You'll also find it, of course, in Evelyn Waugh. I've not borrowed it from them. It's just the general Catholic view of the priesthood, which is not admired for character or learning but for its capacity to change the bread and wine into the body and blood of Christ. If you can do this sort of thing, you can be anything, and one doesn't expect goodness from priests. One doesn't expect intelligence, and, my God, one doesn't get it, for the most part.

The position in England—and I call myself an English Catholic—is that the people you do tend to admire are Anglican ministers because they're all graduates for a start. They're all men of some learning. They're all gentlemen, gentlemen's sons. They play cricket. They may not be very profound, but it's very dif-

ficult to portray an Anglican clergyman who is totally unlikable. I tried doing
such a job of presenting almost the main character in a very short novel called
The Eve of Saint Venus: an Anglican clergyman who is up against this problem of
dealing with exorcism. He doesn't have the equipment to do it. Finally he yields,
and it seems natural for him to accept Venus as one of the Anglican pantheon. It
wouldn't be so easy for a Catholic priest. But this kind of anticlericalism is such
a common Catholic property that I don't really have to explain it or certainly I
don't have to excuse it. In Italy, of course, anti-clericalism is rife.

But it doesn't alter the fact that the priest has a certain thaumaturgical gift.
This is really what he's all about. He's an agent of his gift. And that's his function.

Bunting: As an aside, have you ever met Graham Greene?
Burgess: Yes, I know Graham Greene. I used to know him quite well, but I don't
see much of him now because he's living in France and living the life of a re-
cluse and apparently preparing himself for death, I think a little prematurely, but
he thinks he's going to die soon, and so he's trying to get ready for death, with
a good deal of trouble because he's convinced he's going to be damned. This is
a curiously un-Catholic view, but he's been pushed into the position of fornication, you see, ever since his first wife—he's separated from his first wife. His
wife is doggedly still alive, living in Oxford, England, and there's Greene fornicating with the young *au pair* girls, feeling wretchedly sinful about it, aware also
that he's taken up a heretical position, that of the Jansenists, and not too happy
about his future. A very morose and depressed man, but probably a very considerable writer. Well, he's still a gay writer—God, one can't use the word "gay" now
without having the wrong connotations—but he's still a very gay writer in that
he obviously enjoys the manipulation of language and characters. I think the
film—I haven't seen the film yet—the book, *Travels with My* Aunt, is the sort of
thing that novelists should be doing. Instead of writing great earnest texts about,
you know, the problems of American youth or American Negroes, to write something which is meant to be entertainment, which is beautifully structured, which
has interesting, but not too profound characters in it, and entertains and pleases.
Well, what the hell is wrong with that? But the book was condemned. You know,
"Mr. Greene has written somewhat superficially here, etc., etc." I'd rather have
that one book than all these bloody wads of paper that are sent to me. They're
usually sent to me without my wanting them. I don't like earnestness in fiction,
and there's no earnestness in Greene. There's a lot of earnestness in the American
novel, however.

Bunting: It has been said that your comic characters, such as Alex and Enderby, lack essential dignity. Is this a valid criticism?

Burgess: I don't think it's true. I wouldn't be prepared to argue it, but I don't think it's true. I think that what I learned from Beckett was that you portray the essential dignity of man by showing him at his most humiliated. That's the whole point, I think, of the Beckett novels: however much you try and reduce man to a mere digestive tract, which is not working very well—you make him aged, you deprive him, he's ragged, he stinks—yet he is still man, and his dignity is symbolized in the language that Beckett uses, which is a highly intricate, euphonious, creative medium. The dignity doesn't lie in the posture, in an attempt to see oneself as dignified. It lies in being what one is, of being a human being and maintaining certain essentially human standards against all opposition.

Well, all right, Enderby is a ridiculous figure, a dirty, nasty figure, but he holds fast onto the essential principle of his life, which is to create things. And even young Alex in *A Clockwork Orange* does become a kind of martyr. He is a martyr for man's power to choose, although he doesn't realize it; yet he becomes this one figure who suffers for the rest of us, and in that he's meant to be a figure of something else. I don't—God forbid that I should—go to the trouble of dignifying the characters, but the dignity, the essential dignity, should shine out to some extent despite the overlay of squalor and even evil.

Bunting: How do you generally react to critical works about you?

Burgess: I don't normally like to read them now, especially in England. They tend to be too short in England, and the reviewer naturally has to be funny and make epigrammatic points. But in America the reviews tend to be longer and more serious. On the whole, I still await somebody who understands them. It often happens that they're reviewed by Catholic priests, or Jesuit scholars or something, which is not quite what I want, or they're reviewed by agnostics or atheists, which, again, is not quite what I want. I suppose the idea is they want you to review one's own books, and I did this on one occasion. I got fired from the newspaper for it, but I did try it.

The only sensible reviews I get in England are from Frank Kermode and, you know, I'm happy that it is him because he's probably our best scholar, our best critic. I don't know what the American view of him is, but I think that he's admired over here too, isn't he? He was at my own university of Manchester. He is drawn towards Catholicism; I can see that he's drawn towards it, and he understands what a novelist is doing who's brought up as a Catholic. He's becoming in-

terested in structuralism. He tends to mirror my own mind at some points, and
when I get a review from him, it's usually a sensible review. The only good review
I had of my last real novel, *MF*, was his review in *The Listener* in England, and the
other reviews, almost without exception, were totally uncomprehending. This is
very worrying because this was, I thought, a simple enough novel. But what happens when you really try and write a difficult novel? Who's going to understand
it? So, for the most part, I like a little praise. I'm upset by adverse criticism, but
the reviews don't make a great deal of difference to the way I work. They're just
there, and they make no difference.

Bunting: If the reviewers had taken the trouble to read your essay, "If Oedipus
Had Read His Lévi-Strauss," it might have helped them.
Burgess: Well, yes, they could have done that because the material is always available. If the book lives, if the book lasts, they may do that then. They may get
round to it. This was the key to the book. I'm not suggesting they *had* to get the
key, but at least they should not have reviewed the book at all if they didn't understand what it was doing. It's no good if somebody writing is saying, "I do not
understand this book, and I really cannot say very much about it except that . . ."
This is not a review. But this is what we're getting.

Bunting: How do you assess your function as a critic and as a reviewer?
Burgess: Oh, I'm not critic. I'm not a reviewer. I'm nothing at all. I have no pre-
tensions in those fields at all. I'm a very poor, a very superficial, critic. I'm a good
reviewer because reviewing is only journalism. It's nothing to do with criticism.
But, I've sometimes been asked to write seven-thousand-word essays on Herman
Melville and that kind of thing. I could no more do that than I could fly. And it
is chiefly because I don't really like reading very much. I'm not a great reader. I've
read a lot in my time, but if I were told that if I didn't read the entire works of
George Eliot from beginning to end I would have to die, well, I think I'd honestly
have to die. It's as simple as that. I can't reread Jane Austen. I can't reread Scott.
I can't reread Conrad. I recognize the fault in myself, but when you get into the
writing of novels as a career, you tend to read less. You tend not to be too interested in what other people are doing. It's an occupational hazard. I'd much rather
read a work of criticism. I'd much rather read somebody else's book on Melville
than read Melville myself. This is, in fact, my preferred reading these days: other
people's criticism. I'm not a critic, never would be. I might have made a good
music critic, but I've never really had the opportunity to try it out.

Bunting: *MF* is a rather provocative title. Have you encountered much difficulty in getting your books published because of the feeling that the books were too obscene or too violent?

Burgess: Not in England or America, but in other countries, naturally. In South Africa, in Russia. But, on the whole, I've had no censorship trouble, except at the source, except at the publishing office itself. This held back *Enderby*, which is a rather harmless novel, I think, for a good number of years. The first part was completed in 1959, but I couldn't get it published until 1963 because the publishers thought it was ungentlemanly to write a book about a man sitting in the lavatory all the time. It's not obscene at all. I suppose it may be obscene in a sense, but not viciously obscene, and so the book was held back from publication. I've not had this experience in America. I've had rather the tendency for American publishers to say, you know, "This book isn't obscene enough," or "This book is not tough enough for our audiences." This is what happened with *A Clockwork Orange*, which lost its final chapter in America.

Bunting: That had nothing to do with you?
Burgess: Oh, no.

Bunting: That last chapter, of course, is one in which Alex becomes somewhat reconciled to his condition.
Burgess: Well, he grows up. It's simple enough. If I were writing an allegory or a fable, then I should end it up with Alex restored to his former condition, but I was writing a novel, or I thought I was, and the idea was that there should be at least hints to the reader that there was progress still to be made, that he was still an emerging human being, an emerging character, and that he had to grow up. What would he be like at the age of twenty or eighteen, or whatever it is. He obviously would change. He would realize that aggression was just a mode of youthful activity. But the aggression itself meant something in that it probably meant creative fire, and it was not going to be used as creative fire. It also meant a kind of philo-progenitive urge: he wants a son, he wants a wife, he wants a family. He's a human being. He was intended to be a human being, but he's turned out in the American edition to be a mere clockwork figure, I suppose, who's just impelled towards evil by some deterministic force, which is not what I intended at all.

Bunting: The reputation of Vladimir Nabokov in the United States seems to have come about because of a quirk. Americans were probably looking for a porno-

graphic work in *Lolita*. Do you think the fascination for violence contributed to your reputation in America being established with *A Clockwork Orange?*
Burgess: Yes, it has. Of course, it's totally a false reputation. I notice that even Pearl Buck, whose work I didn't like very much, said at some time that she objected to being associated with *The Good Earth*. I think it's true. I don't think *The Good Earth* is a very good novel. She wrote very good novels; some of them were a bit rather old-fashioned, but very good, very revealing about China. Sinclair Lewis had this association with *Main Street* or *Babbitt*. I think this normally happens to authors, but I don't mind this so long as there's not a falsification of approach, so long as it's not assumed that all the novels I write are violent novels. This is the stupid approach.

Again, I had to address the New York English Teachers Association on Saturday at the Americana Hotel, and a woman came up to me to say, "Mr. Burgess, I loved your talk, but why are you so violent? Why are you acting in such an adverse influence on literature?" I said, "Madam, you make me very angry indeed, extremely angry. This is a libel. You have not even read the book, I gather. You're judging from the film. You must not, you must never go to any author and say this to him." I said this very gently, almost like a schoolmaster, and she blushed and went away. But I had to say it, you see. I had to say this. Especially, "Why are you so violent?" I'm not violent, never have been.

Bunting: Were you satisfied with the film version of *A Clockwork Orange?*
Burgess: Nothing to do with me. How can I say? Ask me if I liked *Last Tango in Paris*. I don't know. It's all right, I suppose. It's nothing to do with me. It's rather embarrassing to see your own characters parading on the screen. They're separated from yourself. They're separated from the literary context. But, on the whole, I think he [Stanley Kubrick, the director] made a fairly good job of it. It was a very slow and dull film; very beautiful, but very dull and slow. But, of course, this is typical of Kubrick. The dullness paid off in *2001* because space travel must be dull, the immense ennui of these open plains of the heavens.

Bunting: In *The Novel Now* you called James Joyce "a major prophet." I wonder if you would clarify that a bit. It's a strange phrase.
Burgess: Oh, it's a silly statement. No, I meant that in a sense he looked forward to modes of sensibility which we regard as essentially contemporary. There's a kind of common mode which most men of education and sensibility share. But this was not in existence when he wrote *Ulysses*. I suppose, in a sense, he made it

and imposed it upon us. Writers do that. But I notice when reading *Ulysses* with a class here, they cannot accept it that this is 1904. They say, "This is astonishing." They're saying pretty well what I say there: rather "prophetic." And, I say, "Yes, it seems to be so, but you have to remember that human beings are always the same. Human beings haven't changed much."

What has changed is the method, the approach to them. We often start off with preconceived ideas; we make our human figures conform to those. What Joyce did was to be absolutely frank, absolutely open, and let human beings act on him. In that this is the normal mode of approaching human personality in fiction or in life, in that he was prophetic. He was looking forward to a contemporary way of viewing life and creating fiction. But, on the other hand, this is not prophecy; this may be just what he created and what we're following. I think it was Dick Ellmann—I quote several lines of Dick Ellmann—who said that we're learning to be Joyce's contemporaries, something like that, which is a rather epigrammatic way of putting it.

Bunting: May I ask what is the greatest influence Joyce has exerted on you? Is it the love and power of the language?
Burgess: Yes, but Joyce has never had much of a stylistic influence on me at all. I've never imitated him, but I think it's his tremendous devotion to the art and also this tremendous concern with the language, which also is preceded by a pretty vast knowledge, within a limited field, of music. Joyce knew how close words and music were to each other, and some of the effects he gets in *Ulysses*, which have never been fully explained by English professors, derive usually from the fact that Joyce is trying to make a musical sentence or a verbal phrase obey the laws of music. You can take any number of these sentences in *Ulysses* and see that he assumes that the vowel sounds represent a kind of scale system, and by using the vowel sounds in a particular order, you can get a melodic sense, and sometimes the melodic image is totally contrapuntal to the image contained in the statement. Now this has not been much pointed out, but it is essential to Joyce, and this is the sort of thing I like in him and try to do myself to some extent. But otherwise I can't really be influenced by him, although I read him at an early age. But, of course, I also read Blake at in early age and Gerard Manley Hopkins.

Bunting: If, as you have said, Joyce pushed the English language to the limit in *Ulysses*, what has Nabokov done that has intrigued you?
Burgess: Well, Nabokov has not done anything new at all. In some ways, of course, he's very old-fashioned, and he likes John Updike's work because this, too,

is rather old-fashioned. I don't think he quite sees this. He's writing rather like
Huysmans. It's rather like the *fin de siècle* kind of writing in which you have glorious coruscations of language but a rather debilitated rhythm underneath. The
rhythms of Nabokov are not strong. I like him because, I suppose, he's European
and cultivated. It's principally the cultivation I like. This may be a bad thing. But,
when one of my students brings me a story or a novel beginning "Ah, shit!" I'm
not squeamish, but I get a bit fed up with this earthy approach to life all the time.
You know, "He passed the reefer to the man next to him." I get a bit tired of it, and
I appreciate this world of hotels and cuisine and ancient monuments and other
languages and literature, this kind of cultivated sensibility that you get in Nabokov and to some extent you get in Updike, although Updike is trying to be sort
of grass-rootsish American, concerned with blow jobs and all that sort of stuff. I
also like the restraint of Nabokov. I also like the word play and the cryptograms,
which, again, is very old. And more and more obviously he's beginning to see, as I
am, that novels are structures, that it doesn't matter what the hell the meaning is,
as long as the structure conveys the meaning. I think he was trying to do this in
Ada. But whether I like what he's doing at the moment, I don't really know. This
last novel that he wrote, I don't really know whether I like it. Still, he's not afraid
of being snobbish, which is a good thing because now he can afford it.

Bunting: Have you ever considered yourself doing what Nabokov did in *Lolita*,
that is, having the cultivated European gentleman look at America from his point
of view? I think the strength of the novel is really the second half.
Burgess: Oh, yes, I think so. I've never contemplated writing a novel about
America and for a very obvious reason: I don't feel qualified to use the American
language. I have to have characters speaking and being American, and it is very
difficult to master a dialect or a series of dialects which is so close to one's own.
It's easy enough to master, say, Provençal French, but to master New York English,
Yiddish English, is quite difficult. I have this problem in writing a musical on the
life of Houdini. I'm a bit scared of doing it.

The little book I'm going to write, which replaces *A Clockwork Condition*, is
about this character Enderby, who's in New York just a day. Just a little book; I call
it *Enderby and the Clockwork Condition* to satisfy everybody. But he just has a day
in New York, and I see it very much from his point of view, and he just faces these
difficult questions that New Yorkers ask. He'll probably end up getting mugged or
something that will form a useful plot out of it. But a short book, probably with
photographs in it. This is about the only American book I feel like writing. I sup-

pose I have to make the effort one of these days to write about Minneapolis or somewhere.

Bunting: There was some time between the publication of *Inside Mr. Enderby* and *Outside Enderby*. I believe you wrote *Nothing Like the Sun* in between.

Burgess: Oh, several things in between. *Inside Mr. Enderby* was one of the five novels that I wrote when I was supposed to be dying. But if I hadn't had this death sentence, I would have written this book that you have here in America. But I didn't have the time, so I just completed the first part. I lived, of course; I went on living. And the difficulty of getting *Enderby* published then rather turned me against writing a sequel. But when I got it published, other things came along, other jobs to do, and I delayed the writing of a sequel until about 1965, I think; or even 1966, I don't know. It was published just when my first wife died, so it would be 1968. I don't want to do any more with this character. I quite like the character, but I might do this little New York thing, and that's the end of him. Get on with something else.

I've got this Napoleon novel to write, and I've got a very long novel—I think it may be a very long novel—about the Papacy, really about Pope John, and this has to be told. The narrator is Somerset Maugham, taking the character, Somerset Maugham, as the narrator at the age of eighty-one, and in his divagatory way tells a long story. It's all about whether Pope John was really a saint or whether a miracle, an alleged miracle, really was a miracle. That's the root of the thing. It's all done from a rather urbane, man-of-the-world point of view. One doesn't know what it's really going to contain until the thing is written. Those are my plans.

Doing What the Hell You Like in the Novel

Lemuel Reilly/1973

From *Delaware Literary Review*, vol. 2 (Spring 1973). Reprinted by permission of University of Delaware Library, Newark, Delaware.

Reilly: Since most of our contributors are at the beginning of their careers, I'm sure they'd like to hear something about what it's like to be working on a sixteenth, rather than a first, novel. Do you, for example, find yourself doing the same thing over and over again? In other words, do you find yourself simply refining the same technique?

Burgess: No, every novel is a different thing, a different artifact. Each requires a different technique, embraces a different subject matter. It's always as difficult to write, say, a twentieth novel as it is a first since in a sense the twentieth novel is a first novel. If you're going to repeat yourself in novel after novel—as many writers do—there's not much point in doing it. Except for money. I try to make every novel as different as I can; otherwise why bother? You must set yourself new problems and try to solve them as best you can. In that sense, I suppose every novel is a failure insofar as you want to "perfect" a given technique. But if you're doing something you know you can do already, well, why do it? It's the things you don't know you can do that are important.

Reilly: I suppose that's what motivated Joyce to spend all those years on *Finnegans Wake* rather than write another *Ulysses*.

Burgess: Well, that's what he said, of course. Once he had done *Ulysses*, there was nothing for him to do except write *Finnegans Wake*. He'd exhausted the possibilities of the "waking" day and all that was left was the sleeping night. An interesting question is what he was going to write after that. He said he was going to write an epic on the sea, but I don't believe that for a moment. I don't think he was going to do anything. I think that to a great extent a writer's works are coterminous with his life. Proust's *À la recherche du temps perdu*, for instance, just about lasted his lifetime. It's hard to imagine Proust writing anything after that. I don't think it was possible for Joyce to have done anything after the *Wake*: night and day, that's it. An exhaustion of the possibilities of both approaches, both techniques.

Reilly: You seem to be in a unique position to speak about modern literature since you've established yourself as a scholar as well as a creative writer. Do you see any particular trend in modern English fiction? Or modern American fiction, for that matter?

Burgess: Well, America is certainly "where it's happening" today; there's not much happening in England. One has to say that because there are so many social changes occurring in this country and, well, we English have had our social changes. (You can still walk around London at night without getting mugged, for example—at least I think you can.) But here the "ethnic minorities"—a terrible phrase—are lending a new vigor to the language. I think Phil Roth, for instance, is a very interesting writer indeed. People are still trying here. They're attempting to produce "big" works of fiction, attempting to grapple with contemporary problems—and grapple with the problems of language! I find it very elating.

Reilly: Is that why you left England?

Burgess: In England, there's something rather weary about the way language is being used, and there are very few situations to write about. That's one of the reasons I got out. I didn't want to get enmeshed in a world of literary cocktail parties and literary cliques. I didn't want to be an English writer any more; I wanted to be an international writer. Or even an American writer. Although I must not become an American writer because then I would have to become an American as well. And that would mean starting very late in the field.

Reilly: In your most recent novel, *MF*, you demonstrate an extraordinary ear for American dialects. The two "halves" of the main character, for example, are worlds apart culturally, but you manage to bring both of them off perfectly.

Burgess: Actually I have great difficulty with American speech because it's so close to English speech that you can trip up if you're not very careful. I don't know how to use, for instance, a simple phrase like "at that" in a sentence like "You're right at that." I have no idea as to what precise tone to use, or even when to use it. And in England we are bedeviled by old "visions" of American speech that stem from magazines like *Punch* in the 1850s. We're forever being asked to believe that you're saying things like, "Wall, ah calculate" and "Ah reckon that." So I'm quite wary about American speech. I'd much rather invent an American speech of my own, which is more fun anyway. Always invent your own dialects if you can.

Reilly: I was struck by the fact that both you in *MF* and John Barth in *Chimera* turned to ancient mythoi for at least part of your plots. Do you see some sort of "neoclassical" movement in modern fiction?
Burgess: I think there's a tremendous interest in myth today, and I think this getting back to the world of myth will be the salvation of us all. Barth is on the right track in trying to synthesize myth: the idea of synthesizing Scheherazade and Greek myth is admirable. What I'm trying to do myself at the moment—and this is not primarily my own idea, it's Beethoven's—is synthesize Prometheus and Napoleon.

Reilly: You're referring to your novel-in-progress?
Burgess: Yes. What I have to do in the novel is evoke the idea of the Greek Prometheus but make it work in a realistic framework. It's fascinating, but very difficult. The section of the book, for instance, in which Napoleon literally meets his Waterloo is done in about thirty-five pages, which corresponds to a Beethoven scherzo. Napoleon, in a great triumph, is borne to a Paris opera house which is showing a new version of the Prometheus myth in his honor. But he objects to this: if he is Prometheus, why is Prometheus having his liver pecked out? (But then there's his Austrian wife pecking out her own liver with Wiener schnitzel and God knows what else.) Then the narrative abruptly shifts from this stage presentation to a presentation that's going on in England where Prometheus has become a comic figure. It's all done very rapidly, of course, as would be the case in a scherzo, and it's done also through the agency of the myth. With the myth you're free for the moment; you can soar outside reality.

Reilly: Is this flight from reality typical of modern fiction?
Burgess: Not really, for you can only soar so far. The novel is primarily a naturalist thing, you see, in which the writer can do what the hell he wants only as long as he holds fast the character. That's Joyce's great achievement: you can read *Ulysses* backward because of Bloom; you can read *Finnegans Wake* upside down because of Earwicker. This is not avant-garde writing; this is good, traditional, solid, character writing. You can do what the hell you like: tear it into diagrams, into mathematical symbols, as long as the characters are strong enough.

Reilly: One final question: you've said that you would rather be thought of as a musician who writes novels than a novelist who writes music. I guess your use of the scherzo technique exemplifies your impulse toward musical composition.

Burgess: That's a good question. I like to think that I'm bringing to the writing of my novels something I learned from the writing of music. I structure them in a musical manner, using leitmotifs, that sort of thing. But I'm not writing as much music as I used to. I'm composing a fair amount, but not enough to render me a genuine musician. The fact of the matter is I make the sort of statement you asked about just to upset people.

Working on Apocalypse

William M. Murray/1977

From *The Iowa Review* 8 (1977). Reprinted by permission of William M. Murray.

Murray: Mr. Burgess, I understand you are working at the moment on an apocalyptic theme. Are you thinking about apocalypse in terms of film or novel?
Burgess: What happened was that I was approached by two big men in Paramount, or rather Universal, but Universal working along with Paramount for this particular project, Mr. Brown and Mr. Zanuck, who made a lot of money out of these disaster films, you know, *Earthquake* and *Jaws* and so on, and they want to make the ultimate disaster film about the end of the world.

Murray: The ultimate disaster film!
Burgess: The ultimate disaster movie about the end of the world. Indeed, this is of course paradoxical, ironic, and typically Hollywood: End of the World I, II, and III. What we'll do after it, I don't know yet. It may not be my concern. And they approached me to see about the writing of this film chiefly because they were well aware that although they were drawing in a lot of money from the box office, with these earlier disaster films, they were not getting a good critical response because of lack of interest—lack of human interest—in the film, lack of character interest, and they thought that I might conceivably do some version in which the characters were interesting and the disaster itself was there in the background. Now, in the 1930s, I think about 1932, Philip Wylie, American novelist and, I think, a scientist in a way, wrote a book called *When Worlds Collide*, which Paramount has already turned into a film in the 1950s, a very bad film, about a couple of planets coming toward the Earth, one planet remaining within orbit somewhere outside the Earth and the other actually hitting the Earth, and people were able to get off this planet of ours into this untouched planet before the other planet collided. This is a very improbable notion. It was useful for me to come to Iowa because I'd already met Brown and Zanuck in New York, and I could see a

very great man, Van Allen, who is here in Iowa, and he would be able to tell me actually what will happen if an asteroid or some other heavenly body comes into our orbit—what would happen in terms of the physical apocalypse. He was able to tell me what it would be like if the moon was smashed up and so forth. But this is mere window-dressing; this is mere background material. The interesting thing is how would people behave in these circumstances and how can we present little creatures behaving in a particular way. So I suppose my interest is not primarily in apocalypse at all, in that sense, but rather in people facing any great disaster.

Murray: Are you thinking of disaster in terms of an accidental event?
Burgess: More or less accidental. Although naturally in the film there's bound to be discussion as to the asteroid possibly coming because God decided he had had enough of man and wants to punish him or destroy him. A parallel with Noah and the Great Flood. And naturally one has to have some great Billy Graham kind of character who thinks this is so. This is one useful dramatic conflict to begin with.

Murray: Why are people fascinated by disaster films? Is there something special in the air now? We seem to be obsessed with disasters.
Burgess: People are interested in disasters, especially here in America, because there hasn't been a great deal of disaster here of the kind that we've had in the West . . . I beg your pardon, in Europe . . . you know.

Murray: Not since 1929—here.
Burgess: Yes, but one hasn't seen in New York, in actual fact, what one has seen often on film, the actual destruction of a city; in London one saw the destruction of the city, it was actually happening, the Nazis were bombing the city, and down the city went. And people were living underground in tube shelters; the fascination of that period, of course, is not the mode of destruction, but the way the people responded to destruction. In a sense it seems that a city is a kind of spiritual entity. It's not only approachable in terms of an accidental urban aggregate but in terms again of its soul, and I think possibly New York has this soul but has not had a chance to demonstrate it and show it exists; no disaster has been big enough yet to explore its soul. It's as though—this is a cognate of what I've already said—the time between the First World War and the Second World War was comparatively short—how many years was it?—from 1918 to 1939—about twenty years; well, much more than twenty years have passed since 1945. Thirty years

have passed, and we have not had a major world war, and people are going to see these films—they want disaster because history has told them in a sense that we always have disaster every twenty years or so and we haven't had a disaster so we're going to assume that there will be no disaster. . . .

Murray: Do you think that as the year 2000 approaches we will get that sort of millennium apocalyptic Zeitgeist that always comes about? You know, the year 1000. . . .

Burgess: Oh, yes, the only records we have, you know, of the last millennium are the records of Anglo-Saxon literature with Bishop Wolston's observation on sin and his talk about the Danes being the Anti-Christ. The year 1000 has come, this is the end of the world, the Anti-Christ is here in the form of the invading Danes. Of course, a lot of people believed it. That will happen—the kind of chiliastic superstitions which sprang up. But I think it's too early for that now. People are rather more strongly influenced than one would have thought possible by *1984*; of course, 1984 is coming closer. It is going to be like Orwell has pictured it. It is now. There's a sense that things are moving in a direction of some great showdown, but I think probably because we have not had a war. I think there is a genuine, unconscious desire on the part of a lot of people to have a war. Unfortunately, we don't know who the enemy would be, but it's even been put forth, has it not, by the economists that the only viable twentieth-century economy is a war economy. And history seems to prove that. We in England in the 1930s with masses of unemployment, here in America too, we got out of our depression by preparing for war, eventually by having a war. There's an end to the peace banners, the genuine desire now on the part of man to go to war.

Murray: Of course, this provides excitement in boring times.
Burgess: The times are a bore. Korea wasn't a real war. Vietnam wasn't a real war. But a great war with bombs dropping on great cities, it's a most stirring image. And, of course, there's a bit of sexual freedom; wars are very sexy. Very true; Aldous Huxley said, did he not, "battles and ruffles, wars and whores." And it's very true.

Murray: Tennyson, I believe, was stirred by the idea, also.
Burgess: Tennyson saw all these things in "Locksley Hall." I think that's what it is. A desire for the kind of sensations and emotional experiences one associates with a major war or disaster. People like getting them at a kind of surrogate level from these films.

Murray: You're thinking in terms of disaster rather than apocalypse, then?

Burgess: Disaster . . . well, it is apocalypse in that the Earth is destroyed, but of course one can't take into account, one cannot envisage the destruction of man; it always has to be a human mind to envisage the destruction of a human mind. The whole thing is contradictory so we have the rather corny image of people getting away from the Earth. I've been aware of a television series already on the issue, called "Space: 1999." It's a British series, I gather, so I discovered the other day, it would be the planet destroyed, people living on the moon. But man and the social structures that are typical of man must go on. We cannot envisage a situation in which this is not happening. I can't.

Murray: Do you think watching disaster movies—or people's desire to watch them—has any moral effect at all?

Burgess: Yes, I think it has a certain effect. I think people like to undergo the emotions at a second remove, and they get a certain titillation out of it. But I don't think they have any moral effect whatsoever. I don't think films of that nature ever do. I gather this week on television they are doing a program about Orson Welles's radio program.

Murray: Oh, yes, right, *War of the Worlds*.

Burgess: *War of the Worlds* did in fact cause a genuine panic in parts of America, but it wasn't followed by a desire to stop backfighting; people went on drinking and fornicating, I think people always do. And I don't think any film or any book of this kind can modify people's patterns of behavior—I don't think they ever do, never could do.

Murray: You'd think if you made a terrifying enough apocalyptic movie and somehow it were shown throughout the world. . . .

Burgess: It might make 'em behave better? I can't believe it would. I think you might even find the opposite. We know that the bad time is going to come. So let's have a good time. I cannot even begin to think that any work of art has ever had, ever could have a moral effect on the auditor or the reader. I don't think it's ever happened yet, that a great work of art has had a moral effect—oh, possibly *Uncle Tom's Cabin* did, probably it's almost unique in the annals of literature. Abraham Lincoln said that Mrs. Beecher's story was the actual cause of the war, that it was the little lady who made this great war.

Murray: You'll probably have to do some research if you're going to get involved in this kind of film. What kind of research do you envision doing?

Burgess: Very little. We rely ultimately on what we know of people; it's an intuitive art, it doesn't involve research. I'd like to say at this point that I have written one novel about the future, in 1962, called *The Wanting Seed* which is, I think, now showing as a film in Italy. It's a Carlo Ponti with Sophia Loren in the lead. *The Wanting Seed* was an attempt to envisage the future, not from the viewpoint of the distant future but the viewpoint of the fairly immediate present, the population explosion and the increasing difficulty in balancing the population with the food supply. This was more or less a comic attempt to show what might happen in the future, how the social patterns would change as the begetting of children became a taboo thing, how homosexuals would reach the top—they are already in England reaching the top—how people who castrate themselves would get the highest jobs of all, and what would happen when the balance was no longer capable of being sustained. The great famine followed by a return in a rational society to a kind of superstition which would take the form of a new passion for the Eucharist. The Eucharist is, of course, symbolic of the flesh-eating process, is the sublimation of it, in which through that process you stop sacrificing real human flesh, the initial process in reverse. After this I'm going back to the sacrifice of human flesh, the ingesting of human protein, and finally the arrangement or fabrication of a warlike situation with no enemy, in which human corpses could be brought about by fighting and these corpses could then be turned into sustenance, and thus the balance would be maintained. This is a possible answer. I put it forward comically in 1962, but I think increasingly we are becoming more and more fascinated by cannibalism, as Piers Paul Reed's novel, rather his study, of the Andes survivors shows. People are fascinated by cannibalism. I think we're going to get it before long. I honestly believe we are going to get it. And with little trouble. We don't know what we're eating most of the time. When we buy things in supermarkets we don't know what we've got. Oh, we get the breakdown, the ingredients on the can, it's usually something like "animal protein," "animal fat." What is the animal? We don't know. We're going to get things like "mensch." This is going to happen, I think.

Murray: When you talk of either disaster or apocalypse, you get quite mythopoeic about the whole thing.
Burgess: It's not only books. . . .

Murray: Films—*Metropolis*, for example. This film is very much flirting with disaster as a mythopoeic event. The destruction of the city.
Burgess: Very mythopoeic. But even visually the city of the future is "metropo-

lis." The city of the future was made back in 1926. I've been looking at some slides of New York that my wife has taken of present-day New York. These cannot touch these studio mockups that were made in *Metropolis*, they cannot touch them. This is the city of the future—we have to approach it through a myth, and myth means mostly film these days. Visually. Provided by film.

Murray: Most of the sets for that film were manufactured, weren't they?
Burgess: All done in the studio, all done with reduced models. Tiny cars going up and down, aeroplanes dangling and so forth. Yet I saw that film first in 1926 when I was a young boy, and that has been a very powerful part of the structure of my mind. Seeing it was traumatic; I was nine when I first saw it. You can imagine the impact it had on a child. My whole generation has been partly made by the film. So when we think of the future, I can't help feeling in some measure it's got to go back to *Metropolis* sooner or later.

Murray: When one thinks of writing disaster or apocalyptic movies, one wants to make allegories or myths out of them. Lang made a modern fable in *Metropolis*. He was not against control, he was not against the master of Metropolis; he wanted a mediator between the machine and man.
Burgess: Yes. He was quite content, I think, with that kind of message. He was very soft, I think, finally. But I do obviously believe that the kind of situation which I and probably many other authors attempt to envisage in fiction—like the one I just mentioned, *The Wanting Seed*, vaguely comic but also vaguely serious— is closer to contemporary disaster myth than the one in *Metropolis*. Suddenly one wakes up in the middle of a traffic stream in Rome or in London, and God! we are overpopulated. These are all people. We can't move. Or you get jammed in a tunnel and the fumes start coming in, and you have a feeling you'll be choked to death or asphyxiated. This is it, you see; we're suffering already now, and then we read about the Andes survivors eating human flesh, with fascination . . . is this a way out, possibly? We turn against, at least I turn against the Vatican II, because they don't make much of the Eucharist anymore, whereas one of the links between our own activism and possibly our future was in the Eucharist; I was taught as a child in the Catholic Church, and you too, we're eating the body and blood of Christ. With all these other bodies around . . .

Murray: I find it repugnant now.
Burgess: Well, no, I find it less repugnant. I feel the Church was missing the spirit of the age in making it symbolical. If you want it to be, Christ is there in spirit.

But it's not the great, incredible thing that Christ, according to the Gospels, ordained—you're going to eat Me and you're going to drink My blood.

Murray: I know some homosexuals who really get a kick out of taking the Eucharist. . . .

Burgess: Oh, sure they do. . . . I hadn't thought of that. . . . You've gotta accept the fact that society is changing, the fact that society has something to do with this particular issue, what we are going to eat. And as to sex, a full quiver is no longer desirable—sex is totally separated from generation. We have the prominent unisex in which you can't tell whether you're looking at a boy or a girl from the back, and even from the front sometimes. You can't be like each other in sex. Homosexuality is coming out in the open, both kinds. We'll end up with societies for castration, back to origin, back to the Church fathers. And these are all patterns which stem from a feeling that it is obscene to beget children. That is a kind of the will not to live, of apocalyptic motif. The beginning.

Murray: Hardy in *Jude*.

Burgess: Yes, very prophetic book.

Murray: If they are castrated early enough, they'll come up with nice tenor voices, counter-tenors that will last all their lives. Music will replace sex.

Burgess: I should have thought of that. Choirs of castrati highly likely; I hadn't thought of that.

Murray: You know the story of the lemmings . . . they go beserk? . . . Old Norse word . . . commit mass suicide from stress . . . overpopulation . . .

Burgess: They're not *trying* to destroy themselves, they believe there's something out there they've got to get to. . . .

Murray: And at certain periods every four years . . . you know the lemmings breed like mad . . . well, they take off looking for a place where they can have some privacy and reduce stress . . . and of course, they end up in the sea. Idea for a disaster movie.

Burgess: Yes, this has often haunted me. I sometimes wake up in the middle of the night thinking of lemmings, especially a film I saw, a BBC film, where millions of lemmings, rush into the sea. No, it does seem to me the kind of pattern through which the future is going to manifest itself; maybe in the sexual mores, it probably is already. That our view of the nineteenth-century mother bearing twenty-five children as a great virtuous woman is replaced by a much thinner, more masculine image of woman who is not going to beget children at all unless she wants to, in which sex is becoming a kind of game. Sex no longer leads us to the great imponderables. Sex is a little game we play. And of course, it's lost a lot of its intensity; sex is not now an intensive experience. It's going to become less and less intense as time goes on. And it's going to get tied up with our sense of the population explosion. I think man will find a means, a way out of the population problem. One way will be through artificial wars; I think men have now artificial wars, and I think we're going to have an ingestion of human flesh. We'll get used to anything. That's more or less as far as I can go.

Murray: Infinitely adaptable man!

Burgess: We must adapt. The most adaptable creature in the world. I don't think if we are hit by an asteroid or by another planet we are going to survive. However, I can't see the end of man. I suppose it's another way of saying I can't see the end of life. I can't see the end of any kind of life, but human life is the only self-conscious life we have, and this is so tremendous an achievement; evolution has been working towards it, the achievement of life understanding itself. We've achieved it to some extent. This cannot be destroyed.

Murray: They tell me there are people in California now buying little hideouts, you know, for $20,000 or $30,000; in the event of disaster they've got this little secret place where they can survive. Self-conscious life lets us look ahead . . . but we can't stop the disaster.

Burgess: Well, of course, California is a great place for an apocalypse, isn't it? It always has been—well, not always, but it's always been associated in my mind with apocalypse and magic and astrology and the like. A few years ago I was in California and went to a great Thanksgiving dinner which was given for the local astrologers of whom there were several thousand, amateur and professional, and the subject under discussion that night was the astrology of the line of the *Queen Elizabeth*, or rather the *Queen Mary*. The *Queen Mary* was treated as a human being and the zodiacal significance of when it was launched, its life, its death, and so forth. It was treated with immense seriousness. And this is the place where the prophets boom or bloom, it's the place of Aldous Huxley and yellow gold, and it's the place where when a disaster is coming we'll know about it there.

Murray: One final question, Mr. Burgess. Why do you want to write a disaster film?

Burgess: For the money, for the money. . . . We end up always with the concern or preoccupation with human beings. I suggested to these two great film moguls that the film we ought to make is Daniel Defoe's *A Journal of the Plague Year*, which is what disaster is all about, how the soul of a city survives, and you know the plague is a pretty bad disaster so it is as bad as any great planet zooming down from outer space, this disease facing you everywhere. You come home and you find your wife and children have got it, and you don't know what to do about it or what caused it, and can you survive as a human being, can you survive as a city? I think nobody has touched the genius of Defoe. I think it's worth going back to. Nobody really reads it; they read *Robinson Crusoe*, but not this. That is the film to make. This is how a city responds to a great plague. I can think of nothing more horrible than the great plague. Nor could Camus, of course, the same idea.

Murray: When one talks about disaster and apocalypse one can't help thinking about one's own end.

Burgess: Well, there's one thing—we both have the same background—there's one thing we haven't touched and really daren't touch, and that is the real Christian end of the world as prophesied by Christ and as depicted by Michelangelo in the Sistine Chapel. I had the job a few months ago of giving a talk in the Sistine Chapel on the Day of Judgment. It was a batted-out thing; the Day of Judgment was behind me, you know, cameras were on us both, Michelangelo and me, there you see so-and-so, and there you see so-and-so, and hoping I was pointing at the right direction. This was one image, it's the most terrible image in the world. This great muscular Christ who is no longer Christ but a Prometheus, a huge monster; his mother is begging him not to condemn these people. And all the saints around are saying, "Don't, for Christ's sake . . ." and off they go, swirling down, Charon waiting with his boat, down to the fires and the pit. And of course that terrible sermon in Joyce's *Portrait of the Artist as a Young Man*. That's the real apocalypse, that's the one thing we daren't believe. We feel it's incredible, impossible to believe. Supposing it were true? Supposing there were a Last Judgment, and there was Christ . . . there's no reason it shouldn't. Without heaven, hell is as Joyce described it. Catholics have this; Catholics have this all the time.

Murray: In time of apocalypse, you don't need the sense of judgment from the outside; if I were to think my life were going to end tomorrow, or the world was going to end, automatically I begin thinking—did I lead a good life? . . . at a time of disaster, I imagine one judges oneself. One performs that day of judgment on oneself.

Burgess: But don't you do that all the time? It may be so. Christianity may be the true religion! Jews feel this, Protestants feel this, about their own faith, that the Day of Judgment may happen; but if I ate meat on Friday when I was a child and was not sorry, that's going to be there . . . the judgment—why not? There's no essential logic in it; why should I not have this? It's a complex problem. Judgment and apocalypse. Intertwined.

Guilt's a Good Thing

Samuel Coale/1978

The following conversation is an abridged and restructured version of an interview with Anthony Burgess that took place on 7 and 11 July 1978 in Monaco. From *Modern Fiction Studies* 27:3 (1981), pp. 429–52. © Purdue Research Foundation. Reprinted by permission of The Johns Hopkins University Press.

Coale: What about your parents?

Burgess: My mother and my sister died in the same week. Have you read Katherine Anne Porter's story, "Pale Horse, Pale Rider"? That's the image of the influenza epidemic at the end of the [First World] war. This was terrible, part of a terrible war. It killed everybody. My father came home and found my mother and sister dead in the same room and myself on the bed alive. I was only about four months old, less than a year. So I never knew her, never knew my sister either. It's not uncommon in England.

Coale: Did your father remarry?

Burgess: He remarried, yes. He remarried an Irish woman who kept a pub.

Coale: What was her name?

Burgess: My step-mother's name was Maggie Byrnes. She had married into the Dwyer family, which produced George Dwyer, the Archbishop of Birmingham. The Dwyers were one of these interesting Irish families that had settled in Manchester. They ran a green grocery business and were determined to shove their kids into the priesthood. But George very quickly became Monsignor and was in charge of missionary services, and then at length became Bishop of Leeds and finally the Archbishop, which is what they wanted, which is what the family was after. That was the family my step-mother had been married into. She was a widow. And then my father married her. They had this huge pub in Manchester. You don't see pubs like this anymore. The pub was called "The Golden Eagle" on Lodge Street. I don't know whether the pub is still there. I know that the eagle itself, the huge golden eagle outside, was taken, was bought by the Anglican Church for use in front of a pulpit. I don't think you'll see those pubs anymore. Those pubs were huge, tremendous size. They had three singing rooms with a piano

115

in each one of them, concerts every night. Before the Defense of the Realm Act began to limit the opening hours of pubs, these were open at six in the morning and were open until midnight. Meals were served, free lunches, a colossal lot to drink. . . .

Coale: What about your real mother, Elizabeth Burgess?
Burgess: The beautiful Belle Burgess. My mother had no living relatives. Family disappeared. Didn't know her at all. Lot of us are in that situation. An unusual woman, judging from the photographs, a very beautiful blonde. I'm trying to dig up some of the stories now, recently. Those were the great days of something that's disappeared, the music hall. It's kept alive artificially in England. She was involved in the old music hall as it was in Manchester. She was a dancer and singer. She was for a time understudy to Josie Collins. The name will not mean anything to you. She was also a singer and dancer in her own right. I can never take those kids you see on the radio with their microphones. I can't take this anymore. Forcing it on you, each with a microphone. There were no microphones in those days. You had to do that with your voice. You had to bat it out.

Coale: And your father?
Burgess: My father was a cinema pianist. I've written a little novel about him called *The Pianoplayers*, which I've not published yet. I think it's too short. It's a kind of structure which I'm surprised hasn't turned up more in fiction, the structure of a man who is thrown out of work by the advent of talking films. My father had been a pub pianist. He'd been other things. He didn't teach me. He never taught me a thing. I heard him play, and I wanted to play like him. So I taught myself, the hard way. When I was about fourteen I began to teach myself, began to compose. I wanted to be a composer. It was a slow way. If I'd had training, you see, it would've been quicker. It always is, if you'd get a decent teacher. Music had been my first love. It struck me as being a better discipline in some ways for an artist than words. I feel anybody can master the technicalities of putting a scene together, and I've always prided myself on that—you know, the carpenter prides himself on a particular skill—so I'd begun as a musician. I taught myself—I never had any technical training—everything.

Coale: Why were you so interested in Christopher Marlowe?
Burgess: I wrote my thesis [Senior Honors Thesis, Manchester University, 1940] on him. It was partly [that] I discerned in Marlowe a kind of Catholic quality. I was very interested in Marlowe's career, about which we know so little, and about

the possibility that he was acting as a double agent. I could see the picture very clearly. There he was at Cambridge, possible because he was a student-scholar from Canterbury, having to take Divinity, and divinity students were visited occasionally by emissaries from France where the Catholics were and at the same time emissaries from [the Church of England], saying, "Right! We know you've been contacted by [the Catholics]. You've been asked to work for the Catholics. You've been asked to become an undercover priest. But we want you to do that, or we want you to pretend to be a Catholic. But at the same time we want you to do so and so and so forth." I feel—this is romantic—but I feel there must have been some element in Marlowe's life . . . he must have betrayed somebody, possibly a friend. He must have seen this person hanged or executed in some way, and there's a tremendous flood of guilt in Marlowe, which is there in *Doctor Faustus*. At the same time, this huge conflict—I think he had a name called "The Over-Reacher." That's the name, "The Over-Reacher." There's no limitation on his appetites. There's a strong desire for both damnation and a kind of sensuous, sybaritic salvation. It's total, most fascinating character of the Renaissance. I was the more impelled to want to write my thesis on Marlowe, because it was 1939–1940, and the bombs were dropping. You know, the Nazis were overhead. One was writing one's thesis with the bombs going over. Indeed, we did our examinations with a raid in a huge glass-roofed gymnasium, looking at the bombs going over. So literature, then, wasn't a pretty game. You were tied up with the matter of life and death. So I felt that Marlowe, certainly *Doctor Faustus*, had something to say to us then. You know the moment was coming when whatever you felt reality was like, the bomb would drop and there it was. I wrote with some fervor on Marlowe. I felt that this was not purely an academic subject. [Burgess served with the British Army on Gibraltar (1943–1946). He returned to England to teach in the Adult Education Corps in the Army, involved in vocational and nonvocational training for demobilized servicemen (1946–1948), and taught teacher training for the Ministry of Education (1948–1950).]

Coale: What were you teaching at the Banbury Grammar School [1950–1954]?
Burgess: I was teaching English. I was doing literature in the higher levels, fifth and sixth forms. I was one of the pioneers of phonetics, elementary linguistics. I was also teaching Spanish and some music.

Coale: When you went to Malaya [1954–1957] and Borneo [1957–1960], was this really a chance to get out of the grammar school in Oxford?

Burgess: I didn't mind it. I was very happy in many ways. I'm a good teacher, I think. I enjoy teaching. I do it well. I still do. I enjoy going to the States.

Coale: Were you just excited by the chance to try a whole new outpost?
Burgess: No, it came accidentally. My first wife, who's now dead, of course—we were finding it hard to live, but we were by dint of, you know, a bit of private tutoring and evening classes and that kind of thing. We managed to keep going just about. I applied for a job on the Island of Sark, which is one of the Channel Islands, and this is very ironical, comically so. We had a collie bitch at the time who was a bit restricted in the village where we lived, so we thought it would be nice for her to go live on an island. Of course, we didn't realize at the time that this was the one island in the world where you couldn't import a bitch. The only person who was allowed to have a bitch on that island is the Dame of Sark. At the same time I must have got drunk on Saturday evening and applied for a job in a Malayan school and forgot about it and posted the letter drunk. Then I was summoned for this job in Sark. They sort of looked at me open-mouthed. Since when have the Channel Islands been under the Colonial Office? But then quite accidentally I was given this job in Malaya as an Education officer . . .

Coale: That must have been an incredible change . . .
Burgess: Well, it affected my first wife more than it affected me, selling everything, the library, every damn thing, and starting again. And knowing we were going to a country where there was a war on, which was stupid, because we'd had one war for six years—I was in Gibraltar; my wife was in London. But we went straight into a war, straight to the part of Malaya where the war was strongest and when, if you went to the nearest town, you thought of the danger of being ambushed. It was back into a bloody war. They called it an emergency with fingerprints, and if you had a gun, you were automatically shot and all that sort of thing. Communists infiltrated into the suburbs where I taught. But it did me good, because it enabled me to write. I got a bit of leisure and a bit of money, and I had a couple of servants. I had a car. I'd already been writing, but now I published for the first time. I published a novel, *Time for a Tiger* [1956].

Coale: Can you tell me what it was like when you were told in 1960 that you had an inoperable brain tumor?
Burgess: I can give you a picture of that year. I remember it fairly well. I still don't know what all this was about but—it is crazy—I don't know what to say about it. I was not popular in Brunei [1957–1960]. At least I was not popular with the ex-

patriates, nor was my first wife. She drank too much. She was already on the way to getting cirrhosis. She died in March 1968. I can remember the date because it was the first day of spring. She died on March 20, 1968, of cirrhosis, which we all fear we're going to get, but very few of us actually do. I don't know whether to feel guilty about that. I think we all choose what we want to do. A woman's liver is too small, and they suffer more from the shortage of vitamin B in the tropics. My first wife had been rude to the Duke of Edinburgh when he visited us. This was not well liked, and I was associated with the liberation movement there, a kind of revolutionary movement. I was friendly with the revolutionary leaders but no more. I've never been politically minded. I kind of collapsed one day in the class-room. I was just finished, and I couldn't go on—so fed up and so bored. They were only too glad to get me onto a stretcher, shove me into a hospital, and diag-nose a possible tumor on the brain. God knows how they do that.

Coale: How did they ever come to that conclusion?

Burgess: Well, this is something of great interest. The first test that you're always given—we used to have a series on television called *Ben Casey, M.D.*, neurologist, and it was pretty accurate. I knew it all from the inside. The first thing they do is give you a spinal tap. It is pretty unpleasant. You feel the whole vertebrae struc-ture collapsing. And if they find too much protein in the spinal fluid, this is a sign there's some organism at work, like cancer, which is causing this. But what the norm is I don't know. How can we tell what the norm is? We can only tell the norm if everybody has a spinal tap. I was rushed back to England and sent to the neurological institute in London and given all the tests, Ben Casey tests. These disclosed nothing. They said there's probably a tumor or some kind of growth, which we can't see, which the instruments themselves aren't able to show us. It may be masked by living tissue or something. So the thing to do is discharge you and give you a year to live.

Coale: How the hell did you find the gumption to write five novels under sentence of death?

Burgess: Look at it very practically. One is sent out. One's car, one's possessions, one's books are still in Borneo. God knows who's looking after them. The ter-mites are getting them. One is discharged from hospital. One has no money, and one has got to do something. And so we took a flat in Hove, which is near Sus-sex on the south coast of England. What do I do now? I've no money. How'd I earn a living? I can't teach, if I've got a year to live. So I write, and I didn't feel too bad. I couldn't really believe I was going to die, so I just got down to write with great pleasure. There's no mystery about being able to write five novels in a year. They're not very long novels. If you write two pages of typescript a day, you've got *War and Peace* practically. You've certainly got *Ulysses.*

Coale: What happened to your wife [Burgess married a Welsh student, Llewela Isherwood Jones, whom he met at the University in Manchester, in 1942]?
Burgess: She attempted suicide in 1960 and had a fairly steady decline from then on. She was highly neurotic, and I couldn't leave her alone. I couldn't say, you know, I've been invited to go to America. I couldn't go to America, because I couldn't leave her.

Coale: If she died in the spring of 1968 and you left in October, it was really a chance for you to start a new life . . .
Burgess: I'd known Liana [Liliana Macellari] before, because she was down at Cambridge. She was in the linguistics department there. She knew my work, because it was her job to do an annual report. We met, indeed, we begot a child, my son, Andrew. This was a bit of a problem. He's fourteen. We were married in 1968, so that means he was begotten four years before the marriage, August of 1964. So that means we had been consorting together since 1963. I didn't . . . I had to have some sexual outlet, because I was having none with my wife. It was all guilt. This was kept absolutely quiet. The liaison was not a regular one. It was very, very clandestine. And we didn't feel free to get away. But then we married. We were living together openly from about April on, caused a scandal, wife hardly cold in the grave, etc. And then we were married in October 1968. Here's a wedding picture . . .

Coale: Because you were a Catholic in England to begin with, did that already give you a sense of exile?
Burgess: That still has a lot to do with it. That's something I'd still like to work out in fiction, in a piece of autobiographical fiction. Throughout the history of my family, such as it is, and throughout my own career, I've always been aware of this inability on my own part—and the part of my own people—to come to terms with the Protestant establishment in England. This is something you can sort of laugh off and say it isn't really important, but it *is* important. It means that no Catholic could have a university education. We had land. We lost land. We got poor. None of my family could ever enter the professions. It was only with the Catholic Emancipation Acts that things began to go right. It's all right if you're a Catholic convert like Graham Greene or Evelyn Waugh. You can have the best

of both worlds, but if you're a cradle Catholic with Irish blood, then you're auto-matically a renegade to the outside.

Coale: And yet, I'm not a Catholic, and I can identify totally with your books with their sense of Original Sin.

Burgess: I think that in the North [of England], and this includes Ireland, there is a kind of puritanical element in Catholicism, which you don't get in the South. You don't get it in Spain, for example. You certainly don't get it in Italy. To some extent you get it in France. You can call it an Anglo-Irish brand, because no North-west English Catholic could sustain the faith in terms of family—in terms of breeding a family to keep the faith going—unless he imported an Irish wife. The process has been going a long time. My grandmother was Irish. She was a Finne-gan. This was just part of the process. Probably my own grandfather was already half-Irish. So I should imagine that there's more Irish in me than there is English. But, of course, you don't define a nation in terms of blood. It's in terms of cul-ture. So I am an Englishman, in that I speak like an Englishman and was brought up in England.

Coale: You refer to yourself now as a lapsed Catholic . . .

Burgess: When I was at the Xavierian College in Manchester and was in the sixth form—I was seventeen—we had a Liverpool Irish Catholic history master, and we were studying the Reformation, and he put the case for the Reformation a bit too well. I'd done a lot of reading on my own about Luther. I wrote a play about Lu-ther, long before John Osborne's play. It was pretty agonizing, chiefly because of the sacramental element in Catholicism. One can throw away certain of the doc-trines, but one can't throw away the Eucharist quite so easily. And of course this was Joyce's situation. I read *A Portrait of the Artist as a Young Man* when I was about sixteen . . .

Coale: Do you think that really affected you?

Burgess: I was *horrified*. The effect of the book was to put me in the position of Stephen Dedalus himself, who's horrified by the sermon on hell. I was so horrified that I was scared back into the Church. I swore I'd never read Joyce again, which was really very ironical. I was so scared of this damn book. The book was dyna-mite. Almost picked it up with tongs and shoved it in the fire. Gradually I got over this, but now I find in early old age I recognize that you can't throw Catholicism away. It's the only thing there is. There's nothing else. I mean, you know, literally.

Oh, in the East, there's Buddhism or what you will, but as far as the West is concerned, there's nothing else. Protestantism, as Joyce, as Stephen Dedalus said, it's an illogical absurdity. You can't justify it in any way.

Coale: Well, did you at university stop going to church?
Burgess: Oh, yes, I stopped when I was seventeen.

Coale: Said to hell with it?
Burgess: I used to go out in the morning on Sunday morning, and say I was going to Mass but actually sit in the park or something like that.

Coale: Was there a lot of youthful bravado against all the traditions . . .?
Burgess: Oh, yes, a great deal of that, but when I joined the Army, then I had to declare myself, and I declared myself a Catholic. Then I went to Gibraltar for a time [1943–1946] and began to feel, you know, once more, that whatever I did about it, I was still Catholic.

Coale: What about all the ceremony and aesthetics of the Church itself?
Burgess: Any provincial Catholic doesn't go to St. Peter's or doesn't go to cathedrals but goes to his local church. He tends, as I did, to turn against that magnificence and want to move to the Society of Friends or Calvinism or something which is austere, because when you get debased Baroque, debased Rococo, then you get the small church with its incense, with its horrible little paintings, and horrible little statutes. That's what we turned against. Then you welcome the Congregationalist aspect, the bare church, with a little wind blowing through. . . . I've never had any feeling for Buddhism at all. Never had any feeling for Hinduism. I cannot go along with the California Vedantists. I cannot go along with Hinduism at all, nor with Buddhism. But I can go along with Islam, because it's pretty close to us. Indeed the whole of Europe could have been Islamicized— the whole of Spain certainly was—and if you're living in the East, if you're living under hot skies and desert sands and camels, you can see the attraction of this very austere religion. You can see the attraction of abstention from food during the hours of the day, in case the enemies strike. It's a very simple religion, but unfortunately the Koran is a very bad book. There's nothing much to read in the Koran. It's most austere. There's no decoration in a mosque. You're not allowed to represent the human figure. So the art is totally calligraphic. There's no music. It's terribly austere, and of course rather attractive. . . . Most of the Muslims I knew were living in a British protectorate and had been corrupted or influenced by the British way of life. I mean, most of them drank, for example. Most of them kissed

women, which is terribly taboo, but they'd seen it in the films and tried it out and liked it extremely. Some of them would go to obscure eating places and eat eggs and bacon, ham and eggs. You couldn't find this in Saudi Arabia, obviously. The news about people whipped publicly, being beheaded, I mean, they really take it seriously there. But there's a charm about Islam in a country like Malaya or Borneo, where it has to stand on its own and jostle up against other religions. See how it gets on. And it's very amusing. It's very touching to see how it gets on. You know, up against Shintoism and Buddhism and Christianity and atheism and what you will. But when it becomes monolithic and a genuine state religion, as in Saudi Arabia, then it's rather repulsive. It's very much like Calvinism in Geneva, very similar.

Coale: Do you attend church at all today?

Burgess: I don't go to Mass. When my cousin was elevated, or whatever the term is, as Archbishop, I went to his Mass in Birmingham. This was the first reformed Mass I'd seen. I was horrified. I was horrified by the turning of the altar around for a start. It was like a butcher's shop. The man was preparing some meat. There were laymen participating, and there was the Kiss of Peace. . . . I was asked to deliver the commencement address at Fordham University in New York, so I attended there. I expected we'd go down the aisle with an organ or orchestra playing Handel or Purcell, but they had a little black girl with a combo singing something from *Godspell.* Then she sang, "Reach out and touch somebody's hand," you know, "make this a better world if you can," which was not exactly literate. Then you had, "Go ahead! Reach out and touch, folks!" We all had to sort of reach out. Bugger! I'm damned if I'm going to do it! So I destroyed my prepared address and said, "This is typical of vulgarity." "BOOO! Throw him out!" But this is typical of the vulgarity which has been brought into education. Once you can allow this, once you can allow your priest to go around in flamboyant neckties, that's the end.

Coale: You said at one point that the good is some kind of existential sense, which is not merely ethical conduct. "There's a good beyond ethical good which is always existential. There's the central good, that aspect of God which we can prefigure more in the taste of an apple or the sound of music." That sounds almost romantic.

Burgess: It's not really romantic. It sounds it. I've always been worried about the tendency of people writing English to confuse the two kinds of good. George Steiner, the biggest bloody fool who ever lived, a man in a responsible situation, a man miraculously equipped with languages and learning, who is so foolish as to wonder why Nazis, why a concentration camp officer could listen to Schubert and at the same time send Jews to the gas. . . . There are two different kinds of good. This is a horrible thing. A bad man listening to Beethoven. The man is going to kill his dog in a few minutes. It's impossible, but this is the romantic heresy, the assumption that a work of art has some kind of moral content. This is very American too . . . moral content. How about Baudelaire? How about *Les Fleurs du Mal*? There is a sense in which a great work of art will seem to touch good in the other sense, but that's only because the great work of art is neutral. It's fairly harmless. It's not committed to the world of action. If God exists, the goodness of God is not seen in ethical terms. God is not good to us. He is obviously not good to us, because He's in no relationship with human beings. He's removed from us. God is good. The experience of God is the experience of Beethoven's Ninth Symphony, infinitely magnified . . .

Coale: Can you comment on the connection between Catholicism and Manichaeism? You said at one point that Manichaeism is an easy heresy to fall into. St. Paul divided everything in twos. Everything was dualistic. I think St. James at one point says anyone who has a dualistic mind, something's wrong with him. Paul still says you have to make a choice between, and *that* choice is obviously spirit. Now Manicheism says in effect the two are equal . . .
Burgess: That's right.

Coale: And so interpenetrate. They can't be separated.
Burgess: That's right. This is a duality that is fixed almost from the beginning of the world and the outcome is in doubt. The forces of light can only win if you help them. Christianity says differently. But you can only justify the notion that God is omnipotent. He set Satan free or set the principle of evil free in terms of a game. To some extent that I'll accept, because this is quite orthodox. St. Thomas Aquinas said that. Why should God—God had no necessity to create the world. There's no necessity for God to create men, except possibly his huge capacity for love, which needed objects. But there was no real need for him to create the world. He must have created it to amuse himself, not out of any necessity, because the ludic element has nothing to do with necessity. It's just an extra. This I accept. The important things in life are games, are ludic, I mean. The American business ethic has obscured this, but what else is there? I mean, nature gets on with her own, or of sustaining us, but as for the rest of the things we do, it must be ludic. This is not a duty. You write a book. It's only a diversion.

Coale: Do you think that the split is healed, is brought together in some cases, by your own use of language, the idea of syntax or metaphor or something like that where both flesh and spirit . . .

Burgess: Yes. It's done through a ritual of some kind, I think, probably language. But of course language is a shaky thing. I was with Buckminster Fuller in Denmark a few weeks ago, and he said to me in a taxi apropos of nothing, he said, "The universe has no nouns. It only has verbs!" Suddenly it dawned on me that he was absolutely right. We'd been playing around dealing with totally unacceptable theses, theses on a fixed object, like a noun. Language is extremely dangerous. Language probably bears no relation to ultimate reality. It's a ritual-making device. You can make rituals out of language. And it is in the ritual that opposites are reconciled, of course. Nobody knows the answer, but you can know there's always a struggling to find something you can work on. That's true of Joyce certainly. In Joyce it is all ritual. It's a substitute for the Mass all the way through, all the way through. Try to find the means of stilling the conflict through ritual forms of language.

Coale: The modernists, some critics suggest, used myth to give coherence to a world they found incoherent . . .

Burgess: No, I don't think it's true at all. I think that Joyce never said anything stupid. He was merely using it for a structural purpose. He wanted to play around with language. He wanted to use a kind of musical pre-fantasia. I believe that whatever he said, the basic elements of that book are the "Circe" and "Nighttown," which nobody denies, and the "Oxen of the Sun." He wanted to do that parody of English literature. The only way he could justify doing it was in those terms. So I think that the myth is a mere justification for what people nowadays probably call self-indulgent expression, not self-indulgent, because it's bloody difficult to do. He's justifying the different modes of technique through the mythical structure. The myth element is not in the least important. I don't think it matters in the slightest. It's mere nonsense.

Coale: Define modernism.

Burgess: In the first place, there's a kind of ethos in modernism which relates it to a particular period in history, I think, the First World War. We can't forget it, even if some of us didn't experience it. It's one of the most traumatic experiences the world has ever had. The Second World War was nothing compared to that. The First World War was a more terrible war, because it was a meaningless war. You have to find the meaning of the war in a myth or something, the old men against the young, anything will do. Some say about the biological motivation of war. It was a biological thing. It was an attempt of the genes to change. Modernism is associated with that, with the breakdown of the nineteenth century, the breakdown of nineteenth-century language . . .

All important literary movements have as background some kind of philosophy. Even behind *Tom Jones* you'll find David Hume or somebody. Certainly behind Proust is Bergson. Behind Shaw is Bergson and Nietzsche. In our own days it's the phenomenologists. Now we're setting the notion of the discontinuous universe behind these people. Well, the universe is not discontinuous. Your job is to create a structure. There's no such thing as anti-art. It's not art. You can't create anti-art and call yourself an artist. This is what these people are doing. [William] Burroughs is a great name. I think he deserves it for the actual content of *Naked Lunch*. But this folding and cutting stuff he uses is not very important. I can see the real reason for doing it is because he wants to make his book have the quality of a newspaper. McLuhan, without mentioning Burroughs, has said the newspaper is a specific literary structure, which mirrors the complexity of the mind, because there are marginal elements, peripheral elements around the thing you're reading, which you're taking in. You know, you're reading in columns, and you can't help taking in the neighboring columns. Well, what Bill Burroughs does is to cut things in the same random way. But the mood itself is not random. I don't think it can be. In a sense a newspaper's not random. A newspaper is unified by being diurnal, by saying this is what's coming today.

Coale: You'd consider yourself, then, to be more a modernist than a postmodernist?

Burgess: I think postmodernism, as it's called, which is a ridiculous phrase, is contained in modernism. I think that the process that began, say, take 1912–1913 as the key years. This is not to do with literature. This is to do with music. Schoenberg's *Pierrot Lunaire* came in 1912 and [Stravinsky's] *Le Sacre du Printemps* in 1913. There was nothing in literature doing anything like that at the time, but the impact of these two works on the sensibility of any artist was very, very great. It must have driven, say, a woman like Gertrude Stein, in the direction of trying to do some prose in the same way. I think this process is still going on.

Coale: And yet discontinuity today seems to be the main vision of things . . .

Burgess: They may say it's discontinuous, and they may talk about random selection—that kind of thing—but they're not reckoning with their own un-conscious part of the creative process. The unconscious may well be impos-ing a coherence, which they're not consciously aware of. I remember in Buffalo, last year or the year before. . . . I attended a class on surrealism. Let's try the ex-periment of writing on the blackboard a completely random set of words: key-board, cognac, feather, dog, anything that came up. So I looked for a structure there. There *was* a structure. There was even a prosodic structure. The words were rather disyllabic or trisyllabic, and they tended to alternate. The words could be put together into a coherent sentence without too much trouble. However hard you try, you see, the unconscious will tend to impose . . .

Coale: In modern fiction, there seems to be a certain arbitrariness . . .
Burgess: Well, I feel this is outside art, and of course this takes us back to music again. Writing a symphony or concerts on something, there's no room for that. There's no room for arbitrariness. There's a concerto by Tchaikovsky, a rather popular romantic—in the second movement, No. 1 in B-flat minor, there's a mo-tif: dah-dah-dah-dah. When this is repeated, for some reason the thing is changed by one note, and this is a frightful experience I always find. Why has it happened? It's arbitrary. He may have not checked when he was writing his repeat what the original melody was actually like. But this is—you know, nobody notices—but any musician will say, "Oh, my God! Why? Why?" If you can't allow arbitrariness in music, you certainly can't allow it in prose. I don't think he could've chosen it. I think it was a mistake in priority. He may not have overseen the proofs . . .

I don't think you can talk about arbitrary elements in fiction, I don't think it's possible. It depends what you want to practice. I've been toying with the idea for a long time of writing a novel which is based on an alphabetic taxonomy, which uses a structure in which all the characters begin with "A" or something like that or all the events have "C" like eating cheese or riding in a car—something like that—but this would only be a help to a writer in aiding him to think of themes, forcing himself to limit himself to themes and, hence, giving the impressions of coherence.

Coale: Would the structure that you choose for a novel be somehow the same as the kind of motif you get in music?
Burgess: Pretty well. We've got a long way to go, I mean to say, with modernism. We've got a hell of a long way to go with modernism. People think *Finnegans Wake* is the end of modernism, which is not arbitrary, far from arbitrary. I've lived with it since the thirties. I understand it. I know what it's doing, but I can't

pick up all the references. When we understand that, then that may be the end of the modernism. I think we're still in a modernist phase. . . . We're only at the beginning of learning what music and literature can do together. We're still in the modernist period.

Coale: In most of your books, you so obviously love the things you can do with language . . .

Burgess: There's a bad man, I think a mediocre man, in England called Malcolm Muggeridge, who's known in America, and he made a declaration a short while ago which horrified me. He said, "I thank God for my mastery of the English language." I thought, my God, this is one thing that no man has ever said, because when you say you've mastered the English language, you've mastered a dead thing. In other words, it's there. I've got it, so there's no possibility of ever changing. What happens in England I find, when I'm criticized adversely, I'm told I write English clumsily. Now if I'm told this, I take this as a compliment, because once you start writing clearly contained, well-thought-out, periodic sentences, you're not being true to the subject matter. You're not being true to the flow. One should go through a great deal of trouble to be cunningly clumsy. Joyce is cunningly clumsy. . . . In fiction there should be an element of doubt in the sentence. It shouldn't be sure of itself. It should tail off a bit, or it should get tangled with itself. If you're depicting the movement of a man's mind or what he's doing, what he intends to do, the sentence should not be too well made. And this is what the British for the most part cannot be brought to realize. Evelyn Waugh wrote extremely well—a very fine prose writer, in my opinion—but it's not appropriate to the novel. It's appropriate to satire, because there's somebody looking down, making a declaration, but he's not in with the people, suffering with them and making the language suffer as well. Joyce knew all about that. When Joyce wrote, the world made sense. He imitates, satirizes the banal, well-made sentence. You can't write fiction that way, and I've never been able to persuade the British to accept this point. . . . With D. H. Lawrence you can feel the thing being made. He repeats himself; he repeats himself again; he's got to get the thing right; you're in the process of watching it happen. This I advise. Of course, Lawrence has never been liked in England very much, except by [F. R.] Leavis of course, who obviously got the wrong thing out of him. Thought he was a great moral master. [He's a] very great pagan writer. . . . One of the surface qualities of most British novels is this, this conflict between accents, which represent cultures, which represent classes. For so small a country, it's amazing, but the division is immense. It's one of the main differences between America and England. You'll never get over the class barrier, because nobody wants to get over it. It's maintained on both sides, you see. It's partly a game, it's partly a joke. In the film of *A Clockwork Orange*, Kubrick, or probably it was young Malcolm McDowell, had the sense to realize this was part of the story. For instance, "Oh, I was just coming around to collect some money for the parish magazine." He got it right, and this is it, and it can annoy a genuine number of the upper class. It can infuriate them, for they feel you've grabbed the one weapon they hold, which is the use of the voice.

Coale: American writers tend to "make it new" each time they write. For example, Whitman called his *Leaves of Grass* a "language experiment."
Burgess: Absolutely right, and this is the greatness of Ezra Pound, whom I will not have disparaged, because whatever they say about the *Cantos* or "Homage to Sextus Propertius," these are immensely important, supreme examples of the development of an ideolect, a personal language, which became in fact the language of an entire generation. Also "The Love Song of J. Alfred Prufrock." That is the seminal work, in my opinion, for all modern literature. Now all that the British could do, all the people like Robert Graves could do, was to point out that Pound's Latinity was bad, and it was meant to be bad. It was meant to be bad. It was meant to be a schoolboy's mistranslation.

Coale: Is this why you're drawn to Hopkins, too?
Burgess: This is true of Hopkins. The language that Hopkins writes with, it's not upper-class English. It's a kind of multiple dialect, which is drawn from my own region in the North, where he was a priest, being a Catholic region, obviously from Wales and all over the place. Blasphemous people give a kind of cant recitation of Hopkins, showing that he's a homosexual. It's not the point. With Hopkins, as with Pound, there's a remaking of the language, and Hopkins' remaking has ironically ended up with a particular mode of commercial advertising—an advertisement for cornflakes or those horrible menus you get in a place like Howard Johnson's. They're based on Hopkins; they're based on the use of compound adjectives and that sort of thing. But Pound is the key.

Coale: You say character is central to the novel and that one of the main thrusts of each of your books is "a slow and cruel stripping off of illusion."
Burgess: It's not really cruel. Strip off the illusions and see what left. . . . Get rid of as much as you can and see what's left, and what's left is the essential human.

Coale: Does the basic element include free will, or is that left mysteriously complex?
Burgess: You can't get rid of that, whatever happens. I don't think you can get rid of that. You can try, but in any case I don't think there would be any point in

writing a novel about a man who loses free will. I don't think there are any such novels. You can't make a novel out of a character without free will.

Coale: One critic wrote somewhere that many of your characters, that many of the books showed man's inability to act at all.
Burgess: No, I wouldn't say that. You can act. You can act. There's no point in writing fiction if you can't present a free character, except in the Soviet Union. That's why it won't work. There is no Soviet history.

Coale: Is the ability of man to choose or to use his free will a kind of answer to the dissolution of things around us?
Burgess: It really is, because I think too many people, Americans and British alike, are prepared to deny it. They deny the existence of free will. You know, they say we can't do anything about it. We can't choose anymore. We've delegated choice to the state or to the directors. I don't think this is true. You can allow it to happen. Probably the only kind of fiction one'll have any time to write in the future is about the individual free will against the collective. It's probably the big theme of the future.

Coale: But with this idea of free will also comes a good, healthy sense of guilt. You can't escape that either.
Burgess: Guilt's a good thing, because the morals are just ticking away very nicely. You know it's bubbling over. It's when you get rid of this very human quality of guilt that you lose a great deal of humanity.

Coale: When you write a novel, would you have extra incidents and events, which wouldn't fit because of the theme or whatever, that you would cut to save the general pattern?
Burgess: You might take a chance on it. You might find yourself impelled in the writing of a chapter to do something you didn't intend to do, to start a party. A man sitting in his room and somebody comes in, then other people, oh, let's bring in some more people. Before you know it, you've got a party. This may seem like arbitrariness but, on the other hand, there may be a very profound unconscious reason for doing it, which may be justified later. You just don't know. You've just got to watch it all the time. In this book, *The Right to an Answer*, I didn't intend the book to be as it was. I'd been told a story by my first wife about two couples who swapped wives on weekends, and the game went wrong. You know, Mrs. A. fell in love with Mr. B., so what did the other two do? It was based on that, but I felt there had to be some atavistic element coming in who would break the thing down. And so I invented an Indian character or Ceylonese character. Of course,

I did this, and the character dominated the book. This I didn't intend. But once this happens you have to . . . you never really know how long it's going to go until about the fifth chapter.

Coale: You write a few pages each day and perfect those pages before going on to the next?
Burgess: Yes. Pretty well, yes.

Coale: So you don't have much rewriting at the end . . .
Burgess: I don't do any rewriting if I can avoid it.

Coale: Does it bother you to be associated so much with *A Clockwork Orange*?
Burgess: Oh, yes, I think so. It's a damn nuisance, but it always happens, I'm afraid. It happened with Nabokov. He was good-humored about it. *Lolita* is a book any man should be proud of, but I'm not particularly proud of *A Clockwork Orange*, because it has all the faults which I rail against in fiction. It's didactic. It tends to pornography. It's tricky. It's gimmicky. One may excuse any author for writing what he writes, because he's primarily earning a living, you see. He's turning out an artifact which will, he hopes, sell enough to pay the rent. It's Balzacian. It's almost, indeed, it's Shakespearean. Nothing wrong with it. But I do object very strongly to these theses that are written on the damn book. The book is not all that interesting or important. It's had a mythical impact of some kind.

Coale: Some critics regard *Enderby* as your best work.
Burgess: I've always liked it, the character. People tend to say, this is you, you are the character. This is not really true. But for some reason I took to the character. It came out of a curious hallucination. I was in Borneo. I'd probably had something to eat and drink, and I opened the bathroom door and found a man sitting on the toilet writing poetry. Of course, there was nobody there. Just a pure hallucination. And out of that came the whole image. It's very curious how a purely imaginary character can suddenly emerge. I could have spent my life with this damn character, quite happily, sending him all over the place, bringing him back to life again. I had to kill him off eventually. Enderby's guilt-ridden. He's Catholic. That's a nuisance in England, because if you write any very Catholic character, it's always assumed you're imitating Graham Greene. Well, look back at Chaucer. They're all Catholic characters. One's merely following that tradition.

Coale: What about *The Wanting Seed*?
Burgess: In *The Wanting Seed* the important thing to me is the revival of artificial war. This I think will happen someday. Also I was interested in what was already

apparently happening in England. Homosexuals were rising to the top. Indeed, we had a homosexual prime minister, Edward Heath. He's been very clever about it. He's never been found accosting little boys. It may have been hushed up. There's no doubt that there is a homosexual mafia, not only in England, but also in California. Santa Monica: that's the biggest homosexual conclave in the world.

Coale: In your latest novel, *Earthly Powers*, how did you happen to choose a Somerset Maugham-type character?
Burgess: Because it struck me as being a most bizarre kind of narrator, someone who's a rationalist. To imagine Somerset Maugham as being related by marriage to the Pope. Of course, it could happen, you see. The sister could marry the brother. There you are. Before you know it, you find you've got a Pope in the family. You as a homosexual, who's rejected the religion of your mother, who's French, now dead, and are called upon to make a definitive declaration concerning a miracle, which is valuable, you know, because if any credulous peasant offered it, it wouldn't be very believable, but if a rationalist and an ex-Catholic made it, it gives it a certain rigor. That's what the novel's about.

Coale: It's almost as if homosexuality is something which is really extremely different from the true faith.
Burgess: Yes. This is the contrast. Here's a man who once belonged to the true faith. He cannot use the word "home" or "faith" or "duty" without crying.

Coale: Is your "lapsedness" beginning to lapse?
Burgess: No, I'll never go back to the Church, because of the changes that have been made by the Second Vatican Council. But, on the other hand, I think the only future for the West, the secular future for the West, lies in some kind of Christianity.

Coale: Do you see homosexuality as a kind of metaphor for the absurdity and grotesqueness of the modern world, which so often appears in your work?
Burgess: It's either taken as a metaphor, or you can take it as something the *élan vital* is doing or not doing. Nature is providing her own checks and balances to a possible population explosion. One saw this in unisex. You couldn't tell a boy from a girl. You still can't in some ways. The manner in which homosexuality is on the increase: I mean, it's actually fostered. It's not purely a biological thing; it's fast becoming very interesting, very glamorous to be a homosexual, a kind of radical chic. This may be nature's response, means of checking the population. It is obviously some kind of quirk. . . . A boy's body is rather beautiful. Some-

thing attractive about it. You know the slim, straight, the Greek shepherd boy. I can see the possible attraction of it, but to grab hold of one of these boys' bodies and perform an act of buggery or fellatio is a horror to me. In *Earthly Powers* the homosexual narrator—I'm on very shaky ground here—is not happy about being a homosexual, because the homosexuality he indulges in is furtive. There's betrayal on the part of the other partner. It gets tied up with people who bugger sailors when they're vomiting, that kind of thing. He tries to get out of it. He's a Catholic. His mother was French. His father is dead. He regrets that. He sees that from any theological, indeed any biological angle, homosexuality isn't right. It's a perversion. The novel's set in 1919. He cannot write novels in which there's frank candid exploration of homosexuals. So he has to pretend it's men and women, and he's sick of the whole business. God has made him like this. Therefore, he must resent God. This gives him particular attitudes toward his brother-in-law, the Pope. I think that homosexuals should feel that, but of course they won't, it *is* a curse. Obviously it's a curse. Definitely a curse. It's the sin of Onan. The seminal fluid is for getting children. We don't always use it for that purpose, but that's its primary aim. To be put in a position of being cut off from begetting and cut off from the guilt that goes along with not begetting. I think this is terrible. But this is probably a very old-fashioned view.

Coale: What's your personal vision?

Burgess: I suppose, a set of personal predilections, isn't it? If you've read Joyce, you have a fair idea of what Joyce was in, often very small things like lady's knickers, what do you call them, drawers. Nothing wrong with that. He was obviously interested in drawers. And in cocoa and wine, not haute cuisine but Irish food, and, of course, in theological disputation, in theological niceties. It's a mass of little things that make up what the hell vision is. I don't know. It's too complex to be easily summarized. You're pretty well formed by your childhood, aren't you? The vision is formed in your childhood, and it's often a very materialistic vision. And it often has a lot to do with food. Joyce was right in making so much of food in *Finnegans Wake*. *Finnegans Wake* is an epic of food, really. He was quite right. A man's patriotism is determined by the kind of food we ate in childhood. Very childish thing to say, but it was probably very true, I think.

Coale: Would you ever like to write something as morally straightforward as a Grimm fairy tale?

Burgess: Yes, I've done that on occasion. I think very highly of that way of telling a story. I think Grimm fairy tales are . . . once you open that big book, you can't put it down. There's no self-consciousness. The thing is ritualistic, because, you know, the Grimm brothers themselves said in their introduction that we heard these stories in various parts of Germany and if the telling—it was usually an old woman—deviated by even one word from the way she'd told it before, she would correct herself. Ritualistic entirely. Children are sensitive. I think that this is still the best way of telling a story, but what worries me about *Grimm's Fairy Tales* is we're absorbed, although none of the fundamental requirements of a novel are fulfilled. There's no description of place. There's no description of people. Don't even know their names sometimes. And yet the things work. Now why? I don't know. They are grim stories. The morality in it is quite uncompromising. Too many kids think that Snow White is Walt Disney. What happens to the Queen at the end? At the wedding she's made to put on shoes, which have been heated to white heat in the fire. She must dance in these shoes, dances until she collapses of a heart attack. And everybody's happy, drinking, the marriage is consummated. It's pretty terrible. Very inhuman. But it's a fulfillment of a moral law. If you do bad, this is what's going to happen to you. It appeals to children very much. They don't see it in immediate terms. Purely ritualistic. There's no blood. I don't see why stories can't be told that way. One of the books I idolize is—it's a kind of novel—Swift's *Tale of the Tub*. I think it's one of the great books of all time, because it reads like a fairy story, yet it's so sophisticated, so subtle, so allegorical. He's telling a straight story.

Coale: Maybe this has to do with the author's authority . . .
Burgess: The authority's in that Grimm book. You know the story. You don't give a damn. You know the story. You're going to tell the story. You don't have to doubt it. You're not like Borges, doubting the medium. It's a story. You're going to damn well listen to the story. . . . I'm falling into the trap of most contemporary novelists, telling lies. And I think one has to get over this, because I think Borges has done his work, and now let's get back to telling stories. I suppose, the point is we don't read enough in the past. If we read enough in the past, we find that all of these new things have been done. *Tristram Shandy*. I started rereading it recently, and, of course, it goes far beyond anything we do, how the set-up on the page affects the track of the eye . . .

The Sense of an Audience

Pierre Joannon/1984

The following conversation took place 9 January 1984. From *Fabula*, vol. 3 (March 1984). Reprinted by permission of Pierre Joannon.

Joannon: You are a professional writer. What does that term mean to you?

Burgess: Well, it is a matter of juggling with two balls. You have to earn a living with the fiction you write. This means I have to pay the rent, to look after my wife and son. I have to live. This means I cannot practice novels in the manner of Nathalie Sarraute or Robbe-Grillet. I dare not experiment too much. I dare not appeal to too small an audience. So I have to juggle between pleasing an audience and, at the same time, pleasing myself. This is the difficulty. Writing a novel, professionally, can be a matter of producing an artifact to a formula which will make a lot of money, or else, it can be producing a work of literature, an aesthetic artifact which at the same time will sell enough copies to enable you to live. I feel that I cannot be as bold or audacious as the French *anti-romanciers* are, because I cannot afford to appeal to a very small audience. At the same time I cannot afford to appeal to a very large audience, because that will kill any artistic integrity I have, so I manage to balance the two balls, the ball of commercial viability and the ball of aesthetic viability, and the problem is keeping the two balls going.

I have managed to do this for some years and I think that now I shall be able to carry on doing that, but one cannot forget that the novel is the primary commercial literary form that we have. I think Balzac would agree with me there . . . Hugo. . . . Flaubert to some extent . . . but there are several novelists in France who regard the novel as a very rarefied form which they don't practice commercially. I practice the novel commercially.

Joannon: You speak of the novel as a relatively stable thing, with its past, its present, but you don't seem to be concerned about the novel as a form of expression in the future.

135

Burgess: I think—and I am probably very orthodox here—that the past, the present, and the future of the novel find a common element in the fact of *character*.

Here I travel very dangerous ground because the whole point of the *nouveau roman*, the *anti-roman*, was that character, the *personnage*, was a bourgeois concept essentially false. When the *anti-roman* began, it was saying in effect that once you rid fiction of character, what you are producing is "anti-fiction." Therefore, I assume that the basis of fiction is character. Even with an *avant-garde* novel like Joyce's *Finnegans Wake*, the strength of the novel does not lie in experiment or the use of language; it lies in the existence of certain characters. This is also true of *Ulysses*. Leopold Bloom is so solid a character that Joyce can do anything, he can turn him upside-down, he can make him speak Anglo-Saxon. I think the strength of the novel lies in this solidity of character. It goes back to the *Satyricon*, to the *Golden Ass, Daphnis and Chloe, Don Quixote*. All the way through to the present time, the strength of the novel has been characters. I take it that this must be the strength of the novel in the future . . . not language, not ideas, not new formulations, but *character, character, character* . . .

Joannon: Regarding the novel, there are other means of communication. In your opinion, what are the relationships between the novel and these other means of communication? You have a particular relationship with music. How do you balance your role as a novelist and that interest in music as an art?
Burgess: Yes, of course. One of the reasons why I thought that the practice of musical composition was comparatively limited was because, whatever we say about music, it is divorced from life. We talk about the humanity of Beethoven, the eroticism of Wagner . . . and so on. But the music is notes, music is sound, music is structure. The reason why I turned from musical composition to the composition of novels was that I wanted real life, I wanted to represent real life. I wanted the smell of life, the taste of life and, more than that, I wanted people. I do feel however that music and fiction have a lot in common. What they have in common primarily is the exploitation of sound. Joyce saw this very clearly. Joyce was a musician himself. The novel is a world of sound. It is the world of what people are saying, the sounds they hear. It is also a world of structure. What we can learn from music is something about the importance of structure. This was realized, I think, very clearly by Flaubert, not quite so much by Balzac to whom life was . . . *tranches de vie* . . . slices of life . . . but with Flaubert, the shape of the novel was important. We are not getting life, not getting chunks of life, but life shaped into a structure. This is something that you find in music. I feel that a

well-structured novel should be like a symphony: it should have a beginning and it should have an end; it should have time-axes.

I find that having studied music and practiced it, this knowledge is invaluable to me as a novelist. When I say I'm going to write a novel, I immediately see a structure, I see climaxes, I see a *dénouement*, I see a beginning, I see an end. This is what a novel is. It is a structure. I don't know how far the writer of a novel is communicating *himself*, his ideas, his feelings. This is probably what makes the poem rather different from the novel. The poem is a means of communicating emotions to the world whereas the novelist is not communicating himself at all. Although I would say this, when we judge a novel, we tend to judge the quality of the mind of the creator. Do we like the *mind* of the person who wrote the novel? Do we like the *mind* of Flaubert, of Balzac? In that sense the novelist is communicating a personality, but not ideas, or emotions, or feelings.

Joannon: If I understand what you are saying, the new novel would communicate more than the traditional novel in which the novelist is obliged to step aside in favor of their characters so that their novel will live, while in the new novel, on the other hand, the novelist empties the whole space of the novel.

Burgess: Of course if the *nouveau romancier* has to obliterate human character from his fiction, he must obliterate his own character. I believe Robbe-Grillet has achieved this; I am not aware of his personality when I read his work. What, however, I am aware of is a certain philosophical theory that he is presenting in his fiction. This is a kind of communication. I think that he and Nathalie Sarraute are communicating a philosophical idea, rather blatantly, because they are not hiding it sufficiently. With Marcel Proust, for example, you have a huge novel, communicating philosophical ideas, about Time, chiefly, but Proust creates his characters so beautifully, creates the physical world so magnificently that the philosophical background *remains* the background while with *nouveaux romanciers* it is too much in the foreground. I do not think you can allow that in fiction. In fiction, you've got to confront people, eating, making love, walking in the streets, doing things and, of course, this is what Proust gives us. It is the greatness of Proust, it is the greatness of life lived. When I remember Proust, I do not only remember the *madeleine* dipped in tea but also the smell of the urine of young Marcel when he has eaten asparagus. This is life, the smell, the feel, the taste of life, while in the *nouveau romancier* you are smelling Husserl all the time and not life.

Joannon: Then you recommend instead a deepening of the humanity of the characters.

Burgess: I think it is a humane form. In some ways, perhaps, this is an old-fashioned form. I don't think it's possible to produce fiction in a community which does not accept the importance of individuality. The job of the novel is to maintain this old humanistic view that the individual is important. The novel is an old-fashioned humanistic form. It has nothing to do with the new philosophies of Machtpolitik or of communism. The novel hangs on to old standards which are being menaced by modern political systems.

Joannon: Looking at your career which is very full and yet splintered into very diverse directions—music, film, literature, journalism—one gets the impression that being a novelist hasn't been enough for you and you've felt it necessary to glean elsewhere, enriching your novels with music, as with *Napoleon Symphony*, or adapt them for film in order to give a new dimension. Do you feel imprisoned within the novel, or on the other hand is being a novelist for you a matter of borrowing all the other forms of expression to enrich the novel?
Burgess: One has to say that practicing other forms such as journalism or the film-scenario is an aspect of the novelist's life, seen in commercial terms. Very, very few novelists have been able to make a living out of writing fiction. What happens to most of them is they publish one novel, two novels, three novels, and then someone asks them to review novels, and you then find yourself in the world of journalism, without having sought it. I think the same thing is true of film-scripts. To do nothing but write novels is almost impossible nowadays, but the more I practice these other forms, the more I see the novel does contain practically everything. It has emerged as the literary form which contains other forms. Joyce helped here but so did Flaubert.

When he wrote the *Tentation de Saint Antoine*, Flaubert was writing a kind of play, a kind of Freudian fantasy. He was bringing new elements to the novel—certainly—which Joyce was very quick to pick up on when he wrote *Ulysses*. They taught us that the novel can contain other forms. The novel is certainly the most satisfactory form we have. It worries me when the French tend to limit the novel. The number of novels that come out in France these days which are very thin, have about 100 pages, 120 pages. This is not what the novel is about. This is not what Balzac or indeed Flaubert or Dickens thought the novel was. The novel to them was a big thing, a big panoramic view of life which contains everything. I hate to bring up this business of commerce again, but in the twentieth century it has not been possible for a novelist to write in the manner of Dickens or Tolstoy because the commercial circumstances have changed. Dickens could write a long novel in installments; he could publish it in fortnightly parts. This was wonderful for him. He'd publish a couple of chapters of *David Copperfield*, and we would immediately know what the response of his readers was. This was wonderful! He could change the novel as he went along. . . . In *Martin Chuzzlewit* he sent his characters to America. His readers did not like this so he brought them back again! This was a marvelous *rapport* between reader and writer. And, of course, this is true also of Tolstoy. *War and Peace* is a big novel only because it came out in fortnightly parts. We don't have this any more, unfortunately. I think Joyce was the last writer to have published in this form. We can't do it any more. *Ulysses* was published in installments. We can't do it any more; therefore we cannot produce the big novel in the Dickensian sense, because we are not earning. Dickens was earning as the novel was published. We are not earning any more. We cannot give ourselves years to write a big novel unless we are earning something from some other source so the tendency is to write shorter and shorter novels or to write *romans-fleuves* in the manner of—in England—Anthony Powell or C. P. Snow.

In America, the situation is different because the writers of big novels are usually subsidized by universities. And this is being done by John Barth, Saul Bellow, various others. The big novel has disappeared from Europe chiefly because of financial circumstances. One has to do other things.

Joannon: What you say about Dickens and Tolstoy is very interesting because you seem to be implying that the public has its role in the process of producing the form of the novel.

Burgess: I think it is true. Perhaps Dickens was exceptional in a sense. Dickens of course was primarily a performer. When Dickens became a professional performer, late in life, he disclosed himself as probably one of the greatest actors of all times!

A novel is a kind of performance in which you have to have an audience there. What we lack in the twentieth century is this sense of an audience. I find it very strongly in my own work. I publish a novel in England, I read the reviews—of course the reviews don't mean anything—what do the people think? What do the readers think? What do the people who buy the book think? You don't know. They very rarely write to you or telephone you. In America they are a little less *écartés* [reserved]; they will come forward and discuss things with you. The French will too. But the sense of having an audience *there* as Tolstoy and Dickens had! This is why the novelist will very frequently, as I do, get on the stage and talk, and recite. I do this in America. In America they will listen to you and I am getting a response. We need this desperately and in Europe we are not getting it.

Joannon: When you speak of better conditions surrounding the creation of literature in the United States, you refer to the economic aspect: does the fact that a nation might be strong economically favor the novel that is better distributed, better responded to, whereas in France the writing of literature becomes something more confidential . . . ?

Burgess: I do feel, increasingly—and France must feel this also—that America is the country where the novel is finding its most typical twentieth-century expression, rightly or wrongly. I mean, the novel is a European creation, but I think America has taken it over, partly because the financial circumstances of the American novelist are so much more favorable than they are in Europe. I don't think that American novelists are any better than French writers or British writers, but they do have opportunities which we lack. If we think about the progress the novel has made during the twentieth century, the major progress—certainly— of the last thirty years has been made in America. I don't like this. I'm patriotic enough to want it to have been made in Europe, but, you see, we suffered the war, the second World War, and we produced no great war novel. The Americans did. There was young Norman Mailer, in his twenties, entering the army with the intention of writing a novel about it. And he wrote a big novel, *The Naked and the Dead*, while we, in Europe, have not produced anything like it. It is not a question of American energy; it is a question of American opportunity. The novel itself in America can become the raw material of other forms, the television serial, the TV series, the big paperback sales. These commercial factors make novelists of America potentially very powerful people, and very rich. I don't think this is good for the Americans. We hear too many stories of American authors achieving success and then committing suicide or dying of drink or despair. There is something perhaps wrong with this cult of fame and wealth in America, but on the other hand it has produced for us an image of America as the country where the novel is still a big, living, energetic, panoramic form. It is not so in Europe. We produce these exquisite little things, little novels. American novelists have this sense that writing a novel is big business, that it is not just something you do quietly in your spare time, as the French writer will, as the French *homme de lettres* does it. Big Business. And it was big business for Dickens, it was big business for

Thackeray, it was big business for Balzac. And, probably, the novel has something to do with big business.

Joannon: The big circulations of French editions today, it is very clear, are historical novels or even histories, and I use the plural. Think of the success of a man such as Le Roy Ladurie or other historians. One has the impression that historical literature, whether it is romanticized or raw, has conquered the field conceded to it by the "literature of the laboratory" which abandoned that human nature you spoke of earlier.

Burgess: I think this is true. The primary task of the novel may well be to explain what history is about. When Balzac undertook the *Comédie humaine* his aim was not merely to entertain, only partly that, but to show what a particular phase of history was like. An interpretation of history . . . possibly this is what the novel is about. What I am trying to do at the moment is write a novel which deals with the first century after the death of Christ. This will be a surprise, and it will shock a lot of people. It is a comic novel. It will make them laugh. If one reads the acts of the apostles, St. Luke, St. Paul, solemn characters, and the persecutions of the Christians are terrible. But look at it from another angle, you find it's rather comic. It's a comic study of human beings trying to adapt themselves to a change. Everyone is aware that an ending is coming, the Roman Empire is finishing.

I was writing a passage in Switzerland, before I came back here, last November, and this made me laugh. Peter is in the town of Jaffa with a tanner called Simon, and tanning is a dirty business, it smells, they use camel dung. So he gets on the roof to get away from the smell. Because he is on the roof, they forget he is there and don't give him any dinner. So he is hungry. So he dreams of food. He dreams of everything, of pork, goatmilk, and a voice says: "Eat, all is good." And he wakes up and he's had a vision from heaven and the whole of Jewish dietary taboos have been broken. This is a comic circumstance. When we read the Scriptures we are told to look at it solemnly. The novelist can make it more human; he can show it in comic terms. The novel is a comic form; it shows men trying to cope with problems and not succeeding very well. It is like Charlie Chaplin, trying to cope and not succeeding. That's the novel.

Joannon: That endeavor to rewrite history which is the honor of the great novelist, from your point of view, and that interaction between the comic and the tragic, you have just attempted to accomplish in *Earthly Powers*.
Burgess: I tried that, yes, but this is old as the novel itself. If we go back to what I

always regard as the first three novels, the *Satyricon*, and the novels of Longus and Apuleus, they are comic. *Satyricon* is a comic novel. It is historical. The Neronic period. Homosexuals trying to cope with a heterosexual morality. The novel does not end, unfortunately. When we come to *Don Quixote* that is definitely comic— a man trying to cope with mad ideas, trying to cope with a sane world, or perhaps he is sane and it's the world that is mad. I think that even *War and Peace* is a great comic novel. Napoleon is to some extent reduced to a comic figure trying to cope with destiny, with forces of history which he does not quite understand. And if one forgets that the novel is a comic form and is made to make you laugh, one is lost. I was very upset about my friend and colleague William Golding who got the Nobel Prize recently, because if any man has gone against the spirit of the novel, it's Golding. The novel with him has become a kind of grim theological tract in which man is evil. You don't laugh at Golding's books. There is nothing funny in them. And I think the novel is a funny form. Balzac is funny, Flaubert is funny, even Zola is funny . . . *comme la vie elle-même* [as life itself].

Joannon: Then you think that the novel is eternal, that it ought to embrace life, even if it transforms life into its own image, but that eventually creative writers, whatever their historical era, have a common language, understood across the centuries.

Burgess: I think that's true. The novel is not like poetry. The novel can transcend languages. The essence is always there. The same characters. The novel travels through history.

What we are hearing more and more is that the future has no room for the novel because there are so many substitutes for it. We are living not only in the age of television, but more and more we are living in the age of the video-cassette. Like other people, I have succumbed to that. I don't think this has taken the place of the novel because the novel has one tremendous advantage, it is portable; it does not require to be plugged into the wall; it does not require the help of exterior forces like electricity or electronics. The greatest invention of all time is still the book. Incredible invention. You can put it in your pocket. You can put in your pocket a paperback of *War and Peace* and take it out and read it whenever you will. I don't think we are going to throw this over in a great hurry. As people are learning, when they see video versions of great novels, there is more in the novel. In the novel you can get inside the characters, when you see the characters you can't get inside them.

The novel is here to stay, I'm quite sure of that.

Getting Your Day's Work Done
Before Breakfast
Don Swaim/1985

The following is a transcription of Don Swaim's interview with Burgess in 1985. Printed by permission of the Donald Swaim Collection, Mahn Center, Alden Library, Ohio University (Athens, OH).

Swaim: You have two new books out in the United States. One is the biography of D. H. Lawrence, *Flame into Being*, and the other is *The Kingdom of the Wicked*. Now I want to ask you some questions about both of the books and about yourself. Let's start with Lawrence for whom you obviously have a great affection. Why is D. H. Lawrence such an important literary figure in your life?

Burgess: Well, in my life particularly because he belongs to the same class as myself, had much the same sort of experiences as myself, as a writer and as a man. We have to remember that literature in England is still pretty much in the hands of the Bloomsbury gang, rather their successors. You know, Virginia Woolf, E. M. Forster, Bertrand Russell, and T. S. Eliot—these were the great figures. They were all vaguely aristocratic, connected with the great universities, whereas Lawrence was the son of a coal miner, had a brief education at Nottingham University, ran away with his professor's wife, who was a German baroness, and lived mostly out of England, was accused of being a spy during the war, had a hell of a bad time (I'm rather similar to this); he was never a member of the Establishment, always a rebel, always lived on the outside, badly treated, sometimes deservedly, and of course he ends up with the biggest literary scandal of all [*Lady Chatterley's Lover*]. Which I think is nice for the writer. I don't like writers to be too respectable. He was *not*.

Swaim: Do you see yourself cut from that same mould? The more humble origins, and also the literary rebel. Are you also a literary rebel?

Burgess: Well, he came from Nottinghamshire, right in the middle of England, and I came from Lancashire. Whereas Lawrence's father was a coal miner, my father was a tobacconist; he sold tobacco to the poor, in a mean street in Manchester, so that's my background. Again, I did not go to Oxford or Cambridge; I went to Manchester University. I *also* married a foreign aristocrat. He married a German baroness; I married an Italian contessa. And I live abroad. So there is something in common. And I've had trouble with books, too.

Swaim: What kind of trouble did you have?

Burgess: Well, I wrote a particular book—which I don't really like talking about too much—*A Clockwork Orange.* When the book appeared, it fell into a great silence, as many books do, but then a film was made of it ten years later, and then my trouble began. I was accused of fomenting violence, rape, mayhem, as it were, because of this film and because of the book it was based on. And I still have to live it down. And Lawrence, of course, was accused of fomenting sexual desire, lust, fornication, and, dead though he is, he still has to live that down.

Swaim: I suppose in most respects D. H. Lawrence was well ahead of his time in writing so explicitly about sex.

Burgess: Yes, I agree with you, but I don't think it was solely about sex; it was the whole philosophy he tried to teach. Which has not really been accepted yet, not even here in America. He said that the intellect was less important than the capacity to feel, the instincts, the sense of belonging to nature. This was rather new at the time. And in a curious way his prophecies have been fulfilled: he said we can only start to live when we overcome the horror of the industrial age, which in a sense we are now doing; we can only start to live when we feel ourselves part of the ecology. We must regard ourselves a part of the cosmos, which is what we're doing. Which again came up from various sources—from Zen Buddhism and other oriental religions. He was a prophet, a genuine prophet. I think he did foresee something of our own age.

Swaim: It's interesting what you said about *A Clockwork Orange.* You've been quoted as saying you'd like to "live down the novel." And *yet* I was talking to a writer a while back by the name of Sloan Wilson, who has not been successful in turning out the kinds of books of literary quality as his first book, *The Man in the Gray Flannel Suit.*

Burgess: Yes, I know that book very well.

Swaim: He was twenty-five or twenty-six when he wrote that book. And he spent the rest of his life writing. He still writes. His books are not widely praised at all. But I asked him, "Aren't you afraid of being categorized as a one-novel writer?" He said, "Well, I don't think that's *bad.* If I have to go to my grave being recognized for my accomplishment in writing that one book, I think that's fine." You take the opposite approach, not because it's your best-known book, but because there are moral ramifications here.

Burgess: Well, yes, I think that really applies to *The Man in the Gray Flannel Suit,* which was greatly admired in England. I remember reading it very well, and often indeed wondered what Sloan Wilson had done after that. If that sort of thing's happened to anyone it has happened to Nabokov, conceivably the best writer America produced in the twentieth century, although he was a Russian. *Lolita* has followed him to the grave—and beyond. Oh, I think it happens to everybody, possibly even Saul Bellow, too, with *Herzog.* What we really want is people, if not to read, at least to be aware of the whole lot as a kind of general progression, of trying to write better, trying to mature. I don't think I would go along with Wilson. It's a pity, but it's what people do.

Swaim: You certainly have produced an enormous quantity of work.
Burgess: By American standards.

Swaim: By any standards!
Burgess: The tradition of doing your job as a writer, as a carpenter does his job, is the old tradition, the tradition of Honoré de Balzac in France, writing all night long on black coffee, trying to pay his debts, and producing an enormous volume of work. And H. G. Wells who never published fewer than four books a year. Arnold Bennett. Dickens himself. And then we began to get this sort of constipated attitude toward literature—*in England*—through the influence of an American, T. S. Eliot, who wrote very little and got all the awards. It was regarded as a gentlemanly thing to write little. It's a blackguardly thing to write too much. H. G. Wells, I think, was a very great writer. He was published by Macmillan in England. Macmillan never invited him to dinner when he was a best-seller because he was scared this "counter-jumper," as he called Wells, would steal the spoons.

Swaim: *A Clockwork Orange* deals with another preoccupation in your life, which is the conflict between good and evil. Apparently this is a renewed conflict in your book, *The Kingdom of the Wicked*, in which you trace . . .
Burgess: Yes, this is an obsession, I suppose, in some ways, and I ought apologize for it. But it seems to be the major theme of our age, the war between good and evil. The fact that evil exists, I think, was spectacularly shown by the Nazis. But people were scared of using the term. I remember when we had this "little" My Lai massacre in Vietnam in the sixties *Time* magazine used the word *evil,* I

think possibly for the first time in journalism, and people began to consider that such a thing did exist: it wasn't just a question of people being deprived, lacking good education or a good environment, which if improved would, even if they were poor, make them *good*. There is substance in life, which we call "evil," a kind of theological substance, which we have to fight against. I believe this with all my heart. A lot of people don't. The chemistry of the socialist, the communist, of course, is to deny it. Everything depends on the environment. I think it's *there*. The pogroms and the Holocaust during the Nazi regime prove it. It is there. It's something that gets into people.

Swaim: You trace the development of Christianity in the early days of the Roman Empire, in *The Kingdom of the Wicked*, and guess you have portrayed Christianity as good and the Romans as bad—good and evil.
Burgess: That's too simple. The title of my book is a translation from the Hebrew. The Jews called the Roman Empire "The Kingdom of the Wicked," and during that period—the first hundred years after the death of Christ—it did manifest *considerable* evil in the Emperors and finally during this period the destruction of the Jews. The Jews were destroyed: their city was pounded into the dust, they were massacred by the Romans, followed by the great diaspora, and the trek in the wilderness began again. I was interested in that period because I felt nobody had yet written a novel about it, although we had had both sides of the story in the New Testament and we have the Gideon Bible in our hotel rooms so we can read about Paul's voyages, but we never read about what was going on in Rome. It's rather like America and Europe: if you sneeze, we catch cold. When Rome sneezed, Israel caught cold. But it is a comic book; I must emphasize that. It's meant to be a funny book. God is always playing his big practical jokes, as ever.

Swaim: So do you!
Burgess: Of course, I create God. What a terrible thing to say! But if you're writing about God, you're creating God.

Swaim: You're a lapsed Catholic according to the publicity materials.
Burgess: Oh, yes.

Swaim: One of your most endearing characters is F. X. Enderby, the poet; he has been running through your literary life for many years now. Another preoccupation, I guess.
Burgess: It's a very curious thing. Some things can't be explained. I was living in Borneo in the late 1950s and suffering very badly from sand fly fever, a kind of

malaria, called dengue. I remember opening the bathroom door in the bunga-
low where I lived, and seeing a man seated on the toilet writing a poem, and the
image lasted for a microsecond, but the figure stuck in my mind so I felt I had to
write a book about a man, stuck in the toilet—the smallest room in the house—
writing poetry. And the figure stuck, I couldn't get rid of him; I killed him off in
the little book about Enderby in New York, in which he dies of a heart attack after
a hefty New York meal, and then I had to write another book in which he comes
back to life, again hearty and vivid as ever, in Indianapolis. This I can't explain.
But some characters get in your mind from nowhere, and there they stay.

Swaim: As I recall, Mr. Enderby was teaching in someplace like CCNY.
Burgess: Something like that. I had to disguise the name of the College.

Swaim: It coincided with your own year there.
Burgess: Yes, he went through my own experiences.

Swaim: You did not paint a very pretty picture or lovely landscape of the upper
west side of Manhattan.
Burgess: Yes, it's not very beautiful, unfortunately. I think it may have improved,
but that was ten years ago. I had to go through Harlem, and those were the great
days when everybody had a right to a university education, but they didn't feel
they had to a duty to work. So I had some of these fights. They involved "ethnic"
elements, which were difficult for me as a foreigner. But it wasn't a dull time. Far
from it.

Swaim: You cannot say New York is dull. You can say a lot things about it but not
that it's dull.
Burgess: Ah, no, far from it.

Swaim: I have to say you have infuriated a great deal of readers with your list of
99 novels . . .
Burgess: Yes, that was the intention.

Swaim: . . . and I wish I had clipped some of the responses to the 99 outstanding
achievements of fiction in the English language since World War II. That took a
certain temerity . . .
Burgess: . . . well, it was intended as a joke. All books are game; all books are tricks.
But what happened in England was this: a small body of people had been commissioned by the book marketing board to give a list of the ten greatest novels
since the war, and the list they provided was totally absurd because the list was

partisan; it contained writers I'd never heard of. There was a publisher, run by Nigerians in London, and they said, Let us produce a book in which we present the *real* big novels of the century, and let us do it quickly. You, Burgess, write the book in two weeks and we will publish it in three. And this was done, probably the most swiftly written book ever, the most swiftly published. I would agree for the most part with the people who object to it, because as soon as you set down a list in that way you realize it's wrong, because of those you've left out. Of course, the women were angry because there weren't even women novelists there.

Swaim: I think you made a point. You said that lists that had been published in England had books you vehemently disagreed with and writers you'd never heard of. But there are writers on your list that I've never heard of.
Burgess: Well, I don't think the list is insular. I don't think it's a British list, rather Anglo-American.

Swaim: But it's weighted toward the British.
Burgess: I wonder whether that's true. All your big American names are there: Bellow, Malamud, Styron. It's a fair reading list. Ay, I wrote it, I wrote it.

Swaim: What Styron book?
Burgess: *Sophie's Choice.*

Swaim: Good choice.
Burgess: No, but I think one has to do this kind of thing occasionally to make people wake up a little and start considering what really makes a good book. I consider that Herman Wouk, with whom I have a friendly correspondence, is a very considerable writer. I think the two volumes he wrote about the war—*The Winds of War* and *War and Remembrance*—are very considerable works of fiction, and yet in Europe they are regarded as mere best-selling trash. And yet a novel comes out of Russia like the new one by Grossman called *Life and Fate*, a very pretentious title, and George Steiner says, All Western fiction pales into insignificance in comparison with this Russian masterpiece. They say the same things about Solzenitzen. But I think a man like Wouk is quite as big as they are, and I get worried because the critics take certain standards for granted, and I think they have to look at those standards occasionally, and reconsider them. I put Wouk's *The Caine Mutiny* on my list as an outstanding work of fiction, which it is.

Swaim: Yes, Wouk is a writer whose later work hasn't been received critically, and I don't know why.

Burgess: Well, I asked the question, Why? Well, I don't make any judgment about myself. Why do we not consider Wouk's book a more important novel than many others? He's a best-seller, and he's made a lot of money. But the amount of research that goes into his work, the plausibility of the situation you get, the panoramic picture you get, is quite remarkable.

Swaim: It's interesting that writers fall in and out of favor, that somebody will suddenly be rediscovered, or discovered many years later.

Burgess: I mentioned Wouk, I suppose, in his capacity to produce these *mammoth* novels, of 1,000 pages or more, because in England, my own country, there's a tendency to praise only and give prizes to novels written by nice English ladies who live in Hampstead and write about discreet adultery, at about 200 pages. I feel the novel is not that sort of thing; the novel is a big thing. The novel is *big*, and America's shown us. It's been possible in America to produce big novels. In Europe it's more difficult because we don't have the chance of huge advances; we don't get subsidized by universities. America has had the chance; and I think has taken it.

Swaim: I think you've said that anybody can write a first novel. What do you mean by that?

Burgess: Well, I think that everybody has enough experience of life and more particularly a childhood, which is an allegory of everyone else's childhood, to enable them to have at least enough material for a first novel. I think when you really start writing professionally, you face this terrible hurdle of the second novel and the third and the fourth, and so it goes on. I do believe anybody can write a first novel. They may not do it very well. But everybody has enough inside them to produce one work of fiction. After, as I say, the initial "essay" in fiction, then you really go to work. You have to start using your imagination, and not just your memory. And that's the problem of any professional writer like myself.

Swaim: I wanted to ask you about *Earthly Powers*, which is a novel that was very well received here in the United States. This one has a main character who's an elderly homosexual, and I was interested in that because presumably you are not homosexual.

Burgess: No, I'm not actually, but nowadays I might be allowed to be, I gather. No, I have no homosexual tendencies at all, but I was always fascinated by the possibility that Somerset Maugham—a big best-seller, who was probably a homosexual—had had a brother-in-law who was Pope John. And out of that *bizarre* image came the possibility of a book. You know, we never really know what we're doing; we have to leave so much to the unconscious mind. You sit down at a blank page, and suddenly something emerges. A plan emerges. The book was difficult to write, and now I face in old age the writing of another, even bigger book, which I don't think now I'm sure I'm even capable of. Yes, I think so.

Swaim: Oh yes, *I'm* sure.
Burgess: When I've written my thirtieth novel, I'll shut up!

Swaim: William Styron ran across a problem in writing *The Confessions of Nat Turner*, in which his narrator was a black man, facing execution for leading a rebellion in Virginia. Styron was told he had no business writing this book about a black because he was white. I just wonder if you ran into the same kind of criticism for writing about a homosexual.
Burgess: Yes, indeed; that's a very good point, indeed, because I was working in America at various universities, conducting creative-writing classes, as they're called. (I don't think there can be such a thing. They say it's possible, but I don't think so.) Anyway, I was teaching such a class at the University of New York at Buffalo which contained blacks and women, and I was told the same thing. I was told, No man could write a novel in which a woman was the chief character. I said, How about Madame Bovary, how about Natasha in *War and Peace*? They said, Well, he was a man; ipso facto these aren't really women. Then blacks said, No white man could write a novel about a black. I said, Yes, I could, and they said, No, you couldn't, man. I felt, God, how *narrow* we're becoming. They'd forbid Jack London to write from the inside of a prairie dog because nobody knows what a prairie dog is like. We've got to take a chance at it, I think. We've got to assume that we know what a homosexual is like, even if we don't. Even that a man knows what a woman's like. I think the next novel I have ready is written from the viewpoint of a woman. I leave it to women to tell me whether I am right or wrong. I don't think they will say I'm wrong.

Swaim: Besides, in fiction you're allowed to take risks.
Burgess: Not too many. You mustn't commit errors, if you can avoid it. We all do, of course. If you get a street wrong in New York or a geographical fact, I don't think it matters terribly much. When you get psychology wrong, you're in trouble.

Swaim: I'd like to ask a personal question, if I may. You had a major scare in 1959 when you were told you had a brain tumor. Tell me about that and what happened.

Burgess: It was a curious story. It's so complicated that it's really hard to summarize briefly. I was working in Borneo at the time, you know, in the oil state of Brunei, which has now become very powerful, I gather. There I was teaching American history, believe it or not, to young Brunei Malays, who didn't know what the hell I was talking about. I remember one day I felt frustrated with the heat, the boredom, and the whole possibility of the job; suddenly I just lay down on the floor, and said, Right, I'm a corpse. Take over. And they did take over and I was given certain tests, which seemed to show that possibly I had a brain tumor. I was sent back to England, to the neurological institute in London, and there they said, Yes, you probably have a brain tumor, but we can't get at it so we better give you a year to live to cover ourselves. So I had this year to live, couldn't get a job, obviously, so I just became a professional writer. But it's still to me a mystery. I think there was some political motive behind it; I think that the British government at the time wanted me out of the state, for reasons of their own, and that was one way of doing it.

Swaim: That was the motivation to become a full-time writer?
Burgess: Yes, it was probably a very negative motive. I'd already published a couple of books, but I thought of it as a sort of gentlemanly hobby. Something you could do in your spare time. When I was given this year to live, and had no money, and there was the prospect of leaving behind an impecunious widow, then I had to get down to writing. I wrote five and a half novels in that year, a certain amount of journalism, a couple of television plays, and I felt fine. I felt I was really doing something at last. And I survived. I've still survived, and I may survive a little longer.

Swaim: Why do you feel the British government wanted you out?
Burgess: I think it was partly because my first wife, who was Welsh and very fiery, said something unforgivable to the Duke of Edinburgh, the Queen's consort. It was something she really shouldn't have said. I won't repeat it over the air because it was totally obscene. I saw the frowns of the British Resident and the rest of his staff, and I thought, Right, they're going to be vindictive; they're going to get me out somehow. I was also fairly closely allied at that time to the opposition party, was writing for their little newspaper . . .

Swaim: Which was the opposition party at the time?
Burgess: The opposition party was the Revolutionary Party that wanted to oust the Sultan and take over the state and own the oil for themselves. They didn't suc-

ceed. Indeed, I had a purely friendly relation with the leader. It was assumed by the British I was very dangerous. Which I am, in some ways, I suppose. All writers are dangerous.

Swaim: Do you come under any criticism from fellow Britons who are not living in England?
Burgess: Yes, that always happens. But I had good reasons for leaving England; they had nothing to do with trying to evade taxes because no author can evade taxation because you get taxed wherever you're published.

Swaim: But not to the degree that Britain taxes.
Burgess: Well, Britain is not the worst of the taxers. The Scandinavian countries are by far the worst; they're really Draconian. I don't think America has anything to grumble about compared with the Scandinavian countries, or even Britain. I felt that England, although it has a great literature, doesn't really like its writers. If I was able to work in a country like France or Italy, I would have felt they had more respect for the vocation. I would have felt I was doing something valuable, whereas in England I always felt that people regarded me as lazy, not doing a real job. You know, You want to get out there and work, instead of sitting at your typewriter all day. I'm afraid this is also an American attitude. Americans don't like their writers much, either.

Swaim: Well, they don't think writers work.
Burgess: No, they don't. But as you know it's the hardest work of all.

Swaim: Monaco seems like an unusual place to relocate.
Burgess: Well, I went there by accident because I lived in Malta, where censorship was so gross that it was impossible to do any reviewing; you couldn't get any books. Then we went to Italy because my wife is Italian, but my son was going to be kidnaped so we got over the border and settled in the next state, which happened to be Monaco. You have to live somewhere. I've always been tempted to come back here, you know. I've always been tempted to become an American author, but I probably left it to too late. I shall probably die by the Mediterranean, not by the Hudson.

Swaim: Why would you want to become an American author?
Burgess: Because, I mean, America is an extension of my own country. Let's be honest. America grew out of a rejection of British hypocrisy and British oppression. This is a fact. I have no shame about the disparaging elements of my own

country, because America is a living disparagement of what Britain used to stand for. In 1620 the Mayflower would never have sailed if these people weren't being persecuted.

Swaim: If that's the case, why is it that Britons have such contempt for American intellectuality? Why is it that they characterize Americans in such vicious ways?

Burgess: I don't think it's true. This used to be true, say, in about 1850 in magazines like *Punch*. Jonathan and John Bull, you know, in a perpetual wrangle. If you want to see real British venom, British bile, this is normally directed against the French. No, whether we like it or not, the British and the Americans are the same people; we share the same language.

Swaim: I don't think the British have a *venom* against Americans. I just think they satirize them; they make fun of them. They stereotype us.

Burgess: Well, of course, you do the same with us; to you the Englishman is a man with a bowler hat and an umbrella. I haven't seen a bowler hat in England in many years. I've seen umbrellas, of course. The stereotypical Briton is the man with the thick accent, who says "jolly good, old chap" . . .

Swaim: Colonel Blimp.

Burgess: Yes, the Colonel Blimp type is long gone. But the typical English accent is to be found up in Liverpool with the Beatles. The London accent is something that belongs to the dying ruling class. We all have these stereotypes. We can't help it. But I don't think the British are all that willing to satirize the Americans. We're too much influenced by the Americans, and Britain can almost be regarded as an outpost of America.

Swaim: You're a jazz pianist, and you are a composer.

Burgess: I have been a jazz pianist in my time. I think my fingers are becoming a little stiff now. But I have played in a "combo," and composed music. But I've got to write also.

Swaim: Music must be a second love.

Burgess: Well, I hope when I have written my thirtieth novel that I can get down to what I really want to do, which is the composition of an opera about Sigmund Freud. Which I think is a marvelous idea.

Swaim: Or H. L. Mencken.

Burgess: No, *Freud*. The orchestra can serve to symbolize the unconscious. Wonderful idea.

Swaim: What kind of schedule do you set for yourself? You have an enormous output.

Burgess: I'm a lazy person. H. G. Wells, who had a bigger "output," said the fact he wrote so much was proof that he was a lazy man: he just couldn't get out of the chair. I think it is possible when you reach a certain stage in your evolution as a writer to get your day's work done before breakfast and have the rest of the day to yourself. I think it's possible to write 1,000 words a day—365,000 words a year. It sounds a lot, but it's a very moderate amount.

Reinventing the Language

Pierre Assouline/1988

From *World Press Review* (September 1988). Reprinted by permission of Pierre Assouline.

Assouline: You are not always sympathetic to fellow novelists. Do you ever feel that you are unfair?

Burgess: Never, never, never. I cannot forget what Flaubert said about the novel: It is a heavy piece of machinery to assemble. A novelist cannot forget this when he reviews a book. It is terribly unfair to write a blanket condemnation in a thousand words. If you are a writer yourself, you think about the problems of writing. If you are also a gentleman, you say that a book is perhaps not so great, but maybe next time. . . . I do not rely on any criteria other than esthetic ones. I do not worry about the author's personality, only about his work.

Assouline: Is jealousy common among writers?

Burgess: I believe it is. But I am not concerned with it, for I am a loner in this trade. When I am in London, I hardly see anyone but Kingsley Amis, a friend whom I admire. He is like me: a monster who has smoked and drunk too much. As for my neighbor on the Riviera, Graham Greene, who lives in Antibes, he has become very strange. He has no friends. He goes on and on . . . about me in the British papers. He claims in a book that I put imaginary words in his mouth (which is false), that I have convinced myself that I am in the dictionary (also false), and that I read a lot, but indiscriminately. Not very friendly, all that.

Assouline: What English writers do you like?

Burgess: In England? Not many. Most of the British are not European enough. On the literary plane, France is No. 1, followed by Italy. When the French write, they think.

Céline, a writer of real breadth, has influenced me a great deal, as has Sartre to a lesser extent. I like what Michel Tournier does, and from Italy, I like Umberto

Eco, Leonardo Sciascia, and Italo Calvino. In the U.S., I prefer Saul Bellow and Philip Roth, also John Updike and Gore Vidal. A man like Bellow may come from Chicago, but he is very French, very European. He thinks.

Assouline: And James Joyce?
Burgess: He is the greatest. I put him above all others. In fact, the second volume of my memoirs (*Little Wilson and Big God*), which I have just completed, ends in 1982 with the Joyce centennial in Dublin. It is very symbolic. You know, I did many things for Joyce: books, articles, lectures, and tributes. As a man, he was bad. He neglected his family. He worked without worrying about earning a living for them. Genius is not enough. My artistic admiration for him is intact, but his life is not exemplary.

Assouline: Are you better than Joyce?
Burgess: I consider myself a serious writer and a responsible man. I do my work, and I try to earn a living without compromising too much. I like to write articles and criticism, but I do it mainly because novels do not bring in enough. Literature is a difficult endeavor. Each book poses new problems. Each time, you have to re-invent the language.

Assouline: If you were richer would you slow down?
Burgess: I am a hard worker by temperament. E. M. Forster wrote six novels, and that was enough. Virginia Woolf? Not much more. Me, I have to write an average of 1,000, sometimes 2,000 words a day. That's hard work. Every morning, I begin by drinking a big cup of tea with six or seven teabags, and I compose the expositionary part of a fugue to get the brain stirred up. Only then do I sit down to work. I write fast. So what? No one would criticize a craftsman for being too fast on the job.

Assouline: A Nobel Prize would be your dream come true, would it not?
Burgess: Writers are generally not secure in what they write. They welcome a rational opinion to encourage them. But a prize means nothing to me. My friend William Golding received a Nobel merely because he had friends in Sweden. There is nothing literary in awarding the Nobel; most of the time the [Nobel judges] do not read the books.

Assouline: How about the British Booker Prize?
Burgess: I admit it saddens me not to be accepted in England. If they wanted to make a little gesture, they might give me a little prize. But I have more trust in the

literary judgment of the French, who gave me the "best foreign book" award for *Earthly Powers* (published in France as *Les puissances des ténebres*). England is not an artistic nation. It is not interested in literature.

Assouline: You are a gadfly, are you not?

Burgess: You have to be in my trade. Like Lord Byron, I like a good fight and polemics, but not violence. In *A Clockwork Orange*, I kept the violence in the background. In the movie, director Stanley Kubrick showed nothing else. I do not like the film very much, but it follows me around. Because of it, people in the U.S. take me for the godfather of violence and are always quizzing me about that. In Italy, too. We had to leave the country and settle down in Monaco and Lugano, because *A Clockwork Orange*, or at least what the movie made of it, convinced the Italians that I was rich, famous, and violent. All that made me afraid that my son might be kidnapped. So we moved to Monaco, where there are no polemics, fighting, or violence.

Assouline: That gives you time to work with peace of mind. Do you have as many plans as ever?

Burgess: A movie on Napoleon is still in the works. Kubrick is thinking and talking about it. He is the only one who could do it as I see it, with the battle scenes shot from a helicopter. The problem is the budget. It would be impossible in the U.S. But it could be done in the U.S.S.R., with Red Army troops as walk-ons.

Assouline: And your opera about Freud?

Burgess: That, too, would be a great thing, but it is difficult for different reasons. I began to write the libretto, and Sartre's script on Freud struck a cord. The problem is that I see the hero, Freud, as a very Jewish baritone who loses his voice from throat cancer halfway through the opera. He can no longer talk or sing. In a dream, he becomes Moses, and he witnesses the coronation of Adler, Jung, and others. Do you know an opera singer who would agree to fall silent from the start of Act II?

Assouline: How much of you is an act? If we compared a biography with your latest memoirs, would we be surprised?

Burgess: I do not think so. The truth would be the same. I did not keep anything secret. There are many people, little insular Englishmen and politicians, whom I hate and do not treat with kid gloves. Americans seem to find me a bit tactless, especially when I'm talking about sex.

Assouline: Will your "having said everything" lead you to abandon literature in favor of music?

Burgess: Never, it would be unthinkable. I am fundamentally a writer, whatever the British may think. Literature will always be superior to music, because it is not just a structure. It has a semantic force that gives it meaning.

We Must Be Free

Rosemary Hartill/1989

From the book *Writers Revealed: Eight Contemporary Writers Talk about Faith, Religion, and God* by Rosemary Hartill (New York: Peter Bedrick Books, 1989). Reprinted by permission of Rosemary Hartill.

"Oh, I've never been an atheist," said Anthony Burgess, with vigor. "I don't think I have ever touched that particular abyss. I think it is possible for Graham Greene and other pseudo-Catholic writers to doubt the existence of God. . . . But whether really this affects the way I live, I don't know."

We were talking down a radio line. I was in a studio in Newcastle, hemmed in by a glass window and three panels of switches. He was in London. The briefness of this most international of Britain's composers, linguists and literary figures' visit to Britain from his home in Monaco had made communications problematic. So, I had no option but to imagine his narrowed blue eyes, darting sharp nervous glances from right to left, the long sweep of thinning hair combed round his head, the gestures as he puffed his usual slim panatelas.

We had been discussing whether a good novelist could ever be a holy person. The main character of his epic 650-page novel *Earthly Powers*, himself a successful novelist, had certainly doubted it. Kenneth Toomey is first introduced on page one, line one, on the afternoon of his eighty-first birthday, in bed with his thirty-five-year-old catamite. To write novels, Toomey believes, a writer has to touch pitch and be defiled.

Mr. Burgess couldn't remember putting those words into Mr. Toomey's mouth, but yes, he did think that to take up the trade of a novelist was to some extent to forfeit the right to sainthood. He could imagine a poet like Gerard Manley Hopkins being canonized, or possibly, John Donne. But the nature of the novelist's craft, on the other hand, is to look at life as it is lived—a life more full of sin and squalor than sanctity.

To suggest that a saint couldn't quite look at life as it was lived struck me as a disappointing idea of a saint. But that seems to be how Anthony Burgess believes the Vatican regards saints. If he himself were put in charge of canonizations in a dark, whispering office somewhere in the Vatican, a new wind would soon be whirling the dusty piles of depositions. For a start, a few animals might be canonized. He often felt when he was living or traveling in North Africa that there had to be a heaven to accommodate the donkeys that bore such heavy burdens without murmur.

As for humans, "No," I could imagine him declaring, deleting with gusto in heavy blue pencil the proposed name of some etiolated piety. "Not sufficiently Rabelaisian." But he had, he said, met one or two people he regarded as saints. One was his cousin, the former Roman Catholic Archbishop of Birmingham, George Patrick Dwyer. Archbishop Dwyer's death in 1987 deprived the Catholic bishops of England and Wales of one of their few splashes of old-fashioned color.

"He wasn't ascetic; he kept a good table; he grew fat. But he had a quality of total realism; he accepted evil and good not as mere philosophical propositions, but as real, solid things. He did his doctoral thesis on Charles Baudelaire, and he knew all about sin, all about evil. But his capacity to remain optimistic and believe that good would finally prevail made him somewhat saintly."

We agreed that it is unlikely George Patrick Dwyer will ever be canonized.

Anthony Burgess's belief in God, together with his affection for the Rabelaisian and his detestation of Jane Austen, grew out of his Catholic upbringing in the 1920s in a working-class area of Manchester. His father was a pianist in cinemas and music halls, whose second wife, a pub landlady, seems to have doled out affection for her stepson only in economical packages. He was brought up in the atmosphere of a slightly slummy public house and later of a more respectable off-license. He says now he was then too young really to appreciate it.

"People were wallowing in drink most of the time, fighting each other, singing, and the rest of it. It was life. It was the warm fug of life."

One lasting effect, he says, is that the coarse, the rough, became part of his make-up. "This makes certain lady critics dislike me as a writer." He did not seem to regard this as a great tragedy.

To Burgess, the coarse and the rough are just one aspect of Catholic culture. He feels that the kind of life he has lived has been totally conditioned by the Catholicism in which he grew up. "When Rabelais wrote his great book *Gargantua and Pantagruel,* he was not really glorifying vomit and defecation and drunkenness; he was telling a symbolic story in which we are all thirsty for the faith, and the wine or beer or drunkenness is a kind of symbol of religious ecstasy. I've always had a capacity to see these things as symbols, as something deeper."

This beer symbolism struck me as a shade obscure. So I stayed with the
Catholicism of his youth. It seemed, I said, to have been a pretty miserable sort of
religion, having to do chiefly with eternal punishment for trivial offenses?

That, he said, was Irish Catholicism. The Irish were the truly Catholic people,
and they should probably have the Pope in their midst. The kind of Irish Catholicism which was imposed on his family in Manchester, and was still being imposed on people in Dublin and elsewhere, was a somewhat joyless kind of faith,
very puritanical and scared of sex:

"When I went to live on the continent of Europe and I saw Catholicism of a
different kind, in Italy and indeed in France, I saw that it was essentially not puritanical. But the priests trained at Maynooth in Ireland who came over to England
did bring with them this terrible fear of sex. And this conviction that sex was a
diabolic creation did, in fact, upset us at a very early age. It has been so difficult,
even in late life, even at my advanced age, to overcome totally the notion that sex
may be sinful. This is madness, but there it is—we can't always conquer our early
conditioning. This is what really was wrong with northwestern Catholicism and
probably still is . . ."

Sixty years on, he still retains his early conception of God as not a very pleasant one: "I think that God is somebody out there watching you, prepared to give
you the big stick as soon as he can. There is no question of his giving you love and
the promise of eternal life. The punishment aspect of Catholicism was what I was
brought up with, and I suppose it's still there."

Sixty years on, he still feels it is all about punishment: "It is not about glory
and about eternal rest; it is about going to hell and burning in eternal fires. I think
with later generations this no longer applies. But with my generation certainly it
did, and with James Joyce's generation before. In those desperate pages about hell
in *Portrait of the Artist as a Young Man*—nothing has ever been seen before in literature like it or indeed since—hell is laid out in good Jesuitical fashion, with every detail presented. And this is what I was brought up on."

Could he not throw off that image of Catholicism?

"I think one can, but with great difficulty. Probably you have to go to a psycho-
analyst or something to do it. But I always felt it is something I have to do for
myself."

I remembered that he had once said being a Catholic was like being a member
of an international club where the subscription was not always called for.

"I haven't paid my subscriptions. I am very much in arrears. The subscription is to go to Mass on Sundays and Holy Days of obligation, and to take communion once a year, usually at Easter. These are the minimum obligations—I suppose the maximum obligation is just the acceptance of the whole system."

Burgess's father had come back from the First World War to discover the corpses of his first wife and daughter, Burgess's mother and sister, tragic victims of the 1919 flu epidemic. In his autobiography, published in 1987, Anthony Burgess wrote bitterly that as a result of that event, he had no doubt of the existence of God. Only the supreme being, he said, could contrive so brilliant an afterpiece to four years of unprecedented suffering and devastation in the First World War.

"What I said in the book was probably a little too cynical. It was the way my father felt, probably at the time, and I was just picking it up from him."

Did he himself still blame God for what happened?

"I don't know. . . . I increasingly accept—not as mere myth—that there's an eternal struggle going on between the forces of good and the forces of evil. I have no doubt that the devil exists. I'm not prepared to identify him with God, although in the Judaic tradition it is possible to do that: Satan in the Book of Job is not the devil as we know him—he is the questioner, the troublemaker, who is able to present himself at the throne of God; he doesn't belong to a different kingdom."

"But in the Christian religious tradition," he went on, "there was a sense of opposition between two forces. And if we accept that evil and good are fighting each other forever, we are brought perilously close to the Manichaean position, which is really a Persian religious idea, in which the struggle goes on for ever and there is never any resolution. There is a definite malevolence in the universe somewhere; and in our history this century we have seen it thoroughly manifested, not only at Auschwitz, but in the Russian labor camps, in the violence on our own streets."

Once he left school, Burgess read English at university. But before long, he was called up into the army for the next outbreak of world suffering and devastation in the Second World War. In the army, he learnt something, he said, "vaguely sentimental": "I learned that ordinary people were very good, that the man in the street, the worker, was a good type who was being terribly exploited. I came to see that there was a terrible division in English life, the product of a long, long injustice. . . . It was the voice of Field Marshal Montgomery which made many ordinary British soldiers want to become Nazis. It was the clubman's voice of Winston Churchill. We were dirt."

He never took a commission, though he became regimental sergeant major. He chose, as he puts it, to stick with the mud, not with the upper reaches of society.

He admits that since the war he may have changed his mind a little about the fundamental sanctity of ordinary people: "But that was my experience during six year of war."

After the war, he became an educational officer with the Colonial service. At the age of forty, an event changed his life, and set him on his writing career. He was told he had an inoperable brain tumor, and that he had only a year to live. What effect did that have on him? Was it fear? A sense of freedom?

"No, it was a sense of relief that I knew when I was going to die. I mean, for the most part we don't know this. I had a year ahead of me. I wasn't going to be run over by a truck or drowned in the sea. I wasn't going to be knifed in Soho, and I was going to live for a year. And I didn't feel too bad."

One part of him could not accept the verdict: "It is as we all feel. We don't think much about death except as a very abstract stranger who will eventually come into our lives."

"Was it exhilarating?"

"In a sense, it was exhilarating. Being cut off from ordinary possibilities—you know, getting a job, and living in that job until retirement—I had to do the only thing I could do to earn a living and that was to write. It wasn't a unionized job; I didn't have to be summoned for an interview. I just had to get on with the job and try to get a living from the writing."

"And that's what drove you to write, was it five?, novels in one year to provide royalties for your wife?"

"Well, that was the idea. I'd always been told when I started writing that it was a terrible job, so difficult, you sweated blood and tears. Of course you do, I'm doing that more and more as I get older. In those days it was a great pleasure to see that writing was a job like any other—that, like the carpenter or like the shoemaker, you had your breakfast and got down to work. And I worked every day, as I still do, writing a thousand words after breakfast."

"Wouldn't that become a bit exhausting?"

"Yes, it did eventually become exhausting. I published my thirtieth novel this year, which is rather too much, I'm told. I have a sort of Manchester workingman's attitude to it: this is a job you do. You don't wait until inspiration comes. You get on with it. And I've stuck to that."

It is now over thirty years since his imminent death was diagnosed. Like Mark Twain, he could say the report of his death was premature.

Anthony Burgess's nearest thing to *War and Peace* is his epic 650-page novel *Earthly Powers*, a landmark in modern fiction in its symphonic scope and energy. Published in 1980, and ranging over the history of the century, and its moral and religious challenges, it was voted in France the best foreign novel of the year, though it failed to win the Booker Prize. Mention of the Booker Prize did not go down well:

"Oh, the Booker Prize is neither here nor there. Once we start thinking in terms of the Booker Prize, we're going to lower all our literary standards."

"Is it that bad?"

"No, it's not. What happens with the Booker Prize is something very parochial and something very middle way which in Europe would not be well understood."

Earthly Powers opens with a visit to the protagonist, the novelist Kenneth Toomey, by the Archbishop of Malta. He has come to request information about a healing Toomey witnessed years ago, and so help towards the canonization of a former Pope, to whom Toomey was indirectly related. The book's portrait of the Pope, Carlo Campanati, was loosely based on Pope John XXIII, who called the Second Vatican Council in the 1960s—an event Burgess regards as a disaster. He says it debased and secularized the Church and made religion subject to fashions. The novel's opening, Burgess said, was related to his own experience of the canonization process of John XXIII, which began when he was living in Rome. During the gathering of evidence, for and against, Burgess was called upon to say why he was opposed to the canonization. His deposition, he says, is part of the reason why John XXIII has not been declared a saint.

The miracle in the novel involves bringing back to life a dying boy. The boy in later life becomes the leader of a religious sect in California, rather like Jim Jones who was responsible for the massacre and self-slaughter of his followers in Guyana.

"I was asking the question, 'What was God doing permitting a miracle to happen, saving a dying child so that this child could grow up to become a false Messiah putting all his followers to death?' I was really presenting the great mystery—what is God, who is God, what is God playing at?"

In the course of the novel, Burgess explores a question which to him is the fundamental problem which should affect everyone, whether religious or not. This is "Are we free?" Out of all his guilt-laden religious upbringing, the profound Christian conviction that he has carried on into his adult life is the principle that individuals are free to make moral choices, totally free.

"I don't think it matters whether we are free to choose this make of car, or this brand of cornflakes or cigarettes. That doesn't matter. We can be conditioned to the limit by advertising, and be forced by other elements to do various things against our will. But as far as moral choices are concerned, I think we are free; we must be free. I have to desperately hold on to that belief that we are free to make moral choices. That if I murder somebody, it is not some devil inside me forcing me to do that; it is myself."

The story of *Earthly Powers* is told in the first-person by Toomey, a man who doesn't believe in free choice at all, a homosexual—a condition Burgess admits he doesn't really understand very well.

"I had to take a big chance in building a big novel round the character of a homosexual. Unfortunately, the book in American bookstalls is now classed as gay literature—God knows why. . . . I made this man homosexual so that he could stand outside the normal covenants that apply to normal people. God had made him a homosexual and therefore made him unable to take part in the normal moral debate which exercises Christians . . ."

For me, the most disturbing question raised by the novel was how can violence and evil be dealt with. The book includes a chapter where Carlo, then an archbishop, confronts evil in the concrete form of a Nazi officer responsible for murdering Jews. Carlo holds the man prisoner in a cellar of his own residence, talking to him for hours each day to try and convince him of the evil of his action.

"This is something we have all wanted to do. This is one of our personal dreams—finding out what is there in the soul of this kind of person which can animate him to the kind of things he does. What Carlo finds in the Nazi officer is that there is nothing there. The man is soulless: he is a mere machine, or a mere emptiness, if you like, to be filled up with whatever particular doctrine is available."

"The shocking thing is that Carlo is driven to committing violence on the man . . ."

"Yes, it's not terrible violence. By accident, I think, his arm is broken. And it's probably not intentional. But one can imagine that to bring about a state of mind in which the possibility of evil facing good can be accepted is to put that person in a position in which he has put so many other people. I'm not saying I approve of that, but of course, in a novel, you can get away with a lot of things.

"The people who had power in the Nazi regime never really faced the moral problem at all. I could forgive—as I think my cousin George Dwyer, and his thesis subject, Baudelaire, could forgive, and as T. S. Eliot was able to forgive—somebody who chooses evil deliberately, philosophically, and then proceeds to perform evil acts. But somebody who mindlessly performs evil acts is in a very different position. . . . I think probably, and this is a dangerous thing to say, the greatest sin is stupidity and most of our young delinquents are stupid."

"But if you are stupid, can you be anything other than stupid?"

"I'm an old teacher. I have this humanistic, liberal, conceivably false, belief that stupidity is a condition that can be liquidated. I do not believe that any human soul exists that cannot in some measure be taught.

"I gather that last year BBC TV put on a film called *The Diary of Rita* in which the way a Pakistani family were treated by some East End yobs was presented in great detail. Finally, the girl makes a Molotov cocktail, doesn't she? and throws it at these thugs and kills them. That, of course, is pure sensationalism. It doesn't deal with the moral problem. The existence of this kind of being, committed to destruction, pain and the rest, without any philosophical backing, is what worries me."

In *Earthly Powers*, Carlo believes that people are basically good. His creator does not share this optimism. He thinks people are basically neutral—that they have the power of choice between good and evil; but that before they can exercise that choice they must know what good and evil are. This, Burgess says, is one of the bases of education. It underlies morality, religion and literature and indeed all the arts and life in general. It is also, he says, totally neglected. He used to lecture on this problem in America at the time when students were concerned about whether they should be involved in the Vietnam War:

"Sometimes I was told to get off the platform by the university faculty. But I said, 'You must know what you are doing. You must know what is evil and what is good. Then you must choose. And you must not in any way be affected by the edicts of government and society and your own parents. You must make that personal choice between good and evil. Whether it is right or wrong is neither here nor there.'"

In his autobiography, published in 1987, Burgess portrayed his own life and his own choices. One section described in frank and honest detail his own and his first wife's heavy drinking, their mutual infidelity and his humiliation. Yet despite such experience, he still speaks of marriage as a civilizing thing:

"I think marriage is the fundamental, the basis of life. Within a marriage, you develop vocabulary, you develop a culture which makes sense within that very, very small closed circle. But one also accepts that it can be outrageously difficult. One of the reasons why some people have turned against Jesus Christ, why people are prepared to accept Scorsese's film *The Last Temptation of Christ*, is that Christ didn't do the most difficult thing of all—which was to live with a woman. The new view of Christ is that he should have lived with a woman, and perhaps he did. I believe that when he began his mission at the age of thirty, he couldn't have lived in Galilee without being a married man, but that's my own personal belief."

After the death of his first wife from cirrhosis, Burgess heard her calling to him. He regards this experience as fairly common. After all, Dr. Johnson, who was very rationalistic, heard his mother calling. He rejects the idea that his own experience could have been a hallucination:

"But I do believe that when you've lived with a person for a long time, you can't face that person totally. I still dream that my first wife has come back to life again. She appears fit and well and beautiful, and sees me in bed with another woman and says: 'Now stop that! We're married; we're going to get back to it.' This, of course, is partly fueled by guilt." Burgess's famously powerful memory does not ease the burden.

Guilt seems to be a constant companion. "Some say that the business of writing too much is an aspect of guilt, that I feel I will be punished if I don't use what talent I have to the full (this is almost biblical), that a failure of love will generate guilt almost to the day of your death. I think women are less guilty than men. I think men carry the greater burden of guilt."

Guilt has often been the subject of his fellow novelist, Graham Greene. Earlier, Burgess had labeled Greene as a "pseudo-Catholic." Why?

"Well, this is probably a highly personal prejudice or indeed the prejudice of my class or of my cradle-Catholic upbringing. I have never trusted converts. I know that some of the greatest Catholics of the Church in England have been converts—Cardinal Newman is a marvelous example. Of course, so was the poet Gerard Manley Hopkins. But I think Greene wanted to be a Catholic chiefly because it was useful from the viewpoint of his craft." I could feel tremors coming from the direction of Antibes, Greene's home.

"When Greene wrote the novel *Brighton Rock*, just before the war," Burgess continued, "he presented two systems of conduct. One was based on right and wrong, which is very secular, social and not very profound: what is right one day is wrong the next. The second is based on good and evil as parts of a permanent system. In the novel, he has this young racecourse thug, Pinkie, pursued and finally brought into the hands of the police by a non-believing lady. Greene seems to say it is better to sin than merely to do the right thing. Well, this is highly dangerous. He seems to apply to sin a kind of sanctity."

Evelyn Waugh, the other great Catholic convert and novelist, also didn't smell too sweet in Anthony Burgess's nostrils. Life in the public house in Manchester had evidently not had many links with Catholic life as portrayed in *Brideshead Revisited.*

"I don't think Waugh would have been happy to find his neighbors at Mass were an Italian waiter from Soho and an Irish navvy. He wanted to feel Catholicism was a religion for respectable people, indeed for aristocratic people. I think this makes no sense at all in terms of the kind of Catholicism I was brought up in.

"In later life, Waugh was in great agony, because of the changes made by the Second Vatican Council. He wanted permission to stay away from Mass, during the more vulgar parts of the liturgy. An aesthetic element came in, as indeed it came into my own life."

Like Waugh, Burgess too had difficulties with the changes introduced to the Church in the 1960s by the Second Vatican Council, though he has never doubted the existence of God.

"I have never doubted at all the rationality of the faith, granted the basic premises . . . I accept the humanity of Christ and the possibility as a theory (which of course I cannot prove, but it seems to me extremely tenable) that the only way in which the sins that man has committed against God could be atoned for was by God Himself taking on the punishment. That seems to me to be wholly rational.

"What I have only been able to doubt," he went on, "is the way in which God has been worshiped, the manner in which the Church in which I was brought up has been debased by the Second Vatican Council, the way in which it has ceased to be a universal Church, and the manner in which certain basic tenets of the faith have been argued over, fought over, like cats spitting." As for the Church of England, he's been quoted as describing it as a cricket club where members have forgotten the rules of the game.

One of the changes that distressed him in the Roman Catholic Church was the decision to say mass no longer in Latin, but in the language of the local people.

"To give an example, my wife, who is an Italian, and therefore brought up as more Communist than Catholic, and I went to Mass in Malta in Valetta, and we heard the Mass in Arabic, which is, of course, what the Maltese language is. I was put off by hearing God addressed as "Allah" and hearing that Lent was now to be called Ramadan. The universality was being lost . . . In the sixties we used to have pop singer masses, yobs with guitars on the altar. Religion was becoming secularized. It became subject to fashions. And I don't think that is what religion is about. I think religion is fundamental, it is unified and it is unchanging."

As he got older, did he find the Christian teaching of a final judgment between heaven and hell becoming more and more real for him?

"It becomes less and less what it was when I was a child. We used to believe it was going to happen some day. I believe it is happening now. I believe the day of judgment is here and now. Whether God exists to judge us or not is not the point. The god may be in ourselves—we may be doing our own judging. . . . We can use these terms metaphorically: Christ used the term the "kingdom of heaven"—it is a metaphor. I don't think it refers to a real location. I think it is a state of being in which one has become aware of the nature of choice, and one is choosing the good because one knows what good is."

"So, as you get older, you don't fear hell?"

"I fear death . . . As you get older, you spend a lot of time wondering what exactly is going to happen at that moment of dissolution. Will there be nothing? Will there be total blackness? Or will the ego contrive to go on living? If it was suddenly revealed to me that the eschatology of my childhood was true, that there was a hell and a heaven, I wouldn't be surprised."

Guilty as Hell: Jeremy Isaacs Talks to Anthony Burgess

Jeremy Isaacs/1989

The following is a transcription of a segment of *Face to Face* on BBC *The Late Show* 21 March 1989. It is the last substantial interview in which Burgess participated. "Jeremy Isaacs Talks to Anthony Burgess" (copyright © Sir Jeremy Isaacs 1989) is reproduced by permission of PFD (www.pfd. co.uk) on behalf of Sir Jeremy Isaacs.

Isaacs: Anthony Burgess, thirtieth novel just published. Thirty novels, twenty other books, great readership, vast reputation. Are you content with what you've achieved?

Burgess: Well, I would contest this business about great readership, or the great reputation. I've always regarded myself as someone who has got the job as a living, primarily. But I'm not content. I don't think any writer is content with what he's done. I think the whole business of writing is so difficult that one hopes that one can someday write a good book. I say that with total sincerity. I think we're so aware of the faults in every book that we write. The faults that spring from ourselves, rather than from defective technique, that one hopes someday to present a better self in the book that one produces.

In England, of course, one is always told that one writes too much, but I think that we're subject to the influence of people like E. M. Forster, Virginia Woolf, T. S. Eliot, who wrote so little.

Isaacs: Are there faults in the last book?

Burgess: Oh yes. But I won't point them out. I leave that to the critics. One breathes a kind of sigh of relief when the critics have not noticed a sticky patch, and indeed, sometimes praise the sticky patch as eminently well done. No, I am well aware of the faults of the novel. But this is true of every book I write.

Isaacs: Do you care about the critics?

Burgess: Unfortunately, I do. One never gets over that. I think even Somerset Maugham at the age of ninety-one could be hurt. And I'm especially hurt by a particular review, which I won't specify, in a particular paper in which I write, which seems to me to be a personal attack rather than an assessment of the book itself. That does hurt. A great deal.

Isaacs: Do you hesitate to pick them up? Or do you turn to them straight away?
Burgess: No, I leave that to my wife. I think wives have certain functions and that's one of them, to look at the reviews first. As I say, she's my wife, who's Italian, and she says to me, "Antonio, don't read that."

Isaacs: But then you do read it?
Burgess: One is led to it eventually. Probably a year later, or something like that. But when the book is fire-hot, fire-new, when the reviews come out, one is somewhat hesitant about that. Yes, I've read a lot of reviews from the past twenty years. I'm not hurt any longer, but I sometimes feel there is more personal enmity in reviews in this country than people really know.

Isaacs: You write under the name of Anthony Burgess.
Burgess: Yes.

Isaacs: But it's not your only name.
Burgess: No.

Isaacs: In your autobiography we meet a young fellow called Jackie Wilson . . .
Burgess: Yes.

Isaacs: . . . who was uncertain of his future. Is he still around?
Burgess: He's still around. The full name is John Anthony Burgess Wilson. And there was a very simple reason for adopting the middle name for writing. I was in the Colonial Civil Service in Malaya and—now called Malaysia, I believe—and in general one was not supposed to produce anything light-hearted such as fiction under one's own name. One was in a serious job. You could produce a monograph on local dialects, or something like that, but you couldn't produce a novel. So I chose the two middle segments of the name and more or less stuck with them. I answer to any name you like, sometimes Jack, sometimes John. But more often than not my wife calls me Antonio. That's my name.

Isaacs: But if Jack Wilson is still inside you, as he must be, I mean it's he who's taking this stand, "I'm not absolutely sure I'm this great writer . . ."
Burgess: Yes, I quite accept that. We always have a problem of identity. The Jack Wilson comes back occasionally. I was in Manchester last year, and I was signing a few books in a bookshop and an ancient man came along and said, "I'm your nephew," and another man, equally ancient, said, "I married your niece." And various people I did not recognize, who were very ancient indeed, called me Jack. But the real Jack callers are all dead. Alas.

Isaacs: You have happy memories of Manchester and your childhood?
Burgess: I suppose. It is my town. One really never gets over this kind of local patriotism. We had a rough time. I think everybody had a rough time. Certainly in the 1920s, 1930s . . . a pretty bad time for everybody. I think that what really was the problem in Manchester was the divisiveness. I think being a member of a Catholic family, living in a Protestant city, the first thing I ever learnt about was this divisiveness. And indeed this bigotry which of course still goes on.

Isaacs: Two ways?
Burgess: I think it went one way because the Protestant majority was pretty vociferous and the Catholics were rather subdued, I remember. What goes on in Northern Ireland now was going on in Manchester in my youth. You know, the Protestants called us "cat licks," and we'd call them "proddy dogs," and we didn't really know what the issue was. It was rather like dealing with two different races, and I suppose the association with the Catholics was Irish really. We were supposed to be Irish.

Isaacs: That may be a good thing for a writer to have in his childhood, that sense of division, to make you look more critically at the world.
Burgess: I agree with you. I think it just shows you what the human predicament is. We're a long time getting toward this notion of universality. We're all human beings. Indeed we're worse off than ever we were. But we won't mention the Rushdie business I hope, for the moment.

Isaacs: Tell me about your childhood. Did you ever know your mother?
Burgess: No. At the end of the First World War there was this tremendous pandemic, or epidemic, of influenza. I think it was the sheer vindictiveness of whatever God there be, or was, imposing this ghastly epidemic on a world that had already suffered enough from the war, that lately made me feel that religion was rather dangerous. I'd rather not believe in God.

The fact was that my mother and sister died within days of each other, which was a fairly common occurrence then. My father, I think, rather resented me because I was still alive, somebody he didn't know, whereas these two he did know and love, had died.
And this of course applies to quite a number of people.

Isaacs: Who brought you up?
Burgess: I was brought up by an aunt. A Protestant aunt, strangely enough, who

had two daughters of her own, who was a bad cook and not very sympathetic. And eventually my father married an Irish woman who kept a pub and so I was brought up in a pub.

Isaacs: Noisy pub?

Burgess: Very noisy pub. One of these old pubs which no longer exists. It always amazes me that the poor of those days could always find money for drink. The drinking, the drunkenness, was excessive. Whether this was a good thing I'm not quite sure.

Isaacs: Didn't put you off it though, did it?

Burgess: Not really, no. Again I recognize this was part of the human condition, getting drunk. But being brought up in a slum district as I was, I suppose again, was not a bad thing. Probably better than being brought up in a rather sedate suburb. I felt that when I joined the Army, for example, that I knew these people, I knew these Glasgow toughs, I knew them all already.

Isaacs: Do you think you learned early to fend for yourself?

Burgess: I've not been very good at that. I'm, I suppose, rather cowardly, like most people. I think that I did gain a kind of strain of fairly tough independence and a little cynicism, a certain ironic approach to life. I've never expected too much from life. I've never expected too much from other people. I think this is wise.

My son is different; he's outgoing, affectionate, and has been let down so often that I realize that this vulnerability is the worst possible thing you can have.

Isaacs: But you protect him from that. Can you still smell the smells and hear the sounds and songs of ribaldry of that Manchester childhood?

Burgess: Indeed I can. I am sorry in many ways it's gone. You see, my mother, whom I never knew, had been a dancer and singer in the music-hall, and my father was a pianist in the music-hall, and eventually a cinema pianist. I'm very proud of the fact that he played once for the Eight Lancashire Lads, which in-cluded Charlie Chaplin and Stan Laurel . . . Stan Jefferson . . . in those days. This was a great tradition which has disappeared. We're a little too sedate, mechanized. I look back with nostalgia, a sort of factitious nostalgia, because I was not there; that was his age of course. J. B. Priestly was always writing about it.

Isaacs: But you're actually saying that you felt the family was an entertaining family?

Burgess: Indeed it was. I think the old traditions of everybody played the piano, everybody sang the songs; there was a certain life in the streets. Perhaps we were all ill, undernourished, poverty-stricken. But this notion, it came up. Somerset Maugham, whose new biography I've been reading, talked of this nostalgia. He wrote *Liza of Lambeth* which is about this impoverished East End, but still it was more alive, more vital, than anything that came after.

Isaacs: Getting an education must have lifted you out of that working class background a bit, or lower-middle-class background.
Burgess: Oh, I think that Catholics, in England of course, have always had trouble with education. The Catholics were not allowed university education until 1829 with the Catholic Emancipation Act, and of course there was no tradition in any Catholic family up North of getting an education. If there was talent you went on the stage, like the Beatles, like George Formby and the rest.

I, with some difficulty, managed to get an education. With some difficulty . . . I had to work for a couple of years, save money, and get to the university. This in a sense did cut me off from that tradition. I was in a kind of literary ambiance. I was more concerned with the music of Wagner and Debussy and so on, than the music that my father had played. So, I'm well aware of this danger of education. You cut yourself off.

Isaacs: Catholicism was a very powerful influence on you, was it, as a child?
Burgess: Yes, it was. It was a kind of northwestern Catholicism; it was conceivably Anglo-Saxon. It was Anglo-Saxon Catholicism that had not been touched by the Reformation. But it had to be reinforced by marriage into Ireland and by having Irish priests, Irish bishops, and so forth.

But yes, it meant a great deal to me when I was young. I believed in hell; I believed that the Host was really the body and blood of Christ; I accepted what the priests said. And this fear of hell still persists.

Isaacs: Still persists in you?
Burgess: I've no means of proving it does not exist. I gather our present Pope . . . well, I know that our present Pope . . . John Paul II, before he goes off to Castel Gandolfo for the summer usually comes out with some minor bombshell such as "Hell still exists, don't forget that." It probably does.

Isaacs: Are you a believing Catholic?
Burgess: No, I don't think I am. But I don't know what the term means, you see,

because, if for several generations, or indeed centuries, the religion has been in-stilled into a family it's part of your blood stream. It's very hard to get rid of.

Isaacs: You're not a practicing Catholic?
Burgess: Well, when I got to Italy I met some few priests whom I admire and like, and I go to their little Renaissance churches to hear Mass in Italian.

Isaacs: You hear Mass?
Burgess: To hear Mass, well, to participate.

Isaacs: Do you go to confession?
Burgess: No, no longer. No, this is bad, I suppose. One should go to confession. But I don't know, I don't think that I can. I think that I'm probably right in being a little scared of organized religion now.

Isaacs: Why do you call your, I think marvelous, autobiography . . .
Burgess: Thank you.

Isaacs: . . . confessions? Why do you call that *The Confessions*?
Burgess: That's a very shrewd point to make. I am in fact confessing. This is a kind of literary equivalent of going into the confessional and saying, *Bless me Father, I have sinned* . . . off we go. I think it's rather Graham Greene's character-ization.

Isaacs: But can you get absolution from the general public?
Burgess: Probably not. Not from a Protestant general public. I have odd letters ab-solving me from the crimes I present in the book. I don't know. I think the confes-sional tradition in literature, as well as in religious life, is probably a good thing. We burden our minds with past sins, regrets, all kinds of inhibiting forces. It's probably best to get them out occasionally. The confessional is probably a very good institution. Nowadays we have psychoanalysis, which costs more.

Isaacs: Do you still feel guilty?
Burgess: Oh yes. Guilty as hell.

Isaacs: What about?
Burgess: I don't know. The fact that I don't know what I am guilty about . . . oh, probably for not treating people well, for not treating my wife well and so forth. For not treating other people well. But I think that I am inclined to get back to the old Judaeo-Christian doctrine of Original Sin which seems to me to explain

the guilt. We're born with something guilty in us which then finds its rationale, you know, in Auschwitz, or what you will. The guilt is there waiting for a subject to, as it were, justify it.

Isaacs: Do you accept, and does that help you to an understanding of other people's guilt, as it were?
Burgess: I think it does. It also means that one is never really ever surprised what happens. One was terribly surprised before . . .

Isaacs: Betrayed, ever?
Burgess: Betrayed? I think we're always betrayed. We must always expect betrayal at some time or another. One must not expect too much. But this is because one knows the guilt in oneself does relate to imperfections in oneself which are part of the human condition.

Isaacs: In the autobiography there's a very frank account of your relationship with your first wife.
Burgess: Yes, indeed.

Isaacs: Were you more hurt by that, in fact, than you let on in the book, or not?
Burgess: I suppose, yes. I think you're right. I think one way, as it were, of shedding . . . shedding the sense of betrayal . . . was to get it on paper where it becomes something else. On the other hand we're all free. My first wife was Protestant Welsh. The Welsh, I think, on the whole, are more sexually given than the other Celts. I mean, the Irish drink, the Scots drink. They're not a very sexually minded race, either of them. But the Welsh are given to that. My first wife honestly believed that free, indiscriminate sexual congress was not a bad thing because this prevented one from identifying it with love.

She said love was a different thing altogether. She may have been right, but, as we know when we see . . . then the knife comes out. We can't quite so easily overcome our primitive instincts. Yes, there's a certain measure of, sense of, hurt and betrayal but this is all over now.

Isaacs: You say somewhere that one of the reasons that you live in Monaco is that it's a Catholic place and that there's a sense of homing about it. Is that serious?
Burgess: It's one of the reasons. When I married again, I married into Europe. Yes, there's a certain sense in which that's true, that if one hears the Angelus bell at twelve and sees people occasionally making the sign of the cross, you feel you're

home. I've never had much pleasure in traveling to the Protestant South of this country. I feel that London is an alien city in some ways. A Protestant city with a Protestant monarch.

Isaacs: Try Kilburn.
Burgess: Well, yes. I know.

Isaacs: But Monte Carlo seems, to some of us, a sort of camp for rich displaced persons.
Burgess: Monaco?

Isaacs: Yes. Rather than a home. Is there not something in that? There are a lot of exiles there.
Burgess: Yes, there are a great number of exiles. On the other hand, it is a genuine Catholic principality where I feel a little at home. Unfortunately, what you say is true. There are too many exiles from Milan. Indeed, from England. People with money. I gather there's one policeman to every five inhabitants. That's to protect wealth. I am not wealthy, being a writer. But one has to live somewhere and to go into the reasons why I am there would take too long. But the fact is, I was living in Italy with my wife and our son, and our son was going to be kidnaped. I was told this by an ex-mafioso, and so we got into the car and ran to the next state which happened to be Monaco.

Isaacs: You said, Europe. Europe, and you have a great sort of sense of that Europe?
Burgess: Yes, I think so. Yes.

Isaacs: And you try to bring that into your books?
Burgess: Yes, I think so. Of course we're all going to be Europeans. We're already supposed to be Europeans. We're all going to be very genuinely Europeans fairly soon. But I don't think the English are ready for it yet.

Isaacs: Do you feel European more than you feel English?
Burgess: Ah, yes, I think that must be so, because my family was never part of the Reformation. We never had any part in the English Reformation. We had no part in Henry VIII's Church, and indeed when James II was driven out of England, we lost our Catholic monarch. My father always said to me, "Son," he said, "don't give allegiance to any monarch: Hanoverian, Protestant. Your last monarch was James II." This ran in the family, and it may seem romantic and stupid. Auberon Waugh would certainly say so. But I can assure you it was genuine.

Isaacs: What do you enjoy about living in Monte Carlo?
Burgess: Not very much. I enjoy going to the Casino. I enjoy seeing the Ballet. I enjoy breathing in the polluted Mediterranean. But the Principality itself is becoming full of skyscrapers. It's becoming, as you suggest, a bolt hole for people who . . .

Isaacs: Do you feel English still?
Burgess: Oh, yes. I think the more one lives abroad the more one tends to emphasize one's Britishry, or Englishry. I come back to England for very small things like English sausages, English cheese, English beer, pubs, and the like. As simple as that.

Isaacs: Might you come back and live here?
Burgess: To die here, undoubtedly. I suppose the time is coming to think about that, and my family is buried up in Manchester . . . Moston cemetery. I might be buried there, I don't know. But this is a problem that faces one in one's seventies. One obviously, by any actuarial standards, has not long to live, so one had better start thinking about death. Wasn't it Jung who said, "It's stupid, it's neurotic, to avoid the subject of death in old age." I think he was right.

Isaacs: Do you think about death a lot?
Burgess: A good deal, yes. A good deal.

Isaacs: Everyday?
Burgess: Every morning, yes. I think . . . one has stupid ideas . . . I feel sorry for my heart. My heart has been beating for seventy-two years without a break, without a rest. It seems unfair to a heart. I mentioned this to a doctor who said, "Don't worry about your heart; your heart likes doing that."

Isaacs: But in the press release about *Any Old Iron* you actually tell us that your heart is thumping away quite merrily.
Burgess: It's thumping away, certainly.

Isaacs: And you tell us that your sex life is still going strong.
Burgess: Strong enough, yes. Not so strong as that of younger people, but yes. I think the sexual instinct is very slow to be killed.

Isaacs: In your three novels that you wrote when you were in the Colonial Service in Malaya, there's a very particular sense of being in a particular place at a particular time. Has that gone from your writing with this search for a wider scope?

Burgess: Hard to say. I must leave that to you and the critics. But indeed you're right to mention this beginning because I had a very strong feeling, when I began to write and publish fiction, that here was a place which was going to disappear from the British conscience before long. Namely Malaya, now Malaysia, and it had to be written about, and I suppose there was a kind of deliberate attempt to encase the atmosphere of the place in fiction. I know it had been done by Willy Maugham . . . by Sir William Somerset Maugham . . . already, but as good as he is, and as much as he is recognized as, you know, the real fictional authority on Malaya, he never knew the people. He never knew the language as I did, and I was able to write from the inside.

Isaacs: Was writing that sort of novel a different sort of activity from writing the grand, ambitious novels of your more recent work?
Burgess: I suppose one can say that . . . I suppose every novelist feels that, every young novelist feels that . . . it's great fun. The writing of fiction is great fun at first, because you're inventing characters, you're manipulating them, there's a sense of power. There's a sense of delight at manipulating language too. But as time goes on and when one has, you know, composed one's thirtieth novel one realizes that one has been playing with fire all the way along. It's a very difficult form, a very difficult form indeed, and the disciplines, the techniques involved, are tremendously difficult.

Isaacs: But are you now deliberately choosing to subsume great areas of subject matter into a new book? I mean, *Any Old Iron* has a vast scope, both in time and place.
Burgess: Yes. But of course it doesn't deal with the present unfortunately, except by implication. I think the thing finishes in the fifties. There's a great danger, I think in my own case, that living abroad as I do, and I may instance James Joyce, at a far higher level. Joyce was not able to write about the Dublin of, say, 1922, he had to write about the Dublin of 1904. I think I must hide myself away in some London suburb and get around, listen to the speech, read the papers, and attempt to do what a novelist should do, namely, to live within his own time.

Isaacs: You're saying that's not what you've been doing recently?
Burgess: I don't think I've been doing that recently, but I don't think that matters a great deal. Dickens didn't deal with his own time; he dealt with, you know, about fifty years back. There's nothing wrong with that. But on the other hand, one possibly has a duty to explain to one's contemporaries, one's younger contem-

poraries especially, what the world is they're living in. And the Thatcherian world is a reality, and I haven't touched it.

Isaacs: So there will be more novels?
Burgess: If I live, yes. It's my trade.

Isaacs: When you returned from the East you were told that you wouldn't live, that you would die. Did you believe it?
Burgess: No. I don't think anybody does. Looking back now, I see that I was driven out of the Colonial Service. I think possibly for political reasons that were disguised as clinical reasons. My poor first wife was told that I had an inoperable cerebral tumor, and they gave me, to cover themselves, a year to live. She tried to keep the secret but could not and eventually divulged it to me. I didn't feel too bad about it, I felt that it was not true, and in any case I'd been given a year. I've not been given a year since.

Isaacs: But you sat down and you didn't reach for the bottle; you sat down and started to write.
Burgess: I sat down with a sense of duty to my prospective widow and tried to make a little money. It was very difficult. You could never make much money with writing at all. I fulfilled what talent I had and produced what works I did. It can be done. If you write two thousand words before breakfast you've got the rest of the day to yourself. And I did, in fact, produce very nearly six novels in that year. This of course didn't earn admiration; it just earned resentment and sneers. You know . . . "Have you written your monthly novel yet, Burgess?" That kind of thing.

Isaacs: Do you still write so fast?
Burgess: No, no. But I think that nobody can write without discipline. You can't say, "Oh, let's wait for the inspiration to come." It doesn't come. It doesn't work.

Isaacs: So you sit down at a desk every morning?
Burgess: Yes, sit down at the desk.

Isaacs: Every single morning?
Burgess: Every single morning. Including weekends. Yes.

Isaacs: This morning?
Burgess: Oh, this morning? I'm in London. I'm on a sort of holiday. I'm with you . . . I mean . . . this is not a working day.

Isaacs: Do you rework what you've written, do you go back over it?

Burgess: I don't rework it. The way I write has much to do with the way I write music. Look at it this way, a very simple way of looking at it: the music paper, especially scoring paper, is very expensive. You can't afford to spoil anything. You'd better get it sorted out in your head, in your ear, in your inner ear, before you get it down on paper. Like Sibelius, you know, Sibelius heard the whole symphony and then wrote it down without making any changes. I like to get a page organized, acceptable, and then the next page and the next page, and so on.

Isaacs: And do you think the whole book through before you . . .

Burgess: I don't think anybody can. I think one can roughly proceed up to a point. Wasn't it E. M. Forster who said that, in *A Passage to India* he'd got it as far as the Malabar Caves, but not further? And Joyce said, you know, don't work too much at thinking of what your characters are going to do, they'll take over.

Isaacs: Some people say that when the characters and the story are humming along, you can't resist the temptation to show off a bit, to put in word play, to tell us about language.

Burgess: I don't know why people call this a show-off. Does Rabelais, does Shakespeare show off? Shakespeare's always introducing strange words like "orgils," "they kissed away kingdoms." That's a very daring thing to say. *Antony and Cleopatra* is a show-off play, if you like. But I don't feel that. I don't feel that at all about my own work. I think that Shakespeare's our great model. Always. The man one should read, learn from. And he was a tremendous player with words. Nothing wrong with it.

Isaacs: But they're there for our entertainment, or because they're utterly germane to the story in the particular book?

Burgess: I think it's possibly an unworthy feeling, an unworthy conviction, that in fiction or in any kind of verbal art, words should be one of the characters. Words should be characters, language should be a character in itself. I'm not suggesting that what I write is superior, God forbid, to say, what Freddie Forsyth writes. But it's two different ways of writing. Freddie Forsyth gives you a transparent language; you can look through it and get at the action itself. Whereas with me the language is a bit more opaque. It's just the way we are.

Isaacs: Is autobiography a sort of fiction? You talk as if you . . .

Burgess: Oh yes, I think so. One manipulates the past to some extent. The past doesn't just flow over one. One does make the past to some extent.

Isaacs: How different will the second volume of your autobiography be from the first one?

Burgess: The second volume is written. It's completed, but it has not yet been published. The second volume will deal with the most painful part of my life. The part of my life when I was trying to earn a living as a writer, with great difficulty. In which my first wife was gradually succumbing to the fatal disease of cirrhosis, the period of her death. And then my final resurrection, rehabilitation, and life with my second wife. It ends happily, I think.

Isaacs: Are you writing any music these days?

Burgess: All the time. But of course, it's never heard in England. The music is played abroad quite a number of times. I think there is some idea in this country that you can't be both a writer and a composer. But if I may boast, in this last six months I've had a symphony performed in Strasbourg, a work for orchestra performed in Geneva, a setting of a poem by d'Annunzio performed in Amsterdam and in Cortona, Italy, and, only last Saturday, a concerto for guitar, "Four Guitars and Orchestra," performed in Cannes.

Isaacs: What sort of music do you write?

Burgess: It is what they call post-tonal. It uses a regular orchestra, regular bar lines, the rhythms are irregular. It is not Pierre Boulez, quite; it doesn't avoid melody. It is, I think, occasionally euphonious. It is well-structured.

Isaacs: Are you more proud of that than of the writing?

Burgess: Well, consider, you see . . . sitting in a concert hall in Cannes, in the Salle Debussy in Cannes last week, with an audience of, say, a thousand listening to my work . . . and watch their faces. You get a response, and at the end, get applause. You don't get that with a novel.

Isaacs: Some people have said, looking back at your work, that this society, critics and public, haven't accorded you the recognition that you really deserve. That we don't treat you as a great man living in our midst, which we ought to do. Do you feel that?

Burgess: Oh, God forbid, I never feel myself great. I'm a little worried, I suppose, at the fact that when I produce a book there is a tendency on the part of critics to have a bit of a laugh. You know: "Burgess is too prolific." Too prolific? God said, "Go forth and multiply." As for honors, no, I don't get those. I get them from other countries but not here. It's rather embarrassing, Monsieur Mitterrand made me . . . a *Commandeur des Arts et des Lettres*. I had to apply to Mrs. Thatcher for permission to accept it. But Mrs. Thatcher didn't say, "Oh, sorry," you know, "we'll give you the same while we're at it." But it doesn't matter.

Isaacs: You said earlier in this, that you were still hoping to write something which put the whole of yourself into a fiction in a way that you hadn't yet achieved.
Burgess: Yes.

Isaacs: Is there a hole . . . without a *w* . . . a hole in your work that's yet to be filled?
Burgess: I think we're pretty well fragmented, you know, all of us. I think it's impossible to see oneself as a whole. I think all one can do is to create characters, or try to create characters, that represent some part of oneself. One can never create a single character that contains the whole of oneself. I don't really think even Shakespeare could do that. Characters are always fragments of the personality of the creator. Is Hamlet Shakespeare? Yes. So is Antony.

Isaacs: If Little Wilson bumped into Big Burgess in front of us now, what would he say to him?
Burgess: Oh, I'd say, you know, "Oh, come off it." Or what has already been said to me in Manchester, "'e's turned into a stuck-up, opinionated bastard." Of course, that's the Mancurian response to anybody who's left the city and tried to achieve something in the bigger world.

Index